CULTURAL ANTHROPOLOGY

VOLUME 31   NUMBER 1   FEBRUARY 2016

CONTENTS

Cover and table-of-contents image by Bernard Dupont.

CULTURAL ANTHROPOLOGY
JOURNAL OF THE SOCIETY FOR CULTURAL ANTHROPOLOGY

EDITORS: Dominic Boyer, James Faubion, and Cymene Howe
MANAGING EDITOR: Marcel LaFlamme
EDITORIAL ASSISTANT: Jessica Lockrem
DIGITAL CONTENT EDITORS: Baird Campbell, Víctor Gímenez Aliaga, Susan MacDougall, Ellie Vainker, and Nathanael Vlachos
WEB DEVELOPER: Dave Katten
COVER DESIGNER: Vani Subramanian

OFFICERS OF THE SOCIETY FOR CULTURAL ANTHROPOLOGY
President: Robert J. Foster, University of Rochester
Secretary: Kregg Hetherington, Concordia University
Treasurer: Eleana Kim, University of California, Irvine
Editors, *Cultural Anthropology*: Dominic Boyer, James Faubion, and Cymene Howe, Rice University
Open Access Advisor: Alberto Corsín Jiménez, Spanish National Research Council
Graduate Student Representative: Darren Byler, University of Washington
Elected Members: Laura Bear, London School of Economics; Hirokazu Miyazaki, Cornell University; Ana María Ochoa Gautier, Columbia University; Anand Pandian, Johns Hopkins University; Kim TallBear, University of Alberta

CULTURAL ANTHROPOLOGY
JOURNAL OF THE SOCIETY FOR CULTURAL ANTHROPOLOGY

Cultural Anthropology is the journal of the Society for Cultural Anthropology, a section of the American Anthropological Association, 2300 Clarendon Boulevard, Suite 1301, Arlington, VA 22201, USA.

Editorial Office: Dominic Boyer, James Faubion, Cymene Howe, *Cultural Anthropology*, c/o Department of Anthropology, MS-20, Rice University, P.O. Box 1892, Houston, TX 77251-1892. The editorial office can be reached by email at ea@culanth.org.

Membership: *Cultural Anthropology* is supported by memberships in the American Anthropological Association and the Society for Cultural Anthropology. All correspondence regarding membership, including dues payments and change of address, should be sent to: AAA Member Services, 2300 Clarendon Boulevard, Suite 1301, Arlington, VA 22201, USA; phone (703) 528-1902; fax (703) 528-3546; www.americananthro.org.

ACCESS, COPYRIGHT, AND CONTRIBUTOR INFORMATION

CULTURAL ANTHROPOLOGY (ISSN: 0886-7356) is published quarterly by the American Anthropological Association on behalf of the Society for Cultural Anthropology.

Open Access: Starting with the February 2014 (vol. 29, no. 1) issue, the journal is available free of charge through the *Cultural Anthropology* website, http://culanth.org.

Aims and Scope: *Cultural Anthropology* publishes ethnographic writing informed by a wide array of theoretical perspectives, innovative in form and content, and focused on both traditional and emerging topics. It also welcomes essays concerned with theoretical issues, with ethnographic methods and research design in historical perspective, and with ways cultural analysis can address broader public audiences and interests.

Author Guidelines: For submission instructions and other information, see the *Cultural Anthropology* website, http://culanth.org/pages/for-authors.

Print Issues: Print copies of *Cultural Anthropology*, for the February 2015 (vol. 30, no. 1) and later issues, are available through major online retailers. See http://culanth.org/fieldsights/536 for an updated list. Earlier issues may be obtained from Periodicals Service Company, 11 Main Street, Germantown, NY 12526, USA; phone (518) 537-4700; fax (518) 537-5899; email psc@periodicals.com.

Disclaimer: The Publisher and Editors cannot be held responsible for errors or any consequences arising from the use of information contained in this journal; the views and opinions expressed do not necessarily reflect those of the Publisher and Editors, neither does the publication of advertisements constitute any endorsement by the Publisher and Editors of the products advertised.

ISSN 0886-7356 (Print)
ISSN 1548-1360 (Online)

ON THE PROBLEM OF THE NAMESAKE

MARCEL LAFLAMME
Rice University
http://orcid.org/0000-0002-7489-4233

Names and persons stand in an uncertain relation to one another. A person may use more than one name over the course of a life, and more than one person may be called by the same name. Take my own name, for instance: while it is uncommon in the United States, there is a mining engineer at Université Laval in Quebec who also bears it. When I am vain enough to Google my name, I find his (mine?) among the results: traces of his career at Natural Resources Canada, the research project he has launched with the aim of developing a new tool for on-site mineral analysis.

If the mining engineer and I lived among the Orokaiva of Papua New Guinea, it is likely that we would count each other as *saso* or namesake (see Iteanu 2009). As long as both of us were alive and on good terms, we would be considered *embo wahai*, the same person. As my elder, he would be consulted at every stage of my ritual life, and I would be expected to furnish him with firewood and other provisions as he grew old. If he died before resolving matters of inheritance, it would fall to me to settle them with his family. Our entanglement at the level of a name would thus knit our kin groups together in a network of mutual obligation. In the world of scholarly publishing, though, the fact that the mining engineer and I share a name is a liability: even though we are unlikely to be writing for the same journals, multidisciplinary databases will display our publications side by side. Unless one of us has been scrupulous about publishing with

CULTURAL ANTHROPOLOGY, Vol. 31, Issue 1, pp. 1–3, ISSN 0886-7356, online ISSN 1548-1360. © *by the American Anthropological Association. All rights reserved. DOI: 10.14506/ca31.1.01*

a middle initial (and we can imagine a case in which these, too, would coincide), scholars searching for my work will have to sift through our respective publications and guess at who is who. The reputational politics of scholarly publishing thus encourage me to stabilize an authoritative version of my name early in my career and to distinguish it from anyone else's name. A namesake, in this context, is more bane than blessing.

Following a meeting held in Cambridge, Massachusetts, in November 2009, some twenty-three publishers, scholarly societies, and other organizations agreed to work together on a solution to what had become known as the name disambiguation problem. The result is the Open Researcher and Contributor ID (ORCID; pronounced like "orchid"), a string of sixteen digits that scholars can use to uniquely identify themselves in publications and other research outputs. ORCID is administered by a member-based nonprofit organization that is committed to privacy and interoperability, and scholars can create ORCID identifiers free of charge. To date, more than 1.8 million researchers around the world have signed up, and publishers large and small are beginning to incorporate ORCID identifiers into their production processes. Starting with this issue, *Cultural Anthropology* will require authors with an article accepted for publication in the journal to provide us with their ORCID identifier and will display that identifier in all published versions of the article, including web, PDF, and print on demand.

As much as the editorial team believes that ORCID is an important innovation, our commitment to what Jason Baird Jackson and Ryan Anderson (2014, 236) have called "a critical anthropology of scholarly communication" means that we do not advocate approaching ORCID as a self-evident good. This editorial opens with the example of the Orokaiva name system to make the point that the so-called name disambiguation problem is not universally understood to be a problem at all (see also Pina-Cabral 2012). Even as we have come to recognize it as a problem in scholarly publishing, we also want to honor and engage with feminist efforts to challenge norms of individual authorship that involve writing under the sign of pseudonyms and collectives (e.g., Gibson-Graham 2006, xli–xlii). We welcome such work at *Cultural Anthropology* and, indeed, we would love to see the journal serve as a catalyst for discussion within the ORCID community about the implicit theory of personhood at the heart of the project. Finally, we recognize the linkages between ORCID and audit culture: even as the benefits of a unique, persistent identifier have been framed in terms of seamlessness and convenience, there is no doubt that ORCID also renders research outputs more easily countable and, therefore, amenable to assessment. Our position is that contributors to the journal are likely to be subject to these proliferating regimes of assessment regardless of what we decide to do about ORCID, and that ORCID may make it easier for our contributors to document their productivity in administratively sanctioned ways. However, if ORCID ever starts to become a more active instrument of audit culture (for instance, serving as a mechanism for pre-screening authors or grant applicants on the basis of research assessment metrics), we reserve the right to discontinue our participation.

Although the Society for Cultural Anthropology is not joining ORCID as an institutional member at this time, we have been given ORCID's blessing to incorporate author identifiers into *Cultural Anthropology*. In doing so, we stand to improve our website's search functionality and to strengthen our integration with key infrastructures for data sharing. Yet our aim is also to boost the visibility of ORCID within anthropology as a discipline. The American Anthropological Association's member database now includes an optional field for ORCID identifiers (Liebow 2014), and the unified manuscript submission system that is currently being developed would be a logical point at which to implement ORCID associationwide. For now, though, keep an eye out for the green ORCID icon in the pages of *Cultural Anthropology*, and consider taking thirty seconds to register for an identifier yourself at https://orcid.org/register. The sooner that anthropologists adopt this emerging standard, the more say we are likely to have about where, when, and how it is used in the future.

REFERENCES

Gibson-Graham, J. K.
    2006   *The End of Capitalism (As We Knew It): A Feminist Critique of Political Economy*. Minneapolis: University of Minnesota Press. Originally published in 1996.
Iteanu, André
    2009   "Why the Dead Do Not Bear Names: The Orokaiva Name System." In *The Anthropology of Names and Naming*, edited by Gabriele vom Bruck and Barbara Bodenhorn, 51–72. New York: Cambridge University Press.
Jackson, Jason Baird, and Ryan Anderson
    2014   "Anthropology and Open Access." *Cultural Anthropology* 29, no. 2: 236–63. http://dx.doi.org/10.14506/ca29.2.04.
Liebow, Ed
    2014   "Nuts and Bolts of Promoting Scholarly Exchange." *Anthropology News* 55, nos. 5–6: 19. http://dx.doi.org/10.1111/j.1556-3502.2014.55503.x.
Pina-Cabral, João de
    2012   "The Functional Fallacy: On the Supposed Dangers of Name Repetition." *History and Anthropology* 23, no. 1: 17–36. http://dx.doi.org/10.1080/02757206.2012.649273.

THE FUTURE OF PRICE: Communicative
Infrastructures and the Financialization of Indian Tea

SARAH BESKY
Brown University
http://orcid.org/0000-0003-2353-0074

Surrounded by sprawling gardens and statues of horse-mounted British dignitaries, Kolkata's Victoria Memorial is perhaps the most iconic relic of colonial power in a city filled with them. Today, in what once was the center of the Raj, the Kolkata police arrange diesel-stained metal road barricades to create a buffer between the capaciousness of Victoria Memorial's grounds and the congestion of Kolkata's streets—from the honks of motorbikes and Ambassador taxis to the smells of horse-drawn silver phaetons and fresh *puchka*. Each of these barricades is adorned with hand-painted advertisements. These advertisements, for everything from snacks to steel, are usually unmemorable, but while I was doing fieldwork on Kolkata's tea trade in 2008 and 2009, one stood out. The lettering read "teauction.com," and it was embossed with a little teapot.

Teauction.com named an attempt to change the way Indian tea was traded. Tea—unlike other major commodity crops, including coffee, cotton, and sugar—is still bought and sold in open-outcry auctions, held in former imperial centers from Kolkata to Colombo to Mombasa.[1] In 2002, Indian state and industry reformers launched teauction.com in hopes that its online platform would take the place of outcry auctions. For reformers, online auctioning was a first step toward the financialization of the tea market. Supporters of teauction.com promised that with the implementation of digital technologies, trade would soon revolve around the buying and selling of futures contracts, not individual lots of tea.

CULTURAL ANTHROPOLOGY, Vol. 31, Issue 1, pp. 4–29, ISSN 0886-7356, online ISSN 1548-1360. © *by the American Anthropological Association. All rights reserved. DOI: 10.14506/ca31.1.02*

Figure 1. Road barricade outside of Victoria Memorial, December 2008. Photo by Sarah Besky.

But the shift to digital auctioning, which began with the launch of teauc-tion.com, has yet to spark the transformative break that industry reformers en-visioned. Among my field materials, the photo of the teauction.com advertisement on the Kolkata police barricade sits amid a slew of unfulfilled pronouncements from the Indian and international press about the imminent revolution that finance capital would bring to the market for the world's most popular beverage. At the time of this writing, tea sales have not only not been fully digitized, but the Indian tea trade has resisted all associated attempts at financialization, including the creation of a futures market. The global financial system is more powerful than many nation-states and individual corporations (LiPuma and Lee 2004, 32), but that so prominent a commodity as tea has yet to be financialized provides a unique opportunity to examine the *how* of financialization—the governmental and tech-nical steps that precede futures and other kinds of derivatives trades.

In this essay, I describe how, in 2009, tea brokers in Kolkata experienced a renewed effort by the Tea Board of India, the government regulator of the tea trade, to convert auctioning from a face-to-face outcry process to a face-to-computer digital one. The goal was to break the control that brokers had over the trade. Outcry brokers—a small group of well-educated middle-class men—

embodied a hidden authority that seemed at odds with free and open trade. Anthropologists have documented the cultural and economic volatility of financial markets, tracing the sociopolitical impact of digital trading technologies and new kinds of speculation (D'Avella 2014; Ho 2009; Miyazaki 2013; Zaloom 2006). Financialization does not take the same form everywhere; sometimes, it does not really take form at all. As Donald MacKenzie (2006, 13–15) has argued, following William Cronon (1992) and Michel Callon (1998), the futures market is a key site for seeing how theories about the disentanglement of commodities—a stripping away of the particularities of quality based on production—get put into action. Futures markets rely on a standardized notion of price and of the things (e.g., grain, cotton, or coffee) being priced. This disentangling brings commodities into a rational trading infrastructure. The story of Indian tea's resistance to financialization shows how such standardization requires not just a disentangling of commodities at the level of productive infrastructure but also a reworking of the communicative infrastructure of trading itself.

I am drawing here on Julia Elyachar's (2010, 452) notion of a "social infrastructure of communicative channels." Elyachar describes women's everyday behind-the-scenes communication and movement through Cairo as constituting an infrastructure that is as important to economic life as roads and bridges. Similarly, the outcry auction and its attendant tasting and valuation practices constitute a communicative infrastructure that has proven central to the circulation of Indian tea for more than 150 years, if also largely hidden from public view. It is this infrastructure that Indian tea industry reformers seek to reconfigure, in a process similar to Caitlin Zaloom's (2006) account of how digital trading in the Chicago and London financial spheres was introduced to rationalize pit trading, with its hand gestures and aggressive hypermasculine posturing.

The shift from outcry to digital trading I describe here, however, is also distinct from that identified by Zaloom. While Zaloom's brokers contemplated a move from outcry to digital trading in already-financialized commodities, the Indian tea brokers with whom I worked were trading a commodity that was in the process of being converted, through a combination of applied economic theory and state intervention, into a commodity open to speculation. As I show below, in Kolkata, financialization depended on an understanding of tea as more narrowly commensurable than brokers had previously allowed. In Indian tea, the digital transition was meant to foment commensurability by reforming the ways traders produced numbers—how they, in Jane Guyer's (2009) terms, "composed prices."[2] It is this change in price composition—a change that occurs in historically, technologically, and politically situated ways—that brings commodities into global financial markets.

After the failure of teauction.com, the Tea Board of India hired a consulting firm to identify ways to ensure the long-term viability of the industry. In the firm's own words, the role of an auction was to effect "natural price discovery" (A. F. Ferguson 2004). In what follows, I describe the Tea Board's rocky attempts to implement the consultants' recommendations.

In Kolkata's outcry auctions, knowledge about tea is held and cultivated in a guild-like community of brokers. The brokers who buy and sell tea are nearly all middle-class men, trained through years of apprenticeship and registered with the Calcutta Tea Traders Association (CTTA). They compose price through what Julia Elyachar (2012) has elsewhere described as a cultivated corpus of "tacit knowledge," ranging from tasting to soil chemistry to a specialized vocabulary for describing tea's flavor, geographical origin, and method of production. In the space of the outcry auction, brokers collectively refine this knowledge through shared cups and clipped discussion. Brokers compose price through what I call *price stories*, narratives about value that are tuned to specific lots of tea.

By the time my fieldwork began, the fate of this colonially rooted system, like that of other more recognizable monuments to British imperialism in India, such as the Victoria Memorial, had become a topic of heated debate. The persistence of the outcry auction had come to represent the Tea Board of India's failure to use the bureaucracy to maximize economic growth. The cloistered interpretations of the tastes and provenances of teas by a relatively small group of well-educated Indian men were difficult to regulate. For Tea Board officials, there was no logical explanation for why some lots were aggressively fought over while others needed an auctioneer's coaxing. Brokers' carefully crafted, guildlike pricing methods—enmeshed in what Elyachar (2012, 85) calls "secrets of the trade"—seemed anathema to free markets, much less complex financial systems. Their friendly personal relations indicated an entrenched, even corrupt elite capture of a potentially lucrative global market. While secrets of the trade are classically associated with a bygone era of (precapitalist) guild-based knowledge communities, in India's tea auctions (as in those of East Africa and Sri Lanka, which have also resisted financialization), these secrets emerged within the colonial system of capital accumulation.

In place of stories, the digital auctioning platform set up a method for composing price through scenarios. Scenarios limit the kinds of information available and the kinds of communicative exchanges that can take place. In *price scenarios*, brokers would deploy not trade secrets but the kind of tacit knowledge that, according to Elyachar (2012, 86), liberal market theorists imagine as conducive to quality price discovery (see also Zaloom 2003, 2006). This form of tacit knowledge is held individually, rather than collectively, and applied not to specific lots of tea, but to broad categories that encompass many presumably commensurable lots. This change in the relationship of tacit knowledge to price was a key step to financialization. Reformers wanted to reassert public control over the auction—still a vestige of colonial infrastructure. Like Victoria Memorial's manicured gardens, the outcry auction's esoteric language and embodied practice had to become a public good. Ironically, reformers asserted this public control by embracing a free-market logic based on behavioral economics: a logic that saw a rationalized price system as the key to translating unspoken, embodied knowledge into fungible information (Elyachar 2012, 86).

PRICE AND THE OBSTACLES TO FINANCIALIZATION

Beginning in 2008, I observed the digital transition and interviewed actors on all sides—Tea Board bureaucrats, corporate players, multigenerational small tea businesses, and brokers. The Tea Board's claims that it was creating transparency in price composition were met with brokers' counterclaims that the digital platform itself constituted a corrupting force. These arguments reflect wider anxieties about the shift to market-oriented democracy in South Asia. As William Mazzarella (2006, 476) notes, digital technologies in India deployed in the project of stemming corruption are often productive of their own kinds of opacities (cf. Gupta 1995; Hull 2012). Putting the anthropology of markets and finance into conversation with an analysis of how other colonial forms of enumeration and value stubbornly persist in the present, I underscore a struggle to come to terms not just with the legacy of colonial commodities but with the embeddedness of the colonial order in sensory regimes of gender, race, and taste (Stoler 1995, 2002).

That the outcry auction has been a major target for tea industry reform in India may appear somewhat surprising. Explanations for tea's resistance to financialization can easily be found in its continued entanglement in a colonial infrastructure of production (see MacKenzie 2006, 13). The vast majority of Indian tea is still grown on plantations, from Kangra to Kerala to Assam. As in East Africa and Sri Lanka, tea exported from or sold within India is not a raw commodity (like, for instance, green unroasted coffee beans). Instead, it is a fully finished product. Unprocessed leaves are highly perishable. Each Indian tea plantation contains a factory in which workers wither, ferment, roll, dry, and sort teas to give them particular flavors. A multiplicity of factory finishing methods yields a multiplicity of teas, broken down by geographical location, grade, and season. Further complicating this process is the fact that tea is not an annual or seasonal harvest. Tea is plucked and processed every day for ten or more months of the year. This variability leads to volatility, both in price and taste. Volatility can of course be desirable in finance, but the sheer variety of different styles and grades of tea has created a sense of confusion among would-be speculators.

The Tea Board of India's interest in the auction can be explained in part as an effort to save it. Increasingly, Indian tea is sold outside the auction system. To date, direct trading or private sales have encompassed mostly specialty, fair-trade, or single-origin teas (Besky 2014a).[3] Auctions remain the trading point for most mass-market tea. In auctions, tea is subjected to a complex method of valuation, controlled by professional brokers. The anxieties of Tea Board officials about the potential of this valuation process to hinder market competition can be linked to a key aspect of trade liberalization in India, namely, the tendency of the state to take an active role in the country's move into a global speculative economy (see Sunder Rajan 2005, 25). The Tea Board, in other words, wanted to keep a hand in the composition of price. To do so, it needed to intervene in the auction: to establish that this "time-tested system" still had "inherent advantages" over private sales, including efficiency, timeliness of payment, regularity of supply, and centrality of organization (A.F. Ferguson 2004, 4.4.05). The consultants were explicitly tasked with establishing ways to get more tea into auctions.

Much of the ethnographic material in this essay comes from India's oldest and largest auction center, Nilhat House, located a couple of miles north of the Victoria Memorial, in the heart of old Kolkata. At Nilhat House, a material plantation infrastructure converges with a communicative infrastructure of trading (Elyachar 2010). For more than 150 years, most tea grown on plantations in northeast India has been sold in weekly outcry auctions in Kolkata. Three weeks in advance of each auction, tea plantation companies contract representatives of brokerage firms registered with the CTTA to taste and evaluate their individual lots of tea. After tasting and evaluating the lots, these seller-brokers distribute a list of valuation prices, along with tea samples, to buyer-brokers from firms also registered with the CTTA.[4] Buyer-brokers do their own tasting and evaluation to determine whether they want to bid on behalf of retail companies across the world and at what price. Since its inception, the auction at Nilhat House has been a closed performance, regulated at first only by the CTTA, and after Indian independence in 1947 by the CTTA and the Tea Board of India.

The Tea Board and its consultants determined that the auction was creating a barrier to financialization: that outcry trading was producing *un*natural prices. According to Jane Guyer (2009, 203), the observation—rooted in Karl Marx's (1976) notion of the commodity fetish and Karl Polanyi's (2001) subsequent analysis of "fictitious commodities"—that price is not a "singular amount," but a "composite," a "fiction" resulting from acts of "creation, addition, and subtraction," is now widely accepted by consumers and traders. The task of anthropological analysis, then, is to decompose price: to reveal what prices keep "hidden in plain sight" (Guyer 2009, 205). Classically, these hidden terms, following a Polanyian analysis, would include land, labor, capital, and the state—the trappings of the tea production infrastructure that might easily be foregrounded as the main hindrance to tea's financialization.

In Indian tea, these hidden terms also include the communicative infrastructure of brokerage. As an ideology, price "circumvents . . . moral and political commentary" about these elements of composition, naturalizing their arrangements (Guyer 2009, 204). Proponents of both the old outcry system and the new digital system freely acknowledged that prices were compositions. They differed in their view of how the human capacity to taste and judge—to act on nonquantitative knowledge—should go into those compositions. While outcry brokers mobilized a set of collectively held trade secrets, proponents of digital auctioning favored a cultivation of individually held knowledge. What Michael Polanyi (2009) called "tacit knowledge" needed to move from the collective, storied world of outcry auctioning to the atomized, scenario-based world of digital trading (Elyachar 2012). As Elyachar (2012, 80) explains, liberal market orthodoxy presumes that "quality prices"—a prerequisite for the elaboration of free markets as well as complex financial transactions—only emerge insofar as private individuals, not collectives, wield tacit knowledge. The ideal trading sphere is not a place to cultivate and share ideas about value but act on already-formed ideas.

In her description of the shift from pit to digital trading, Zaloom (2006, 136) notes that the market became not something a trader worked *with* but something he reacted *to* (see also Preda 2006). The Indian brokers with whom I worked rarely spoke directly about the market. They spoke about tea brokerage as a trade: a cultivated craft that deserved to be updated, not abolished. While rationalization and efficiency were certainly on the minds of Indian reformers, outcry tea brokers saw themselves working not so much with a generalized market as with specified kinds of tea. The financialization of tea entailed work by state and industry actors to reconcile the sensory legacies of colonialism with the demands of a fast-moving global financial system.

OUTCRY AUCTIONING AND PRICE STORIES

Mr. Dey, a seller-broker with thirty years of experience, swoops into the auction room, flipping his tie over his shoulder and draping a brown-speckled white apron around his neck. Working his way down a line of cups, he first lifts a saucer filled with steeped tea to his face, burying his nose in the damp aromatic leaves to breathe in the delicate essences. He slams the saucer down, reaches for the cup filled with lukewarm tea, takes three aerated sips—*slurp, slurp, slurp*—and spits the tea in a thin, arching stream out into a dented aluminum bucket. He then turns to his assistant. Drawing from a controlled list of English adjectives that date back to the formation of the auction system in London in the seventeenth century (e.g., "cheesy," "wiry," "biscuity," "knobbly"), he describes the tea's qualities. In addition to this specialized vocabulary, he translates the sensation of that tea—the taste, touch, and smell—as well as his recollections about the color, aroma, and texture of teas that have come up for auction before, comparing this week's lot to last week's, grade by grade, plantation by plantation, to reach a singular number: a valuation price. The assistant follows him, pushing a large easel on which he records these qualitative and quantitative evaluations. Mr. Dey kicks his spit bucket down the line and repeats the procedure with the next cup.

Mr. Dey tells me that tea is unlike coffee or wine, which are annual vintages. In tea, vintages do not correspond to years. Instead, each plantation, or often section of a plantation, on a given day, constitutes a kind of vintage. Each tea, from day to day and season to season, might be fired at different temperatures or fermented for variable amounts of time. This variability ensures that each lot of tea, each week, tastes differently. As a seller-broker, Mr. Dey's job is to narrate this variability to make different lots of tea commensurable with one another through the metric of valuation price. University-educated and a member of several social and sporting clubs, Mr. Dey is a connoisseur of tea as well as of Scotch whisky (he prefers Laphroaig). Company profiles of tea brokers tend to include brokers' interests in cricket, football, and badminton, as well as theater and travel. While some younger brokers avoid alcohol, cigarettes, garlic, and onions for fear of damaging their palettes, Mr. Dey remains a committed gourmand. He has no doubt about his abilities.

A broker's work is ongoing. Tastes and valuation prices fluctuate dramatically throughout the year because of what people in the tea business refer to as "flushes," or seasons: *first flush* (mid-March to mid-April), *second flush* (mid-April to May), *monsoon flush* (June to August), and *autumnal flush* (September to November). There are several grades of leaf tea, all yielding different prices, from the highest grade, SFTGFOP (Super Fine Tippy Golden Flowery Orange Pekoe), and descending to FTGFOP (Fine Tippy Golden Flowery Orange Pekoe), TGFOP (Tippy Golden Flowery Orange Pekoe), GFOP (Golden Flowery Orange Pekoe), FOP (Flowery Orange Pekoe), to OP (Orange Pekoe), BOP (Broken Orange Pekoe), and "fannings" (tea typically found in tea bags and in many cases swept up from the factory floor). Further complicating the price of tea are two production processes. There is leaf-grade, or "orthodox" tea, to which these categories apply, and CTC, or "cut-tear-curl" tea, which is rolled into little balls and sold mostly within India and the Middle East (and graded using a set of terms different than those applied to orthodox tea).

After tasting and valuing the long line of teas, Mr. Dey goes downstairs to the auction room. There, lot by lot, Mr. Dey—now as auctioneer—attempts to fetch something close to the valuation price he set upstairs, a number that he sees as a "natural" reflection of quality and desirability. He sits at the front of what resembles a small university lecture hall, before dozens of buyer-brokers who bid by crying out offers. The valuation price is just one of several numerical devices brokers use to distill the qualities of tea. In addition to the circulars outlining that week's valuation prices, auction catalogs sent out by each brokerage firm connote the grade, age, warehouse location, and number of packages of each lot. The numbers in this thick paper booklet structure the interactions between seller-brokers like Mr. Dey and the buyer-brokers who represent retailers. The paper catalog organizes tea-producing landscapes distant from Kolkata into an order that corresponds to those of grade and flavor.

One by one, Mr. Dey brings up lots for bidding. The sale of two lots of tea sounds something like this. He calls out: "Let's move on to the clonal tip, lot 24."

A call comes from the crowd: "800."
"No, I need 1200," Mr. Dey replies.
"1100."
"Fine. I will start at 1150."
"1150" . . . "1200" . . . "1300" . . .

"No more bids?" The gavel slams.

"Any interest in the China?"[5]

"650."

"No good."

"7, sir, 7 . . ."

"Not on this tea, sir. Let's start the bidding at 8. 800?"

In the front, a buyer nods. Then another raises his pen. Nods again. Pen. The nodding man stares and then subtly shakes his head. The gavel slams.

The fact that British merchants devised this entire auctioning and valuation system (first in London in the seventeenth century and, later, in Kolkata in 1861) is well known and even celebrated. In 2012, a journalist profiling the 150th anniversary of J. Thomas and Company—the largest brokerage firm in Kolkata and the company that managed the first tea auctions held in India—noted that "recruitment to the profession [of brokerage] is based on sound background, schooling and sportsman-like qualities. The job is generally learnt hands-on" (Priyadershini S. 2012). As J. Thomas's vice-chairman told *The Hindu*, "tea tasting even today remains the single most reliable method of evaluating a tea." Mr. Dey and his colleagues trade on their ability to taste in both of Pierre Bourdieu's (1984) formulations: to apply a biological sensibility as well as a social capacity to discern flavor. Taste, historically embedded in the trading system of Nilhat House, constitutes an obstacle that the financial system has trouble surmounting. Brokers understand taste, like price, as a compositional, transactional practice that is integrated with histories of materiality as well as ideology (Atkin 2010; Janeja 2010). The article in *The Hindu* refers to tea auctioning as "the gentleman's trade," replete with "the romance of colonial hangover" (Priyadershini S. 2012). The storied price composition of outcry auctioning requires that Indian brokers perform British taste (that they both belong to the right clubs and can translate sensory experience into the right vocabulary and with the right panache), but also that they cooperate—that they work *with* tea—to see that as many lots as possible find a buyer.

Brokers on both sides of these transactions are motivated to see them come to a satisfying end. Buyer-brokers and seller-brokers collect fees and commissions for completed sales, but there are other motivations. Despite the vagaries of weather, season, and provenance, companies demand a consistent taste in the tea blends they distribute. A tea bag of Tetley always has to taste like the last bag of Tetley you had. To produce consistent blends, buyer-brokers must find teas with certain qualities. Most mass-marketed teas are blended in this way. A given bag of Tetley has different kinds of tea in it. If you were to take two bags of Tetley, the teas that go into it could be from completely different regions and completely different seasons, yet they taste the same. The seemingly abstract numbers in the auction catalog present buyer-brokers trained to read them with the ability to tell the stories of particular teas, to link the differential regime of taste with the abstract regime of price.

Numbers and stories distill social life into order, making things and concepts commensurable and comparable, and they allow people to make normative judgments. By giving tea a story—a chronicity—brokers come to care about each tea's ultimate fate. Chronicity, as Kirin Narayan (1989, 243) has argued, "gives narrative an impression of lifelikeness that can recruit imaginative empathy." Without the stories behind the catalog numbers, seller-brokers and buyer-brokers cannot arrive at a satisfactory (and lucrative) ending: a successful sale. Outcry auctioning is a performance of differentiation whose object is to bring lots of tea from field to cup (Callon 1998). Because of the need for particular tastes, lots are often split between two or sometimes three buyer-brokers. This is achieved by calling out to the current high bidder during the auctioning of that lot to strike an amicable division of the lot, which is broken up into a certain number of packages of variable weights between parties. Lot splitting ensures that each bidder gets at least some of the taste that he wants.

Buyer-brokers and seller-brokers know one another by name. The community of tea trading is a small one, relationships have typically been collegial, and trading decorum has been reserved, unlike the combative and even violent trading pits of Chicago (Zaloom 2006, 111). The gentlemanly repartee of tea brokerage is hidden from those outside Nilhat House. Whereas ideas about the places of production like Darjeeling or Assam have been made increasingly translatable outside the space of the auction, the complex set of descriptive English adjectives, weights, and measures seem opaque to outsiders. Catalog numbers, then, circulate alongside terms like *cheesy* and *biscuity*. To those inside Nilhat House these adjectives and numbers reflect the nature of tea, understood by individuals with a shared embodied sensibility and lexicon. They reflect a composition of price in which the sensory qualities of tea—all the things that make it taste—matter. To those outside, they reflect an archaic and colonially rooted system of secrets, of price-fixing and meddling.

PRICING AND COLONIAL ENUMERATION

The style of pricing I observed at Nilhat House has roots not only in colonial tea trading but also in broader colonial practices of enumeration. In his work on the colonial census in India, Bernard Cohn (1996, 8) examines how the "enumerative modality" of colonial rule created "a particular form of certainty" by putting fluid categories into concrete form. Numbers were used to chart the colonial project of improvement in an array of contexts, from health statistics to literacy rates to agriculture (Arnold 2005; see also Drayton 2000). Census numbers, labor ledgers, and health statistics were effective in charting improvement because they rendered India's melange of cultures, languages, and ethnicities—a melange that was, from a colonial viewpoint, wholly natural—commensurable. A discourse of improvement in colonial enumerating practices had a clear temporal component: bringing the colony out of a backward past and into a suitably modern present. As Arjun Appadurai (1996, 117; emphasis added) suggests: "Numbers gradually became . . . part of the illusion of bureaucratic control and key to a colonial imaginary in which countable *abstractions*, of people and resources at every imaginable level and for every conceivable purpose, created a sense of a controllable indigenous reality."

Thus, while it is possible to see the colonial project as one of cold ordering, colonial numbers can be more usefully understood as analogous to Jane Guyer's (2009) price compositions, numerals that leave the conditions of their production hidden in plain sight. Like prices, colonial numbers turned a differentiated population into an abstract, improvable object. As Appadurai notes, these attempts at ordering and abstraction, elaborated and re-elaborated in spaces like Nilhat House and its analogues in other imperial ports, became their own kind of unruly profusion. The tea auction catalog is thus one site in which the doubling of abstraction and differentiation, opacity and transparency, becomes apparent (Mazzarella 2006; cf. John 2011).

Numbers continue to be powerful signifiers. Sally Merry (2011) describes global human rights indicators as increasingly popular tools for assessing social justice. These numbers represent everything from economic development to women's rights, and they distill social phenomena into discrete, commensurable forms (see also Espeland and Sauder 2007; Guyer 2010). These distillations have local effects, as Andrea Ballestero (2015) examines in the "calculation grammar" involved in water pricing in Costa Rica, and as Harris Solomon (forthcoming) notes in his critique of popular reliance on a global Body Mass Index for the definition of obesity in India. Such numbers also mask the conditions of their own composition. Practices of enumeration reinforce dominant ideas about the capacity of individuals, rather than of collectivities, to manage and mitigate risks, while hiding collective histories of vulnerability. This conversion from collective yet particular forms of vulnerability to individualized abstract risk, calculable in numbers, is a hallmark of so-called market democracy, in which health, environmental, and even political behaviors have been technically and discursively divided into measurable, reflexively felt categories (Elyachar 2005; Paley 2001; Moodie 2010; Beck 1992).

Capitalism, too, depends on numbers to produce a sense of abstract and objective knowledge (Zaloom 2006, 142; Marx 1976; Simmel 1978). In financial markets, numbers attest to the commensurability of both tangible things like corn and intangible things like emissions (MacKenzie 2009; Fourcade 2011; Cronon 1992; Espeland and Stevens 1998). Such markets allow speculation on the future values of commensurable things. Speculation, however, is not a natural outgrowth of commensuration. It must be learned, as I suggest below, through the enactment of scenarios, particularly on digital platforms.

The Tea Board saw digital auctioning as a means of opening and freeing the tea market. Just as colonial bureaucratic enumeration was based on the ideal of rendering a mix of races, ethnicities, languages, and cultures transparent, digital trading technology promised to make the opaque world of valuation transparent. In South Asia, the concepts of transparency and opacity have been threaded into discussions of democracy and corruption (Gupta 1995; Mazzarella 2006). Transparency continues to be an objective of postcolonial bureaucratic governance (Hull 2012). Paradoxically, the Tea Board—a government bureaucracy—used the transparency and free markets promised in the digital auction to reassert regulatory control over the tea industry.

The challenge of financialization—made all the more acute in contexts like India's tea industry—becomes one of how to disentangle economic behavior from (gendered, ethnicized, racialized) affective sensibilities when the very thing being traded (that is, an imperial commodity like Indian tea) is so deeply implicated in the sensory colonialism that paralleled the elaboration of the bureaucratic state. It is the abstractness and numerical legibility of economic categories that makes them seem democratic, yet as Analiese Richard and Daromir Rudnyckyj (2009) have shown, collective affective sensibilities drawn from religious and kinship practices consistently make regional and cultural differentiation central to the making of neoliberal subjects. In Asia, colonial enumeration—from census numbers to ledger books—was entangled not just with religion and kinship but also with colonial ideas about intimacy and embodiment (Stoler 1995, 2002; Bear 2007). Tea plantation production provides a ready example of this. Discourses about the sexed and raced bodies of women plantation workers remain woven into discourses about the taste of tea (Chatterjee 2001; Besky 2014b). The cultivated ability of marginalized yet exoticized women laborers to coax flavor from Indian tea sits in direct relationship to the cultivated ability of male elites to properly consume and judge it (Bourdieu 1984). The proposed digitization of the tea auction, to which I now turn, can thus be usefully characterized as a new permutation on an old project of improvement (cf. Drayton 2000).

AUCTION REFORM AND THE FUTURES OF INDIAN TEA

In a May 2009 interview with a Tea Board bureaucrat in charge of the rollout of the online auction, the bureaucrat explained: "We need to establish a more robust price discovery mechanism, because at present, the price discovery is not actually the *real* price discovery." She pulled the thick, spiral-bound consultants' report from the shelf behind her. "It's all in there," she continued. "They say the outcry system is completely inefficient—against basic auction principles. The auction needs to be transparent. They said go for the electronic auction."

The transition I witnessed in 2009 was not the Tea Board's first attempt to institute an electronic auction. In 2002, the Tea Board had created teauction.com, a voluntary, alternative system to which they had hoped traders would gradually gravitate. Even after years of investments, the online platform failed. In 2004, in the wake of that failure, the Tea Board's hired consultant, A. F. Ferguson, issued a report that described the problems with the outcry system and argued that mandatory, rather than voluntary, digitization would facilitate a move toward futures trading. The freeing of the market in Kolkata required strong government intervention. The report details how the outcry system was not an auction at all in (free-market) economic terms. The outcry auction's very chronicity—with lots coming up one at a time and choreographed by an auction catalog and a list of valuation prices—allowed traders to buy "with market trends" (A. F. Ferguson 2004, 2.4.03; cf. Zaloom 2006). The report pointed out that buyers not only knew other bidders but also that during the auction, buyers knew who the highest bidder was and at what price he was bidding. The tone of the report is one of uncovering the secrets of the trade, which kept outcry transactions gentlemanly and cordial, but which also kept prices low and "worked against auction principles."

In our interview, conducted soon after the mandated reintroduction of digital auctioning, the Tea Board official explained how this latest incarnation was certain to work. Beginning in 2007, the Tea Board contracted the Indian National Stock Exchange Information Technology (NSE-IT) department to redesign the digital auction. The first attempt, she said, had been run by a private IT company that did not have the correct vision for real price discovery:

> One should not drive the proposed auction system on an overwhelming desire to get a consensus, because there are so many different stakeholders. We have the producers [plantations]. Then we have the brokers, or the auctioneers. We have the warehouse keepers. We have the buyers. And after buyers, post-auction, we have a system of traders. And different parties have different conflicting interests. The interest of the sellers [plantations] is completely different from the interest of the buyers. So, there will never be a consensus. . . . The focus on price was never *their* concern.

Echoing the suggestions of the A. F. Ferguson report, the official repeated that "real prices" were not being "discovered" in the outcry auction system because of this complex network of social relationships. The outcry structure, with buyer-brokers making purchases for any number of international retailers, splitting lots with one another, and sharing tea and cigarettes with seller-brokers working for Indian plantation companies, conspired against the discovery of high prices.

The official was sure that this attempt at digitization, five years after the initial failed attempt, was going to work, even if it had to be unilaterally imposed by the Tea Board:

> These buyers . . . they can't accept change . . . and they are *unscrupulous*. The computerized system will be inherently better because it will be impartial. These buyers all go to lunch with each other, and then come back into the auction room. How can that lead to fair prices? They are far too friendly with each other. [The brokers] say that the auction is so personalized; that it is vibrant, exciting. But it needs to be impersonal. The computer is impartial.

For the Tea Board, rich, vibrant social relations constituted the ultimate obstacle to the realization of price. The express objective of the digital auction was to turn a collective process of storytelling into an individualized one of scenario-enactment. As A. F. Ferguson's (2004, 4.4.04) report noted, the "qualitative factors" that went into auction trading could not be ignored: not everything could be done by computer. Brokers had to act on knowledge about the taste and provenance of the tea they traded, but they needed to learn to keep such knowledge tacit. While such knowledge remained vital to the trading infrastructure, it had to be seen as existing *prior to* rather than *emergent within* the transactions themselves.

The introduction of computerized trading would cultivate such a shift in price composition in three ways. First, it would alter tea's commensurability. For the digital auction to succeed, tea grades had to become universal standards. A. F. Ferguson's report criticized the wide variation in grades and types of tea as idiosyncratic and opaque, calling for a more streamlined relationship between grades and prices. Brokers would still buy and sell SFTGFOP tea, for example, but one lot of SFTGFOP should be commensurable with all other lots of the same kind. There should be no need to know each lot's story. A discourse of natural price discovery trumped discussions of a tea's *terroir*, or its seasonal and regional variability.

Second, the introduction of computerized trading would change the temporal orientation of price composition. Whereas price stories were oriented to the collective past experience of teas that had come up for auction before, digital price scenarios would be oriented to individual feelings about tea's future. From millenarian Christianity to disaster management, scenarios are communicative infrastructures and technological practices for tuning individuals to uncertainty. Scenarios are, as Melinda Cooper (2010, 170) describes with respect to weather risk markets, the elaboration of "*multiple future worlds*, attendant on alternative actions in the present." Scenarios work imaginatively as much as they do technically: they force participants to prepare for events, from crop failures to pandemic emergencies, that have not yet happened but that potentially *could* (Lakoff 2008; Briggs 2011; Samimian-Darash 2013).

Third, it was clear in my discussions with bureaucrats that if the digital auction worked as planned, buyers would not need to be in the space of Nilhat House at all. Since tacit knowledge was individually held, they could be anywhere. This constituted the ultimate aim: opening up the auction to more participants. In a process similar to those that Zaloom describes during the digital transition of financial spaces in Chicago and London, trade was opened to any individual with a computer through which they could tap into an externalized market. This was one of the express objectives of the scenarios I witnessed in Kolkata—to make trade look *and feel* like it does for other commodities.

But how technologies touch down, and how they produce imaginative and communicative states, varies with context. The Tea Board's attack on the auction system as unnatural and corrupt elicited a countercritique from traders directed at the artificiality and opacity of the Tea Board's vision. What was being corrupted, they insisted, was the taste and value of Indian tea. Tea needed their collective skill as storytellers to translate between the material and communicative registers that compose price.

THE DIGITAL TRANSITION

The first day of the digital CTC auction in May 2009 started like any other. A few minutes before 8:00 a.m., I walked up to the iron gates of Nilhat House and passed dozens of buyers huddled around the tea stalls, cigarettes in one hand, earthen cups in the other. I greeted each of the guards while the brokers and other officials streamed up the marble steps to the auction rooms. But the large CTC auction hall remained almost empty, except for two unfamiliar young men standing where the auctioneers should have been. At each empty seat stood a black laptop. Brokers were milling about outside. "What's going on?" I asked a few buyer-brokers, who were standing in the corner and lighting fresh cigarettes, right at 8:00 a.m., when the auction always punctually started.

"We will go in when we are ready," one responded with a harrumph. "They are trying to replace us with . . . with . . . those *things*!" he said, motioning back to the auction room with disgust. The lanky, soft-spoken, and well-respected director of the Calcutta Tea Traders had rushed over from his office a few blocks away to usher everyone inside. The brokers tried one last time to convince him that the digital auction was a waste of time. They should just start the analog auction. But the director said that neither he nor they had a choice. This change had been sent down from the Tea Board.

The buyer-brokers went in but would not sit down. Two young technicians from the National Stock Exchange (NSE) IT department tried to reassure the crowd: "It will work this time. . . . We have worked out the kinks." With eye rolls and crossed arms, the sea of middle-aged men sat down.

I sat next to two older buyer-brokers. Without prompting, one of them said: "Years of experience and knowledge, just *tsssss*!" He blew air through his teeth, making a sound like steam hissing from a kettle, and flipped his hand in disgust toward the open computer in front of him. After the technicians had gone around and ensured that each of the brokers had signed in with his unique password, the auction began, just after 10 a.m.

Immediately, thirty-six lots came up at once. Screams and hollers came from the audience:

"What?"
"Why is the whole catalog up?"
"Just take your time and bid," the technicians reassured.
"I don't know how to bid!"
"It won't take my bid!"
"Who's the highest bidder?"

The older buyer-broker I was sitting with was trying to buy tea. He put in a high bid, but didn't get the lot he wanted. He called the technicians over. "It's not me! It's not me!" He pointed to the screen. "It's New Tea Centre [another CTTA-registered firm]. Where did *my* bid go?"

The other man who he was sitting with shut the hood of his laptop and pulled out a snack bag of *bhuja*, offering his companion some. "It's like bidding in a vacuum. Nobody knows what is going on and that is the way they want it. This is what they mean by transparency."

The digital auction replaced the linear structure of the auction catalog and the one-lot-at-a-time sequential order with a website that flashed multiple random lots at one time, for which buyers had one minute to bid. This led to outrage in the auction hall, but according to Tea Board officials I interviewed, the randomness had been instituted to prevent buying with market trends. "It has been proven," one Tea Board official told me, drawing on behavioral economics theory, "that when people don't know what is coming up next, they buy more, and at higher prices."

In the digital scenario, brokers were being asked to take individual responsibility for their bids and, in a very real sense, to bid in a vacuum. The aleatory nature of the bidding process undid the social infrastructure of communicative channels. With no time for open discussion, brokers' knowledge was rendered tacit in a new way.

That new form of tacitness was punctuated by the crunch of *bhuja*, the imitations of tea kettles, and the spontaneous outbursts of emotion. Later in the proceedings, a roar of laughter came over part of the room. The high bid for a lot of low-grade CTC was currently at 10,000 rupees (about $225) a kilogram, instead of the 100 rupees at which it was valued. The current high bidder screamed: "I withdraw the bid! I withdraw the bid!" This plea, however, could not be answered, as there was no longer an auctioneer physically mediating the proceedings. Despite sitting in his seat at the front of the room, the auctioneer could do nothing except raise or lower the reserve price. The usually suave and commanding man just looked up from his lectern and shrugged.

What upset the brokers at Nilhat House was that digital trading scenarios violated an aesthetic and ethical connection between a style of trading, a style of production, and a style of consumption, as well as the very space of Nilhat House. Unlike futures traders in Chicago and London, who had little material connection to the products they moved, tea brokers knew tea—and tea plantations—on intimate terms (Zaloom 2006, 97). The sensory aspects of soils and waters, as well as of aromas and flavors—were as important as the embodied process of calling out lots, splitting lots, and jockeying for particular grades. Brokers felt that tea's idiosyncrasies (the flushes, regions, and grades that caused daily differentiation and took them a career to master) made it a bad fit for a valuation practice based on the spontaneous and individual, rather than collective and recursive, application of tacit knowledge. Tea's particular sensory qualities created a material barrier between India and the global market to which the digital system was supposed to link the nation. When the Tea Board attempted to replace the open-outcry auction with digital trade, tasters and buyers felt not so much a disembedding (see K. Polanyi 2001) as a change in the relationship between knowledge, thing, and price. Knowledge about tea was no longer arbitrated within the transaction, but outside of it. In a reversal of what Caitlin Zaloom describes, tea traders in Kolkata experienced the digital transition as one from storied, sober, collegial interaction under the open-outcry system to adversarial combat under the computerized one. Such a difference in the social experience of financial technologies illustrates how the communicative infrastructures that preexist digital market transitions create variability in the infrastructures resulting from those transitions.

While the storied price composition of the outcry system depended on a polite rendering of an agreed-upon past (of provenance, origin, and embodied memory), the pricing scenario of the digital auction reoriented traders to an uncertain future: a future in which traders were still dealing with actual tea but faced the risk of buying too much or not enough.

Whereas outcry brokers learned to participate in the crafting of price stories through a slow apprenticeship and a social infrastructure based on gentlemanly camaraderie, the imagined participant in the digital auction was not an apprentice, but a trainee. Just as the digital auction was being revived in 2009, private firms began to offer aspiring young brokers a new product: training in tea tasting and valuation. In institutions from the Birla Institute of Management and Futuristic Studies (a subsidiary of the Birla tea company) to Assam Agricultural University, students can now purchase lessons in the secrets of tea tasting, preparing to enter a reformed auction system, based on standardized scenarios, that would welcome a greater number of participants, imagined not as colleagues but as competitors (cf. Elyachar 2012, 88). Whereas particular price stories draw a small community together within a discrete, shared social and ecological space, generalized price scenarios organize large numbers of people over a vast scale. These people need share nothing but a desire either to buy or to sell.

CONCLUSION

It appears, then, that brokers' collectively honed knowledge has been re-packaged as a commodity unto itself. Yet as Julia Elyachar (2012, 90) notes—in line with Jane Guyer's (2009) suspicion of facile narratives of commoditization—the repackaging of knowledge as a fungible commodity is rarely so seamless. While neoliberal theorists have drawn on Michael Polanyi's notion of tacit knowledge in science to argue that rational economic orders must emerge through sponta-neous actions, I have shown in this essay how a move to foment a spontaneous relationship between price and knowledge actually requires a great deal of gov-ernmental and nongovernmental planning.

Through an account of an attempt to financialize tea in India, I have shown how digital technology puts the theories of behavioral economics into action (MacKenzie 2006; Zaloom 2006). Ideas about the transparency, impartiality, and rationality of digital systems reveal how visions of India's economic future depend on the elimination of cloistered expertise and its replacement by a distributed, democratic knowledge, acquirable through training rather than apprenticeship. This elimination replaces what I have called the collective, embodied story of price with the enactment of standardized, individualized scenarios. This shift ap-pears to allow numbers to speak for themselves, because participation in their production is radically distributed, while the possible actions taken to produce them are radically limited. The shift to scenario-based price discovery links Indian tea-industry reform to broader discussions of the social contexts of technological change in global finance (Zaloom 2006; MacKenzie 2006; Preda 2006; Miyazaki 2013), as well as to other technoscientific changes in the global economy of nature and numbers, from bioterrorism to epidemiology to climate change models (Lak-off 2008; Samimian-Darash 2013; Edwards 2010). Putting models into practice through scenarios is a prerequisite to the implementation of new forms of surveillance and control in the future, but it is also central to the elaboration of new kinds of market relationships in the present. Price scenarios work to turn environmental commodities like tea—fickle, particular, and shifting like pathogens, air, and water—into potential financial instruments.

To conceive of finance as an anthropological object, then, we must think about the physical dismantling of auction houses as much as about the physical opening up of goldmines or hydraulically fractured shale formations. At an even broader level, attention to the technologies of market opening puts the anthropology of finance into dialogue with ethnographic approaches to modernity and infrastructure, which are already rich in attention to how planning accounts for (or ignores) spontaneity and "leakage" (Anand 2011; see also Appel 2012; Larkin 2013). Leakages, whether they are what literally flows out of pipe crevices or the outbursts of traders who "don't know what's coming up next," are as common in price compositions as in city water systems.

Efforts to reform India's tea industry are ongoing. Obstacles to financialization in the tea sector exist in multiple locations within the colonially derived production infrastructure. Since 2009, tea brokerage in India has become a hybrid system, with digital technologies wedged awkwardly into the old outcry model. The seller-brokers and buyer-brokers still gather in the auction rooms of Nilhat House. The long list of grading and tasting terms continues to confound attempts to commensurate tea grades for rapid digital trading. Still, the push for digitization in the auction continues, not least because online sales have taken off elsewhere during the past five years. A growing number of direct traders, who use the Internet to cultivate buyers in Europe and America, have managed to circumvent the auction. Direct traders are threatening the status of the tea trade as a national institution. The Tea Board is trying to meld the ethic of speed and seamlessness that marks digital trading with the quality assurance offered by the auction. To do so, the Tea Board has marshaled a new kind of expert authority. The savvy, young (but still overwhelmingly upper-middle-class, English-speaking, and male) IT expert has started to replace the wizened, middle-aged taster-broker. The push for digitization is part of a broader attempt to keep tea palatable in India, both politically and socially. Digitization has come along with bold pronouncements about the beginning of the end of the plantation system, with its variable geographies, esoteric factory processing procedures, and archaic labor process. The taste of tea in the broadest sense—its association with refinement but also with enlightened liberal values—is at stake.

Yet as I have argued in this essay, to understand efforts to financialize fields and factories, we must understand how those efforts resonate with similar moves to transform a more hidden communicative infrastructure of price composition in places like the tasting and auction rooms of Nilhat House. Such an analysis enables the anthropology of finance to join studies of environment and development by critically engaging megaprojects that do not take the form of dams, roads, or other modernist structures.

ABSTRACT

For more than 150 years, most tea grown on plantations in northeast India has been sold in open-outcry auctions in Kolkata. In this essay, I describe how, in 2009, the Tea Board of India, the government regulator of the tea trade, began to convert auctioning from a face-to-face outcry process to a face-to-computer digital one. The Tea Board hoped that with the implementation of digital technologies, trade would soon revolve around the buying and selling of futures contracts, not individual lots of tea. Despite these efforts, the tea industry has thus far resisted all attempts at financialization. That so prominent a commodity as tea has yet to be financialized provides a unique opportunity to examine the how of financialization—the governmental and technical steps that precede futures and other kinds of derivatives markets. Futures markets rely on a standardized notion of price and of the material things being priced. The story of Indian tea's resistance to financialization shows how such standardization requires not just a disentangling of commodities at the level of productive infrastructure (that is, the separation of individual trader and thing being traded) but also a reworking of the communicative infrastructure of trading. In this essay, I analyze this reworking by examining the effort to reform how tea is priced at auction. Specifically, I describe a transition in tea valuation from socially embedded price stories to standardized price scenarios. [brokerage; bureaucracy; tacit knowledge; economic reform; scenario]

NOTES

Acknowledgments   Thanks to Dominic Boyer, the *Cultural Anthropology* editorial collective, and the anonymous reviewers for their helpful feedback on this manuscript. Many other people have also provided comments on it during the past few years, including Nicholas D'Avella and Paige West at a 2012 panel on Enumerating Environments at the annual meetings of the American Anthropological Association, Nikhil Anand and Anuradha Sharma at the 2012 Annual Conference on South Asia, Martha Lampland, Daniel Hirschman, Caroline Schuster, Alex Blanchette, Matthew Hull, and colleagues at Brown University, North Carolina State University, University of Cologne, University of Edinburgh, University of Michigan, and the 2014 biennial meeting of the Society for Cultural Anthropology. Special thanks to Alex Nading for his detailed responses to this article's multiple incarnations. Funding was provided by the Fulbright-Hays Doctoral Dissertation Research Abroad Program, the American Institute of Indian Studies, the Land Tenure Center at the University of Wisconsin–Madison, the Andrew W. Mellon Foundation, the American Council of Learned Societies, and the Michigan Society of Fellows. All errors are my own.

1.   There are seven auction centers in India. In addition to the largest in Kolkata (West Bengal), there are centers in Guwahati (Assam), Jalpaiguri (West Bengal), Siliguri (West Bengal), Cochin (Kerala), Coonoor (Tamil Nadu), and Coimbatore (Tamil Nadu).

2.   In Caitlin Zaloom's (2003, 259) case, the digital transition forced traders to change how they reacted to the numbers that constituted the market.

3.   As William Roseberry (1996) and Paige West (2012) have shown, the neoliberalization of agriculture allows for the creation of specialty markets in which taste—in both of its Bourdieuian senses—is more important than ever.

4.   For the sake of clarity I use the term *seller-brokers* to describe people who taste and auction tea and *buyer-brokers* to describe people who buy tea at auction. In everyday auction parlance, *sellers* are actually plantations, *buyers* are what I call "buyer-brokers," and *brokers* are what I call "seller-brokers."

5.   This tea is not from China, but it is the "Chinese variety" of bush (*Camellia sinensis*).

REFERENCES

A.F. Ferguson & Company
      2004   "Study on Primary Marketing of Tea in India—Final Report."
Anand, Nikhil
      2011   "Pressure: The PoliTechnics of Water Supply in Mumbai." *Cultural Anthropology* 26, no. 4: 542–64. http://dx.doi.org/10.1111/j.1548-1360.2011.01111.x.
Appadurai, Arjun
      1996   *Modernity at Large: Cultural Dimensions of Globalization*. Minneapolis: University of Minnesota Press.
Appel, Hannah
      2012   "Walls and White Elephants: Oil Extraction, Responsibility, and Infrastructural Violence in Equatorial Guinea." *Ethnography* 13, no. 4: 439–65. http://dx.doi.org/10.1177/1466138111435741.
Arnold, David
      2005   "Agriculture and 'Improvement' in Early Colonial India: A Pre-History of Development." *Journal of Agrarian Change* 5, no. 4: 505–25. http://dx.doi.org/10.1111/j.1471-0366.2005.00110.x.
Atkin, Peter
      2010   *Liquid Materialities: A History of Milk, Science, and the Law*. Farnham, U.K.: Ashgate.
Ballestero, Andrea
      2015   "The Ethics of a Formula: Calculating a Financial–Humanitarian Price for Water." *American Ethnologist* 42, no. 2: 262–78. http://dx.doi.org/10.1111/amet.12129.
Bear, Laura
      2007   *Lines of the Nation: Indian Railway Workers, Bureaucracy, and the Intimate Historical Self*. New York: Columbia University Press.
Beck, Ulrich
      1992   *Risk Society: Towards a New Modernity*. London: Sage.
Besky, Sarah
      2014a *The Darjeeling Distinction: Labor and Justice on Darjeeling Tea Plantations*. Berkeley: University of California Press.
      2014b "The Labor of *Terroir* and the *Terroir* of Labor: Geographical Indication on Darjeeling Tea Plantations." *Agriculture and Human Values* 31, no. 1: 83–96. http://dx.doi.org/10.1007/s10460-013-9452-8.
Bourdieu, Pierre
      1984   *Distinction: A Social Critique of the Judgment of Taste*. Translated by Richard Nice. London: Routledge.
Briggs, Charles L.
      2011   "Communicating Biosecurity." *Medical Anthropology: Cross-Cultural Studies in Health and Illness* 30, no. 1: 6–29. http://dx.doi.org/10.1080/01459740.2010.531066.

Callon, Michel, ed.
    1998   *Laws of the Markets*. Oxford: Blackwell.
Chatterjee, Piya
    2001   *A Time for Tea: Women, Labor, and Post/colonial Politics on an Indian Plantation*. Durham, N.C.: Duke University Press.
Cohn, Bernard S.
    1996   *Colonialism and Its Forms of Knowledge: The British in India*. Princeton, N.J.: Princeton University Press.
Cooper, Melinda
    2010   "Turbulent Worlds: Financial Markets and Environmental Crisis." *Theory, Culture & Society* 27, nos. 2–3: 167–90. http://dx.doi.org/10.1177/0263276409358727.
Cronon, William
    1992   *Nature's Metropolis: Chicago and the Great West*. New York: W. W. Norton.
D'Avella, Nicholas
    2014   "Ecologies of Investment: Crisis Histories and Brick Futures in Argentina." *Cultural Anthropology* 29, no. 1: 173–99. http://dx.doi.org/10.14506/ca29.1.10.
Drayton, Richard
    2000   *Nature's Government: Science, Imperial Britain, and the "Improvement" of the World*. New Haven, Conn.: Yale University Press.
Edwards, Paul N.
    2010   *A Vast Machine: Computer Models, Climate Data, and The Politics of Global Warming*. Cambridge, Mass.: MIT Press.
Elyachar, Julia
    2005   *Markets of Dispossession: NGOs, Economic Development, and the State in Cairo*. Durham, N.C.: Duke University Press.
    2010   "Phatic Labor, Infrastructure, and the Question of Empowerment in Cairo." *American Ethnologist* 37, no. 3: 452–64. http://dx.doi.org/10.1111/j.1548-1425.2010.01265.x.
    2012   "Before (and After) Neoliberalism: Tacit Knowledge, Secrets of the Trade, and the Public Sector in Egypt." *Cultural Anthropology* 27, no. 1: 76–96. http://dx.doi.org/10.1111/j.1548-1360.2012.01127.x.
Espeland, Wendy Nelson, and Michael Sauder
    2007   "Rankings and Reactivity: How Public Measures Recreate Social Worlds." *American Journal of Sociology* 113, no. 1: 1–40. http://dx.doi.org/10.1086/517897.
Espeland, Wendy Nelson, and Mitchell L. Stevens
    1998   "Commensuration as a Social Process." *Annual Review of Sociology* 24: 313–43. http://dx.doi.org/10.1146/annurev.soc.24.1.313.
Fourcade, Marion
    2011   "Cents and Sensibility: Economic Valuation and the Nature of 'Nature.'" *American Journal of Sociology* 116, no. 6: 1721–77. http://dx.doi.org/10.1086/659640.
Gupta, Akhil
    1995   "Blurred Boundaries: The Discourse of Corruption, the Culture of Politics, and the Imagined State." *American Ethnologist* 22, no. 2: 365–402. http://dx.doi.org/10.1525/ae.1995.22.2.02a00090.
Guyer, Jane I.
    2009   "Composites, Fictions and Risk: Toward an Ethnography of Price." In *Market and Society: The Great Transformation Today*, edited by Chris Hann and Keith Hart, 203–20. Cambridge: Cambridge University Press.
    2010   "The Eruption of Tradition? On Ordinality and Calculation." *Anthropological Theory* 10, nos. 1–2: 123–31. http://dx.doi.org/10.1177/1463499610365378.
Ho, Karen
    2009   *Liquidated: An Ethnography of Wall Street*. Durham, N.C.: Duke University Press.

Hull, Matthew S.
 2012 *Government of Paper: The Materiality of Bureaucracy in Urban Pakistan*. Berkeley: University of California Press.
Janeja, Manpreet K.
 2010 *Transactions in Taste: The Collaborative Lives of Everyday Bengali Food*. New Delhi: Routledge India.
John, Gemma
 2011 "Freedom of Information and Transparency in Scotland: Disclosing Persons as Things and Vice Versa." *Anthropology Today* 27, no. 3: 22–25. http://dx.doi. org/10.1111/j.1467-8322.2011.00809.x.
Lakoff, Andrew
 2008 "The Generic Biothreat, or, How We Became Unprepared." *Cultural Anthropology* 23, no. 3: 399–428. http://dx.doi.org/10.1111/j.1548-1360.2008.00013.x.
Larkin, Brian
 2013 "The Politics and Poetics of Infrastructure." *Annual Review of Anthropology* 42: 327–43. http://dx.doi.org/10.1146/annurev-anthro-092412-155522.
LiPuma, Edward, and Benjamin Lee
 2004 *Financial Derivatives and the Globalization of Risk*. Durham, N.C.: Duke University Press.
MacKenzie, Donald
 2006 *An Engine, Not a Camera: How Financial Models Shape Markets*. Cambridge, Mass.: MIT Press.
 2009 "Making Things The Same: Gases, Emission Rights and the Politics of Carbon Markets." *Accounting, Organizations and Society* 34, nos. 3–4: 440–55. http:// dx.doi.org/10.1016/j.aos.2008.02.004.
Marx, Karl
 1976 *Capital*, Volume One. Translated by Ben Fowkes. New York: Penguin. Originally published in 1867.
Mazzarella, William
 2006 "Internet X-Ray: E-Governance, Transparency, and the Politics of Immediation in India." *Public Culture* 18, no. 3: 473–505. http://dx.doi.org/10.1215/ 08992363-2006-016.
Merry, Sally Engle
 2011 "Measuring the World: Indicators, Human Rights, and Global Governance." *Current Anthropology* 52, no. S3: S83–95. http://dx.doi.org/10.1086/657241.
Miyazaki, Hirokazu
 2013 *Arbitraging Japan: Dreams of Capitalism at the End of Finance*. Berkeley: University of California Press.
Moodie, Ellen
 2010 *El Salvador in the Aftermath of Peace: Crime, Uncertainty, and the Transition to Democracy*. Philadelphia: University of Pennsylvania Press.
Narayan, Kirin
 1989 *Storytellers, Saints, and Scoundrels: Folk Narrative in Hindu Religious Teaching*. Philadelphia: University of Pennsylvania Press.
Paley, Julia
 2001 *Marketing Democracy: Power and Social Movements in Post-Dictatorship Chile*. Berkeley: University of California Press.
Polanyi, Karl
 2001 *The Great Transformation: The Political And Economic Origins of Our Time*. Boston: Beacon Press. Originally published in 1944.
Polanyi, Michael
 2009 *The Tacit Dimension*. Chicago: University of Chicago Press. Originally published in 1966.

Preda, Alex
 2006 "Socio-Technical Agency in Financial Markets: The Case of the Stock Ticker." *Social Studies of Science* 36, no. 5: 753–82. http://dx.doi.org/10.1177/0306312706059543.

Priyadershini S.
 2012 "A Tea Time Story." *The Hindu*, January 28. http://www.thehindu.com/todays-paper/tp-features/tp-metroplus/a-tea-time-story/article2838319.ece.

Richard, Analiese, and Daromir Rudnyckyj
 2009 "Economies of Affect." *Journal of the Royal Anthropological Institute* 15, no. 1: 57–77. http://dx.doi.org/10.1111/j.1467-9655.2008.01530.x.

Roseberry, William
 1996 "The Rise of Yuppie Coffees and the Reimagination of Class in the United States." *American Anthropologist* 94, no. 4: 762–75. http://dx.doi.org/10.1525/aa.1996.98.4.02a00070.

Samimian-Darash, Limor
 2013 "Governing Future Potential Biothreats: Toward an Anthropology of Uncertainty." *Current Anthropology* 54, no. 1: 1–22. http://dx.doi.org/10.1086/669114.

Simmel, Georg
 1978 *The Philosophy of Money*. Translated by Tom Bottomore and David Frisby. New York: Routledge, Kegan, and Paul.

Solomon, Harris
 Forthcoming *Metabolic Living: Food, Fat, and the Absorption of Illness in India*. Durham, N.C.: Duke University Press.

Stoler, Ann Laura
 1995 *Race and the Education of Desire: Foucault's History of Sexuality and the Colonial Order of Things*. Durham, N.C.: Duke University Press.
 2002 *Carnal Knowledge and Imperial Power: Race and the Intimate in Colonial Rule*. Berkeley: University of California Press.

Sunder Rajan, Kaushik
 2005 "Subjects of Speculation: Emergent Life Sciences and Market Logics in the United States and India." *American Anthropologist* 107, no. 1: 19–30. http://dx.doi.org/10.1525/aa.2005.107.1.019.

West, Paige
 2012 *From Modern Production to Imagined Primitive: The Social World of Coffee from Papua New Guinea*. Durham, N.C.: Duke University Press.

Zaloom, Caitlin
 2003 "Ambiguous Numbers: Trading Technologies and Interpretation in Financial Markets." *American Ethnologist* 30, no. 2: 258–72. http://dx.doi.org/10.1525/ae.2003.30.2.258.
 2006 *Out of The Pits: Traders and Technology from Chicago to London*. Chicago: University of Chicago Press.

BROTHERHOOD IN DISPOSSESSION: State Violence and the Ethics of Expectation in Turkey

KABIR TAMBAR
Stanford University
http://orcid.org/0000-0003-4724-5489

In the summer of 2013, many of Turkey's cities and provinces erupted in protest. Initially sparked by a relatively small demonstration in late May to protect Gezi Park in Istanbul from demolition, the protests grew exponentially in magnitude after police forces aggressively intervened with water cannons, plastic bullets, and tear gas. Confrontations between protesters and the police continued throughout June and into July. The firing of tear-gas canisters alone killed at least two people, one individual was killed with live ammunition, and another died after being severely beaten by a police officer dressed in civilian clothes (Amnesty International 2013). On August 1, 2013, the Turkish Medical Association announced that 5 people had died, 11 had lost an eye, 106 had suffered serious head injuries, and 63 were in critical condition (Türk Tabipleri Birliği 2013).

In late June of that year, as much of the country was convulsing with these events, Selahattin Demirtaş, the co-chairman of the pro-Kurdish Peace and Democracy Party, addressed members of his party. He began not with the Gezi events but with bombings that had taken place in Roboski village in the province of Şırnak in December 2011. Two Turkish fighter jets had fired at and killed what the government claimed were militants of the Kurdistan Workers' Party (PKK) crossing the Turkish-Iraqi border.[1] It turned out that the thirty-four individuals killed were civilians, not guerrillas. They were smuggling goods, such as cigarettes, tea, and oil, and it appears that security forces were in fact well aware of

CULTURAL ANTHROPOLOGY, Vol. 31, Issue 1, pp. 30–55, ISSN 0886-7356, online ISSN 1548-1360. © by the American Anthropological Association. All rights reserved. DOI: 10.14506/ca31.1.03

these circuits of trade. Despite major protests that occurred after this incident throughout many Kurdish-majority cities in the southeast of Turkey, the official investigation did not lead to the prosecution of the guilty parties.

About ten minutes into his discussion, Demirtaş (2013) indicated that this sort of state violence did not only apply to Kurds. Asking his audience to consider the ongoing protests in Istanbul and elsewhere, he continued: "When looking from Gezi Park . . . Roboski is more easily understood." For Demirtaş, many of those looking from the debris of Gezi's barricades were members of the Turkish majority who might not have previously viewed state violence in the Kurdish provinces with much sympathy or comprehension.[2] To look from Gezi, in the assessment of Demirtaş, was to be granted the opportunity for historical insight. Demirtaş was not only alluding to recent historical events or to violence against Kurds; he proceeded to mention the Armenian genocide of the early twentieth century and episodes of violence against Alevis in the 1930s, 1970s, and 1990s. The experience of police aggression in Gezi offered its participants an unmasked look at the violent underbelly of republican statecraft.

Demirtaş did not shy away from supporting the protesters and critiquing the government's intransigent recourse to police violence in the face of dissent. However, in situating this violence within a longer history, his speech worked against efforts to celebrate the protests as spontaneous and novel, and he refused to identify the violence on display as a scandalous departure from the historical ideals of the republic. The scandal of state aggression against select members of its citizenry betrayed an all-too-familiar political form that repeated itself throughout republican history. Rather than simply denounce state violence in Gezi Park, Demirtaş pointed to its generative possibilities. He concluded his history of violence with a gesture toward a possible political future: "Confronting all of these facts [of historical violence], confronting these truths, is an opportunity. It's an opportunity to better understand one another."

I will return to Demirtaş's speech later in this essay; along the way I will discuss other discursive events that also sought to recast the historical significance and generative potential of the violence that dominated the protests. What interests me is less the constructed nature of historical narrative—a point long stressed by many scholars of nationalism—and more the way in which appeals to history act as interventions into imagined futures. As public statements, these contentious histories constitute acts of address that seek to provoke and discomfit those in their audiences who have benefited from the forms of state repression now called into question. These historical discourses not only challenge official narratives of state formation; they also call on those who have been interpellated by official history to question the violence that has informed their own investment in a political future secured by the state.

To understand the relationship between historical pasts and political futures, I find it helpful to draw on Reinhart Koselleck's (2004, 259) distinction between the space of experience and the horizon of expectation. These categories are meant to conceptualize the sinews that bind memory to anticipation. Experience is "present past, whose events have been incorporated and can be remembered." Expectation, by contrast, is "future made present . . . [directed] to the not-yet . . . to that which is to be revealed." Both of these terms, experience and expectation, are open to rival figurations. As anthropologists attuned to the temporal tropes of modernization have insisted, expectations are themselves both objects of political control and vulnerable to historical revision, open to competing social claims (Ferguson 1999; Coronil 2011; Piot 2010; Bryant 2012).

The moments depicted here sought to rearticulate past to future in ways that both exemplified the broader spirit of state critique animating the Gezi protests and that tried to establish distance from them. This estranged engagement might be understood as the tense, dialectical act of leveraging, from within the very terms that structure political life, a reflexive interrogation of its organizing categories. The commentaries I discuss in this essay revisit the history of state violence against populations labeled as minorities or threatened with that designation; at the same time, they position their own discourse as addressed to the putative majority, or those who would identify as such. What results is not primarily a set of claims to rights, resources, or recognition that presupposes the state as the site of political adjudication. Rather, the encounter yields an ethical demand on the would-be majority to recognize the histories of violence that have constituted its own sense of political identity. This essay unpacks that ethical demand.

I follow recent anthropological studies of ethics in emphasizing that any effort to step back from and reflexively evaluate social practice is a historically constituted practice in its own right, one that can be directed toward the task of transforming a subject's sensibilities and dispositions (Zigon 2007; Faubion 2011; Laidlaw 2014; Keane 2014). Traditions of ethical self-scrutiny are often most clearly defined in contexts of disciplined pedagogical authority, under the tutelage of moral guides or exemplars (Robbins 2004; Mahmood 2005). The moments I describe in this essay are ones in which a community of actors invites its addressee (the majority) to inaugurate a process of self-transformation and to disidentify from categories in which it is currently invested. However, the self-transformation in question is demanded not by a recognized authority, but by those who have been historically dispossessed, and it is addressed not to subordinates but to those who have enjoyed political privilege. My analysis explores a form of address in which those issuing the demand for transformation have lacked the authority to set the terms of speech, and where the historical privilege of the addressee manifests above all in the ability to refuse to recognize that a dialogue is even being initiated. Indeed, the inability to enjoin a response from a reticent addressee is not necessarily a product of individual communicative misfires; in the cases under study in this essay, it is a structural effect of what scholars have more generally understood as the state's symbolic and affective regulation of public life (Navaro-Yashin 2002; Cody 2011; Mazzarella 2013).

The ethical mandate I am examining arises in forms of public speech that seek to reorient the conditions of the speech setting itself or what, following Charlene Makley (2015, 454), we might term the conditions of "mediated addressivity" (see also Bakhtin 1986). The actors discussed in this essay are attempting to establish lines of communication that, while neither indifferent to nor satirical of the state's dispensation of politics (cf. Yurchak 2008; Haugerud 2012; Boyer 2013), nonetheless contravene its structuring conventions, even reversing its normative valences. In doing so, they challenge those who have historically benefited from the state's governing rationalities to identify with populations that these same administrative logics have externalized as foreigners or criminalized as terrorists. With the aim of elaborating a highly charged modality of intercommunal ethics, my account pivots around certain types of ethnographic material: moral appeals that, through both admonishment and entreaty, endeavor to transform the conditions in which the claims of the speaker might be heard by his or her interlocutor.

This essay, then, suggests that anthropologists would do well to interrogate the medium of speech and address that gives voice to the critique of violence. As a social practice, the act of criticism presupposes contexts and relations of address that are themselves products of the history of unequal power relations scrutinized by the critic (Tambar 2012; Muir 2015). The ethical force of these speech acts resides in the way they unsettle the institutional conditions of the dialogue they are attempting to commence. These dynamics are paradoxical, though productively so. They enable an ethics of expectation in which the impasses of address and nonresponse become so many indexes of a future not yet realized.

Throughout the essay, I speak of a would-be or putative majority to stress that it is a category of aspiration, rather than simply an empirical designation. The term *Türk* shelters a linguistic ambiguity between ethnic identity and legal citizenship (Bayır 2013). This ambiguity is itself symptomatic of a historical conflation of the demographic concept of majority, which is an ostensibly measurable quantity of population, with the normative concept of nation, which purports to unify political community in the state. The efforts by Demirtaş and others whom I discuss in this essay to address the majority are precisely aimed at prying open this gap, disinterring the demographic from its normative cast to reorient its horizon of expectation.

I begin by exploring how the category of minority has helped scaffold the normative subject of political modernity, the nation. The figure of the minority has been shaped by what I call a *negative historicity*: negative in the sense of being evacuated from the time and place of historical progression that has characterized the national subject. The symbolic space of national sovereignty, as it came to be defined with the birth of an international order of nation-states following World War I, renders the minority spatially displaced—seen as foreign to what may have constituted its historical homelands—and temporally suspended from the narrative tethering of national experience to expectation.

After fleshing out the negative historicity of the minority, I return to scenes of commentary adjacent to the Gezi protests, asking how their temporal interventions redirect the minority question toward an ethical inquiry into the aspiration to majority. Rather than rejecting the temporal suspension of the minority from the historical narratives of the Turkish nation, Demirtaş and others deploying this discursive maneuver summon Gezi protesters to relinquish their own sense of progressive historicity and, in effect, to embrace the negative historicity so often ascribed to the objects of state violence. They seek not so much to redeem the nation from the violence it has unleashed, as to ask whether that very violence might serve as the ground on which to produce an alternate figure of a political community to come.

THE MINORITY QUESTION

The minority question defined the founding of the Turkish Republic in 1923. I do not simply mean that, as with any nation-state, early republican leaders strove to standardize language, history, and cultural heritage in such a way as to marginalize religious and ethnic minorities. That broadly modular process was given sharper definition by the peace settlements that concluded World War I (between

1919 and 1923) and led to the emergence of the Turkish Republic. The historian Eric Weitz (2008) notes that these settlements were premised on a new conception of politics, one focused on discrete populations and the ideal of national homogeneity. He provocatively argues that this conviction enabled two seemingly contrary historical results: on the one hand, a new concern for the legal protection of minorities and, on the other hand, internationally sanctioned, forced deportations of populations from their historical homelands to new nation-states where they were now said to more authentically belong. According to Weitz, the new protections for minorities did not simply constitute a humanitarian response meant to safeguard those communities from oppressive majorities. A certain violence also formed part of those protections and of that new concern for the minority.

The formation of the Turkish state exemplifies the conundrum of minority protection and displacement at the heart of the postwar global order. From the republic's foundation in 1923, Jews, Armenian Christians, and Greek Christians were recognized as minorities and offered legal protections with regard to the autonomy of their religious organization. And yet, in the years leading up to the formation of the republican state, Armenian communities were deported or exiled from Anatolia and killed, and the Lausanne Treaty that promised minority recognition also led to the so-called population exchanges that compelled many Orthodox Greeks to leave Turkey. The category of minority came to index a process of dispossession—from rights to land, from political status, and from a sense of belonging.

In this context, a community recognized as a minority gained certain rights and protections from the state. However, this recognition also carried the weight of an extraordinary historical judgment, one that inheres in what I am calling negative historicity. At once moral and political, the negative historicity of the minority implied that the community in question was in some sense external to the nation and its history, external to the body politic, and so also of suspect loyalty, even in cases where the so-called minority population had deep historical roots in the territory now dominated by the new nation-state. Recognized as a population within the citizenry but distinct from the presumed majority, the minority constituted a figure at once included in and excluded from the biopolitics of the nation-state. If sovereignty in the republican state was constitutionally vested in the nation, those now classed as minorities would always remain ambiguously connected to this project. They were legally recognized as citizens and yet treated as suspect others. As Aron Rodrigue (2013, 44) argues, those classed as minorities "could remain Turkish citizens, but they would never be true Turks."

The ethos of suspicion was amplified by the fact that leaders of the new Turkish republic came to view the very designation of minority as a symbol of Western imperial ambitions: in demanding that the minority clauses be accepted by the new republic, Western powers encroached on the nation-state's sovereign autonomy in the very act of recognizing it (Ekmekçioğlu 2014).

Mark Mazower (1997) argues that after World War II, Western powers shifted their emphasis from collective rights to individual human rights. Yet this change in ideological accent did not lessen the stigma attached to minorities. To consider some paradigmatic examples from the mid-twentieth century, the construction of Arabs as a minority in Israel and of Muslims as a minority in India were broadly comparable to the process that shaped dominant forms of political subjectivity and state identity in Turkey several decades earlier. The histories of state formation in Israel and India were, in many respects, quite distinct: India was founded through anticolonial struggle and partitioned at the moment of independence; Israel was established through settler-colonial practices and, despite U.N.-led plans for partition, never separated into two states. In each case, however, a normative narrative of national belonging was fostered through the forced expulsion and dispossession of many of those now recognized as a minority, and those among the minority who remained had to bear the burden of proving loyalty to state authorities who viewed them as foreign (Pandey 1999; Robinson 2013). Compare also the case of Copts in present-day Egypt: intellectuals and organizations within the community continue to debate the risks of pursuing rights as a religious minority, because such a designation might mean their exclusion from statist narratives of national unity (Mahmood 2012).

The term minority (*azınlık*) in Turkey today functions more often as an accusation hurled at socially vulnerable populations than as a strictly legal-bureaucratic category for allocating resources or ensuring communal rights. It is in this context that the Jewish community, historically recognized as a minority, has anxiously debated the safety of publicly displaying religious signs, for fear of being accused of disloyalty to the state (Brink-Danan 2011). Other marginalized groups who are not recognized as minorities are nonetheless not simply accepted as part of the majority; as a result, they frequently make strident appeals to the dominant ethnoreligious imaginaries of the nation. Undocumented Bulgarian migrants, working under conditions of legal constraint and social precarity, have sought avenues of limited political inclusion by claiming ethnoreligious identification with the Turkish majority (Parla 2011). Some Turkish converts to evangelical Christianity, who remain largely unconstrained by the legal limits faced by undocumented migrants but who often suffer harassment and violence, also seek majority status. They socially distance themselves from the Armenian and Greek Orthodox Christian churches, which were labeled as minorities after Lausanne, in efforts to present themselves as authentically Turkish (Özyürek 2009). Alevi civil society groups have waged struggles for collective rights that are in fact offered to recognized minorities, like exemption from state-mandated religion courses in elementary and secondary schools, but they have overwhelmingly rejected overtures from the European Union to claim such rights under the minority designation. They justify their repudiation of the term with the claim that they are foundational elements (*asli unsur*) of the Turkish state (Tambar 2014).

These examples indicate that what appears to be a simple binary of majority-minority in fact orients a heterogeneous field of unequally positioned identities and claims. Importantly, these examples also exhibit a shared underlying assumption that the category of minority functions not only or even primarily as legal protection; it operates more potently as a mode of social recognition that groups seek to evade, protect themselves against, or overtly repudiate, because it threatens to excise the community in question from the historical past and future of the nation and its purportedly unified people.

For their part, Kurds have long been viewed by Turkish state elites as "prospective Turks" (Yeğen 2007)—that is, because of their predominantly Muslim denominational affiliation, they have often been seen as assimilable to the social, linguistic, and political norms of belonging in the Turkish nation. In moments when Kurdish organizations have been perceived as raising a fundamental threat to the Turkish state, especially acute in the past few decades with the onset of armed confrontation between the state and the PKK, Kurdish political leaders or public figures have faced accusations not simply of committing legal crimes but of being crypto-Jewish or crypto-Armenian—ethnoreligious affiliations whose minority associations mark them almost self-evidently as treasonous (Yeğen 2007; Paker 2010). Applicable even to those once considered prospective Turks, the negative historicity of the minority entails a moral sensibility that sustains ideological exclusions and justifies collective violence.

It is worth noting that the Justice and Development Party (AKP), which has established a dominant position within the Turkish government over the past decade, describes its own history as a struggle against state repression. The leader of the party and prime minister at the time of the protests, Recep Tayyip Erdoğan, commonly asserts that his party represents the oppressed (*ezilen*) who have not only been neglected but also actively marginalized by Kemalist elites. The AKP does not, however, define its constituency as a minority (*azınlık*). To the contrary, it sees itself as the authentic representative of the nation.[3] Prime Minister Erdoğan explicitly asserted this claim during the Gezi protests. Seeking to counter the globally circulating images of popular discontent, he organized a mass gathering of his own under the heading "A Meeting That Respects the National Will." In his speech, Erdoğan mentioned the military interventions that led to the execution of Prime Minister Adnan Menderes in 1961 and the banning of the Islamist Welfare Party in the late 1990s. Politicians from the AKP often reference these events as exemplifying state oppression against the line of parties and organizations from which their own party derives. Erdoğan went on to proclaim that, on each occasion, the nation (*millet*) responded at the ballot box (*Sabah* 2013). The AKP's invocation of a history of state violence contributes to its own rendering of the national subject. We will have to look elsewhere for a frontal interrogation and productive repurposing of the minority's negative historicity.

FINDING AN INTERLOCUTOR

Every week, a group called the Saturday Mothers/Peoples (Cumartesi Anneleri/insanları) hosts a public vigil to remember individuals who were forcibly detained by security forces, disappeared, and are now presumed dead. Many of the disappearances occurred in the 1980s and 1990s in the predominantly Kurdish provinces of the southeast, and so the group speaks from a similar history of violence that provided a context for Demirtaş's speech described above. In most cases, neither have the bones of the dead been returned to their families, nor have the perpetrators been brought to justice.[4] Participants in these gatherings include mothers and other relatives of the disappeared, friends, and other supporters, including lawyers working for the Human Rights Association (İnsan Hakları Derneği). Most participants, whether Kurdish or Turkish, have never been formally classed as minority in Turkey, but in drawing attention to the systematic nature of what might otherwise appear an aberrant practice of enforced disappearance, the Saturday Mothers and their supporters have struggled to expose and stage for public display the biopolitical liminality more commonly associated with minorities (Bargu 2014).

The group started to hold these weekly gatherings in 1995 and eventually stopped in 1999 because of repressive police force. They resumed them again in 2009, and while their gatherings these days by and large do not incur state intervention, police forces invariably arrive prior to their public rallies and make their presence felt by standing about a hundred yards away. Thus, the Mothers' activities have been shaped by a history of police violence and surveillance, long prior to the Gezi events. In Istanbul, they gather on İstiklal Avenue, the central pedestrian thoroughfare where the Gezi protesters were also active.[5]

At these events, participants commonly talk about relatives and friends who were forcibly disappeared, but during the summer of 2013, they connected these histories of detention and disappearance to the authorizing of police violence during the Gezi events. In reference to the latter, one participant said: "The scenario hasn't changed; only the players have changed."

Another participant commented on the fact that the prime minister had recently made a speech in a Kurdish-majority province about the peace process that the ruling government was pursuing with the PKK. In that speech, Prime Minister Erdoğan had reportedly announced: "Spring has come to the mountains and mothers will no longer cry." The speaker at the Saturday Mothers event responded by saying that in only one month, the police had killed five young people. "Are their mothers not really mothers?" he asked. The speaker here again articulated the Gezi events to a longer history of state violence, identifying continuities with an earlier era of state power that the ruling government often claims to have superseded and left behind.

Following one of the Mothers' events in July 2013, I found the opportunity to ask one of the founding members of the group about the current protests. Her brother had been detained and killed by police forces in 1995, and her family had been among the first to begin publicly gathering in protest of the disappearances. I asked her why speakers at these events persistently made reference to the Gezi protests. She responded that both cases—enforced disappearances and the current clashes between protesters and the police—involved the same phenomenon: state terror (*devlet terörü*). The discussion continued, as it often does, at a crowded tea garden tucked away on a passageway that extends from the main avenue. Another regular participant in the vigils, whose brother had also been forcibly disappeared in 1995, indicated why the group sympathized with the current protesters: as a group that has known state violence intimately, he explained, they were calling for an end to the recent acts of police brutality.

This was not the first time the Saturday Mothers had acted in solidarity with a movement dedicated to protesting state violence, especially violence against minorities. Some members of the group reported to me that they had joined annual demonstrations to commemorate and mourn the assassination of Hrant Dink, an Armenian intellectual who had been prosecuted several times for "denigrating Turkishness" and who was gunned down in 2007 by a right-wing nationalist, Ogün Samast. Photographs of Samast in custody, flanked by police officers proudly waving a Turkish flag, demonstrated to many critics that at least some members of the police supported the killer; police officers working in intelligence units have since been arrested as part of the official investigation into the murder. The connection drawn by the Mothers between these different episodes, linked by the rubric of state terror, exposes a form of officially sanctioned violence against communities whose loyalty and obedience state authorities doubt.

The historical sensibility evinced in the Saturday Mothers' gatherings in 2013 was apparent not only in their comments on state violence and its precedents in the Kurdish southeast, but also in a number of comments focused on the gatherings themselves and the mode of address they have been developing for the past twenty years. One participant exclaimed that they have been coming to this location for a long time and that only now, with the Gezi protests, they were discovering to whom they had been speaking all this time. In a more muted tone, an elderly mother asked: "Why have we been sitting here? No one has heard our voice. People come and go [past us], but without hearing our voice, and nothing has been done." Pressing the point further, she later merged her concerns about enforced disappearances in the Kurdish southeast with the Gezi protests: "What happened in Gezi Park? They were sitting in the shade over there. What was over there, was it a war? We say to everyone: Listen to our voices. End this war. Let mothers laugh a little." In her statement, the term *war* references both the three-decade armed conflict between the Turkish state and the PKK and the excessive response of the police to protesters in the park.

Undoubtedly, as with any act of public address, the speech act is heard and taken up by a range of differently positioned actors. In many respects, the Mothers' voices have reverberated more strongly in international settings than in domestic ones: Amnesty International organized sit-ins in Paris, Berlin, Sydney, and London to support the gatherings in Istanbul; the International Human Rights Association awarded the Mothers the Carl von Ossietzky Prize; and they were the subject of a documentary by a French filmmaker (Baydar and İvegen 2006, 696–97). It is nonetheless striking that many in the group, when speaking about their reception in the domestic arena, claim not to have been heard. They indicate that the communicative setting that their vigils presuppose has by and large not been recognized by their presumed addressees in the mainstream Turkish public.

The issue is not only that they have struggled to motivate legislators to reform criminal law or to inspire public prosecutors to raise cases against state officials. Beyond this legal impasse, they point to the fact that members of the putative Turkish majority have largely failed to respond to the ethical claims that the Mothers have sought to make on them. Their acts of address, iterated across years of weekly speech acts, carry the burden of creating a context of interlocution that their intended addressees have refused to recognize. The speech act presupposes a context of communication it must in fact produce. This paradox of performativity, I suggest, is not simply stifling; it produces an ethical charge that enables a sense of expectation. The ethical impetus derives from the gap between the communicative impasses the Mothers have persistently confronted and a dialogical encounter they posit as a possible future.

To draw out this argument, it is helpful to note that scholars who have examined the Saturday Mothers have broached questions concerning the ethics of the group's public presence largely by analyzing the gendered politics of motherhood. If some have argued that the group "revolutionizes the traditional maternal role" (Arat 1999, 376), others have worried that the moral resonance of motherhood risks depoliticizing the gatherings (Baydar and İvegen 2006). The idea of mothers-in-mourning seems to domesticate, within traditional gender relations, what might otherwise be taken as a deeply political protest against the violent abuses of state power. State authorities themselves appear vexed by this performance of mourning, adopting conflicting positions on its legitimacy. At certain moments, they have permitted the Mothers to convene in public with little harassment. At other times, police forces have aggressively intervened, even attacking members of the group, and on occasion detaining some participants on charges of aiding terrorism.[6] Ignored and harassed, permitted and repressed, the gatherings prove unsettling for state authorities and much of the mainstream Turkish public.

The tensions elicited by the Mothers at least in part result from how the Turkish state has invested in the morality of motherhood. The militarized masculinity of Turkish nationalism has presupposed a feminine counterpart, whether in the form of daughters, capable in some cases of participation in the military, or, more commonly, in the form of mothers, who support and "reproduce" the military nation (Altınay 2004). The recursive loop that links the morality of motherhood to the politics of national sovereignty was reactivated in the 1990s when Turkish media outlets began to report on a group of Turkish mothers who met in a cemetery on Fridays to collectively mourn the deaths of sons who, as Turkish soldiers, died as "martyrs" in the armed conflict with the PKK. Zeynep Gülru Göker (2011a, 170) notes that in nationalist media portrayals, the "mothers of the martyred" were explicitly set in contrast with the Saturday Mothers, in effect constructing a "hierarchy of grief."

The Saturday Mothers invoke recognizable tropes of motherhood—of an emotional, moral obligation toward sons—and yet repudiate militarism's gendered narrative of national reproduction. Their public vigils appear uncanny—familiar yet alien—to many in the Turkish public, including state authorities, because they rely on what is conventional in them: the dissident demanding that state officials be brought to justice is at the same moment a mother calling for public acknowledgment of her moral claim to mourn her child's death.[7]

The Saturday Mothers hold out an ethical provocation to those who would identify with the Turkish majority—a provocation to which, according to some in the group, few within that majority have been willing to rise: to recognize the moral claim of the Mothers' mourning and, in doing so, to denounce the violence of the state that acts in the majority's name. If many in the Mothers group have worried about the absence of an interlocutor, the issue only in part concerns the way in which state authorities and media outlets have censored or silenced their voices. More significantly, they are suggesting that the would-be majority can only become their addressee, responsive to their moral claims, if that majority embarks on a process of self-transformation.

The statement mentioned above, that the Mothers are just now finding an addressee, indicates that some within the majority are beginning to constitute themselves as interlocutors for the Mothers' claims, but only after having confronted police violence in the Gezi protests. The Mothers' practices of historical analogy open an explosive ethical question: what encounters with the state's security battalions would the putative majority need to endure, and thus what would that majority need to become, to see the decades-old struggle of the Saturday Mothers as part of its own political experience, formative of an expectation to come?

FROM MINORITY TO MAJORITY

As the Gezi protests unfolded, there was considerable commentary in Turkish news outlets and blogs about the extent of Kurdish involvement. Some protesters, who have seen Kurds rise up en masse to oppose state violence on countless previous occasions, were frustrated that Kurdish cities had not displayed the bold street politics for which they are often known. Many participants with whom I spoke during the protests complained that Kurdish politicians were too ambiguous in their support.[8]

Selahattin Demirtaş was not dismissive of the Gezi uprising, but he did not celebrate it either. Rather than addressing the question of why Kurds were not more forcefully joining the protests, he reversed the frame, stressing that Turks were only now seeing what their state was capable of doing to its own citizens and that they were only now experiencing a historical reality that Kurds had long known. This stance and the distance from the protest that it implied made for objects of considerable critique among Gezi activists. Several Turkish protesters, a few of whom were longtime supporters of the Kemalist Republican People's Party, described this distance to me with some bitterness. They explained that Demirtaş and the Kurdish political party he represented were involved in the peace process that the ruling government was negotiating with the PKK, and that the party did not want to upset that process by openly participating in the Gezi uprising. These protesters maintained that Kurdish politicians, who had long struggled against state authoritarianism, were now allowing realpolitik to blunt any support they might give to an antiauthoritarian protest movement.

Such explanations of political maneuver are plausible, but they underestimate the social significance of this hesitancy among many Kurds. It is important to recognize that this critical distance from the protests, accompanied by the historical sensibility that Turkish protesters were only beginning to witness forms of violence previously applied against Kurds, was not only a matter of tactical cunning on the part of a political party. It resonated with sentiments that I encountered in the course of fieldwork in Diyarbakır (a key cultural and political center of the Kurdish movement in Turkey) with Kurds hailing from a range of age cohorts and class backgrounds.

I asked a lawyer in his mid-twenties to explain the political significance of the Gezi protests, but rather than engage the question, he smirked dismissively, adding only that Turks in the western provinces of the country were just starting to grapple with issues that Kurds in the east had faced under more dire circumstances for decades. Welat, a retired man in his late sixties living in a working-class neighborhood of Diyarbakır, was less cynical in his assessment, asserting that people in his city supported the Gezi protesters. Yet he proceeded to list many of the Kurdish politicians from his neighborhood alone who had been arrested by the Turkish state during the past few decades, indicating that the history of oppression against Kurds has been ongoing for thirty to forty years. The judgment of Delal, a middle-aged woman who worked for the city's municipal government, was more attuned to the mediatized nature of the Gezi protests. She said that audiences in Europe and North America were gripped by videos of police violence against Gezi protesters, but that photographs of the injured and dead in Turkey's Kurdish-majority cities have never been permitted to circulate so widely, nor have they been viewed with such sympathy.[9]

Demirtaş's (2013) speech was grounded in and emerged from this social milieu. It is worth examining the speech in more depth because Demirtaş gave voice to popular sentiments in the form of an address, turning the hesitancy felt by many Kurds into an ethical demand on the would-be majority. It resembled, even if it was not altogether identical with, the discourse of the Saturday Mothers. While Demirtaş did not appeal to tropes of motherhood, he made recourse to a history of violence to recast the space of experience out of which the current conflagration around Gezi Park emerged. Recall that he began by describing the bombing in Roboski village, framing that event as a precedent to the more recent acts of state violence against Gezi protesters. What makes this framing more combative is the way that it serves to ground a horizon of expectation. The contentious character of this narrative tethering of memory to anticipation became apparent in the course of the speech, as Demirtaş's tone shifted from historical description to moral admonishment. This shift was marked grammatically, as Demirtaş began to directly address his audience in the second person:

> As with groups in power in the past, the habit of lying that we find in this [governing] power has a counterpart among the people. . . . I wish to remind especially those who support the prime minister and nourish his lies. . . . He lied that "the BDP [Demirtaş's political party] coercively gathers votes" . . . that "it pays children to throw stones," and you believed it [*siz inandınız*]. . . . He said that during the hunger strike [among Kurdish prisoners in 2012], "they are eating inside." You believed it [*siz inandınız*]. . . . He lied in Roboski, you believed it [*inandınız*]. . . . Now it's emerged that he lied that [Gezi protesters] were drinking alcohol in a mosque [where they were given shelter and medical care], and as if this was the first time he's lied, you started to raise objections.

The repetition of the phrase *you believed it* functions poetically, in Roman Jakobson's (1960, 369) sense: the rhythmical and patterned parallelism fosters "interaction between meter and meaning." Concentrating attention on itself, the phrase builds in importance, even as it rests on the denotationally unspecified deictic "you." To whom is Demirtaş directing this reprimand?

At the start, it is clear that Demirtaş (2013) is talking about supporters of the prime minister and his political party. Yet as he continues, the *you* he is challenging assumes greater proportions.

> Will you still believe the lie that "Armenians went around from one place to another, sometimes along the way, because of some problems, a few people were killed?" Or will you hear the truth that they suffered an officially [organized] genocide, they were officially eliminated? Alevis in Dersim, Maraş, Çorum, Sivas, Gazi were killed at the hand of official state policy. Will you now believe this truth?

The events he mentions—the Armenian genocide of the early twentieth century and violence against Alevis in the 1930s, 1970s, and 1990s—all preceded the rise of the AKP-led ruling government. They involved a constellation of state authorities and political parties that embraces much of the field of mainstream politics, across a landscape of political groups that otherwise claim to oppose one another. When Demirtaş alludes to "lies," he claims to be describing official state policy, the same policy that has been part of the ascription of negative historicity to the minority. Turkey's current government, on this account, is not the originator of those lies but has continued the tradition of adhering to them. For Demirtaş, the elision of these events of historical violence in public memory has been supported or tacitly accepted by secularists as much as Islamists, by right-wing nationalists as much as left-leaning liberals.

Demirtaş's account brings together events of violence that took place at different historical moments and, arguably, it risks flattening into a single narrative modalities of violence that are worth distinguishing—violences of different scale and acts of state repression with different mechanisms and consequences. What interests me here, however, is not simply the historiographical validity of his narrative (for instance, whether the episodes of violence against Armenians, Alevis, Kurds, and Gezi protesters constitute a single continuous history or a more heterogeneous set of agencies, interests, and effects). In line with the argumentative thrust of this essay, I want to suggest that his effort to consider these events together produces an ethical demand worth taking seriously in its own right.

Demirtaş's admonishment extended not only to the AKP's electoral base but even to some of those involved in the protests, including Kemalists and other nationalists. What is striking about the ambiguity of the "you" in Demirtaş's address is the lack of strong distinction between Kemalists and Islamists—the "white Turks" that long dominated Turkish politics and the "black Turks" that have come to power in their stead in recent decades (on the political significance of these categories, see White 2013, 46–48). This seemingly commonsense distinction of contemporary Turkish politics holds no salience here and is actively destabilized. When he says "you believed it," the *you* includes anyone who identifies with a national horizon of expectation without interrogating the experiences of violence that have produced it.

These events of violence were foundational to the history of the body politic. The violence against Armenians mentioned in the speech occurred in the waning years of the empire, in the very years when imperial elites feverishly adopted ethnic nationalism, which proved consequential in entrenching the ideological terms of nation-state formation in the following years. The episodes of violence targeting Alevis that Demirtaş mentions took place later, but in the speech itself, he invokes a string of cities (Dersim, Maraş, Çorum, etc.) immediately after mentioning the "official elimination" of Armenians. The cities become emblems of those episodes of violence and they appear, in the speech, as echoes of the founding genocide of the republic. The speech offers a history of the Gezi protests that begins not with the ruling party and its belligerent leader, nor with the neoliberal turn in state policy, but with the constituting moment of the republic itself. It implicates the form of the body politic as such, including its "counterpart among the people," who have been empowered to speak as a sovereign nation.

The political party that Demirtaş represented was the most prominent voice in mainstream politics to speak on behalf of rights and freedoms for Kurds: cultural and linguistic rights (the right to use Kurdish in elementary schools, political campaigns, and courtrooms); rights for self-governance (in proposals to decentralize certain aspects of governance to provincial levels); and the granting of amnesty to political prisoners and releasing the leader of the PKK, Abdullah Öcalan, from solitary confinement. In this particular speech, Demirtaş was not primarily concerned with these issues, which are often glossed as the "Kurdish question," but with what we might call a Turkish question.[10] He made an appeal to the putative majority not simply to question state violence, by for instance recognizing the killing of Armenians as a genocide. His was not a project aimed at redeeming the nation in a liberal vintage that is more inclusive and less authoritarian. The persistent dilemma with that kind of liberalism, in Turkey as elsewhere, is that it remains premised on the perspective of the majority, which can then offer or withhold tolerance to the marginalized (Brown 2006). The often unacknowledged statist commitments of that sort of liberalism reinforce, rather than scrutinize, the split between the progressive historicity of the nation and the negative historicity of the minority. Demirtaş's demand went further, admonishing the would-be majority for failing to push the critique of violence to the point where it implicates its own constitution as an ethnic majority. He summoned those who would see themselves as part of the Turkish majority to develop a critique of violence that not only condemns the ruling government but one that leads to a self-transformation, where it might question the very aspiration to majority status.

A POLEMICAL ETHICS

We have witnessed a flurry of debates about political futures after Gezi, much of which have centered on how the oppositional spirit of the protest might be preserved or harnessed after its conclusion. Would the uprisings yield electoral consequences damaging to the ruling party? What alternate forms of politics, aside from the ballot box, could be developed to reactivate its energy and its collaborative ethos? Or, scaling up, in what ways were the protests contributing to a global movement of resistance connected to anti-austerity protests in southern Europe, the Occupy movement in North America, or the protests around public transportation in Brazil, to name just a few (see Tuğal 2013)? The materials I have been examining in this essay permit us to remain sensitive to the temporal conditions of possibility for such debates: whose experience matters and to which political future?

The Gezi Park protests could, for instance, be interpreted as a relatively spontaneous uprising against the ruling government, its increasing controls on public sociability, its embrace of neoliberal politico-economic measures, and its intensifying hostility toward political opponents. But if, following the Saturday Mothers, we view the police actions in Gezi Park as continuous with a space of experience that includes the enforced disappearances in the 1980s and 1990s, then how would the target of the critique shift and where would the burden of responsibility for violence fall? In what ways would some of the protesters themselves, including especially those who identify as members of the Turkish majority, be implicated in the tradition of state violence being renewed by the government today? If, following Demirtaş, we wrote the history of the Gezi uprisings by beginning with the foundational violence of the Armenian genocide, how would that alter the horizon of expectation emerging from the current protests?

There is an ethical contentiousness to these questions that would be elided if, with Ernesto Laclau (2005), we rushed to discern the chains of equivalence emerging between different social and political communities. That sort of theorization could offer a plausible explanation of the pluralistic character of the protests, in which a wide variety of otherwise distinct, sometimes rival, political communities contingently articulated their disparate demands with one another, under the sign of Gezi Park and against the ruling government.[11] I am not, however, convinced that, when the Mothers and Demirtaş drew comparisons between historical events of state violence and the current confrontations with police brutality, their aim was simply to help develop a popular bloc of opposition. Rather than investing in the signifier of Gezi Park, their queries interrogated the ethical demands that an emergent political connection should make on the majority—of its responsiveness to forms of political identification that the state has long labeled as terrorism, and its willingness to claim responsibility for acts of violence committed by the state in its name.

Judith Butler (2009, 36) takes us somewhat closer to the matter at hand by outlining a notion of political obligation in terms of shared vulnerability to violence. She not only moves away from historically resonant notions of substantive (ethnic, religious, linguistic) unity but calls for a conception of political relationality that arises precisely when more conventionally nationalist notions of identification are put into question: "What is our responsibility . . . toward those who seem to test our sense of belonging or to defy available norms of likeness?" The commentaries that I have discussed largely avoid drawing on the worn tropes of national indivisibility as the ground of political unity. Instead, they highlight the increasing impossibility for those in the would-be majority to escape the violent address of security forces. State violence is not just under indictment; it leaves in its wake the terrain on which a new political community might be identified.

Certain moments of protest during the Gezi events in fact sought to build new forms of political connection on the basis of a shared vulnerability to the ongoing violence. After Medeni Yıldırım, an eighteen-year-old Kurd, was killed in the largely Kurdish town of Lice while protesting the building of a military outpost, Gezi protesters in Istanbul, Ankara, and elsewhere began to incorporate Yıldırım and Lice into their slogans. Protesters in Kadıköy, a neighborhood of Istanbul known for its middle-class, secular-nationalist Turkish inhabitants, were reportedly chanting the Kurdish phrase *Bijî biratiya gelan* ("Long live the brotherhood of the peoples"), as well as a Turkish-language slogan of solidarity, *Diren Lice, Kadıköy seninle* ("Resist Lice, Kadıköy is with you") (Schafers and İlengiz 2013). As a term meant to promote solidarity, *brotherhood* may be irreparably compromised by the patriarchal ethnonationalism that has defined its dominant usage. However, its invocation in Kurdish and its coupling with a pluralized "peoples" suggest that critical labor is being performed on the concept itself. In a context where the public use of Kurdish has been banned, censored, and discouraged, and where political officials have been accused of aiding terrorism because of their choice of linguistic code (see Jamison, forthcoming), these gestures evince a sense of responsibility toward those who unsettle "available norms of likeness."

These assertions of solidarity claim a shared vulnerability, in Butler's sense, but the question that remains open to dispute is how any such claim indexes an anticipated future. The commentaries I have examined in this essay point to common encounters with state violence, but they also lay bare the historically unequal distribution of that violence. They harbor a polemical ethics whose force derives from the way they recast the temporal valence of the minority. Confrontational rather than conciliatory, Demirtaş and the Mothers' respective discourses convey an ethical charge because they ask the majority to see its own horizon of expectation defined anew, not in relation to the privileged past of the nation, but through an experience of state violence more commonly reserved for the minority. Demirtaş and the Mothers do not present the negative historicity of the minority simply as an outrageous violation of the republic's highest ideals; that outrage stands as a precedent anticipating a political community to come. More than becoming sensitive to the plight of the minority, the would-be majority is asked to see the minority's past as prefiguring the form of its own political future.

If we were to discern in these critical discourses a nascent form of political community-in-the-making, we would have to begin with the unsettling, even paradoxical, notion that the subject of politics they project is formed on the basis of exclusions constitutive of "the people" in the republican state. This vexed reassessment of experience and expectation suggests that the oppressed minority stands as a model for the political identification of the majority. Perhaps we need a figure for political thought that, evoking the dialectical tensions that animate the materials presented here, would summon the ethnic and gendered politics of the nation-state—but only to mark their negation. A brotherhood in dispossession, let us say, which can even incorporate the dominant majority, but only to the degree that it too has faced the violence of the state as a precondition for its entry into politics.

ABSTRACT

The category of minority has been constitutive of the concept of the people in Turkey, distilling those who do not belong to the history and destiny of the nation from those who do. Minority, in this sense, is not simply a demographic classification, nor merely a matter of legal recognition. It carries the weight of a historical judgment, which scaffolds political community by delineating which populations, languages, and religions remain beyond the framework of collective obligation and responsibility. This essay examines comments delivered by a pro-Kurdish political party and a largely Kurdish mothers-of-the-disappeared group during Turkey's Gezi Park protests of 2013. These moments of public address participated in the broader spirit of state critique on display during those demonstrations. They were noteworthy, however, for recasting the Gezi events as a late occurrence in a longer history of state violence, prefigured by a century of dispossession experienced by those who have been classed as minorities or threatened with that designation. The essay asks how these invocations of history enabled interventions into imagined futures. The commentaries were not primarily aimed at repudiating the historical judgment of minority as discriminatory or contrary to law, but instead sought to delocalize the judgment vested in the category of minority, to see in that judgment an increasingly generalized economy of state violence, and to view it as prefiguring a political community to come. [futures; politics of history; ethics; protest; minorities]

NOTES

Acknowledgments   This essay has greatly benefited from the criticisms of a number of friends and colleagues. I am especially grateful to Joseph Hankins, Kelda Jamison, Banu Karaca, and Sarah Muir, who generously read multiple drafts. I also thank Faiz Ahmed, Yeşim Arat, Elif Babül, Fırat Bozçalı, Zeynep Gülru Göker, Heiko Henkel, Cemal Kafadar, David Nugent, Esra Özyürek, Öykü Potuoğlu-Cook, Joan Scott, Kamala Visweswaran, and Jarrett Zigon for their comments on the essay. Sertaç Kaya Şen provided crucial research assistance. I presented earlier versions of this essay at Boston University, Harvard University, Brown University, the London School of Economics, the University of Copenhagen, the University of Amsterdam, Koç University, Sabancı University, and Stanford University. I thank the organizers and participants at those events for their feedback. The editors and anonymous reviewers for *Cultural Anthropology* provided stimulating engagement that helped me develop the arguments. Research funding was provided by the Institute for Research in the Social Sciences and the Hellman Fellows Fund, both through Stanford University.

1.   The Partiya Karkerên Kurdistan (PKK) is a Kurdish organization that has engaged in armed struggle against the Turkish state for more than three decades.

2.   Not all participants in the protest had previously been uncritical of the Turkish state's use of force in Kurdish-majority regions. Some hailed from political communities long critical of the state, including some leftists, Alevis, Kurds, feminists, and anticapitalist Muslims. For one breakdown of class positions and political identities among the protestors, see Yörük and Yüksel 2014.

3.   In their analysis of Erdoğan's populism, S. Erdem Aytaç and Ziya Öniş (2014, 45) excerpt an apposite quotation from one of his speeches: "My story is the story of this people. Either the people will win and come to power, or the pretentious and oppressive minority—estranged from the reality of Anatolia and looking over it with disdain—will remain in power."

4.   The Saturday Mothers saw Argentina's Madres de Plaza de Mayo as a model to follow. On the similarities and differences between the two groups, see Baydar and İvegen 2006.

5.   Other Saturday Mothers groups organize activities in a number of provinces in Turkey,

especially in the Kurdish-majority southeast, where many of the disappearances took place.

6. Police harassment of the Mothers' gatherings spiked in 1998 and 1999. On the two-hundredth week, the group suspended the vigils. At that point, 431 people had been arrested, with some held in custody for up to five days, and 40 participants were put on trial (Göker 2011b, 114).

7. Compare Joan Scott's (1996) analysis of the ways in which key French feminists avowed, even as they sought to undermine, tropes of sexual difference.

8. İrfan Aktan (2013) argues that the very questioning of the Kurds' presence in the protest resulted from and helped reinforce a political framework supported by Turkish nationalists.

9. On the hesitance, even resentment, felt by many Kurds toward the Gezi protests, see also Bozçalı and Yoltar 2013.

10. To the extent that the so-called Kurdish question implicates the formation of the Turkish state and the policing of its material and imaginative boundaries, it is always already a "Turkish question" (Özsoy 2013).

11. Images juxtaposing signs of Turkish and Kurdish nationalism became iconic of this collaborative pluralism. For instance, a frequently circulated photo showed a man holding a portrait of Mustafa Kemal posing with another protester, who was holding a banner that displayed Abdullah Öcalan.

REFERENCES

Aktan, İrfan
    2013 "Gezi, Kürtlerin de parkıdır." *Bir+Bir*, June 27. http://birdirbir.org/gezi-kurtlerin-de-parkidir.

Altınay, Ayşe Gül
    2004 *The Myth of the Military-Nation: Militarism, Gender, and Education in Turkey*. New York: Palgrave Macmillan.

Amnesty International
    2013 "Gezi Park Protests: Brutal Denial of the Right to Peaceful Assembly in Turkey." EUR 44/022/2013, October. http://www.amnestyusa.org/research/reports/gezi-park-protests-brutal-denial-of-the-right-to-peaceful-assembly-in-turkey.

Arat, Yeşim
    1999 "Democracy and Women in Turkey: In Defense of Liberalism." *Social Politics* 6, no. 3: 370–87. http://dx.doi.org/10.1093/sp/6.3.370.

Aytaç, S. Erdem, and Ziya Öniş
    2014 "Varieties of Populism in a Changing Global Context: The Divergent Paths of Erdoğan and *Kirchnerismo*." *Comparative Politics* 47, no. 1: 41–59. http://dx.doi.org/10.2139/ssrn.2261178.

Bakhtin, Mikhail M.
    1986 "The Problem of Speech Genres." In *Speech Genres and Other Late Essays*, translated by Vern W. McGee, 60–102. Austin: University of Texas Press.

Bargu, Banu
    2014 "Sovereignty as Erasure: Rethinking Enforced Disappearances." *Qui Parle* 23, no. 1: 35–75. http://dx.doi.org/10.5250/quiparle.23.1.0035.

Baydar, Gülsüm, and Berfin İvegen
    2006 "Territories, Identities, and Thresholds: The Saturday Mothers Phenomenon in İstanbul." *Signs* 31, no. 3: 689–715. http://dx.doi.org/10.1086/498986.

Bayır, Derya
    2013 *Minorities and Nationalism in Turkish Law*. Surrey, U.K.: Ashgate.

Boyer, Dominic
    2013 "Simply the Best: Parody and Political Sincerity in Iceland." *American Ethnologist* 40, no. 2: 276–87. http://dx.doi.org/10.1111/amet.12020.

Bozçalı, Fırat, and Çağrı Yoltar
    2013   "A Look at Gezi Park from Turkey's Kurdistan." In "An Impromptu Uprising:
            Ethnographic Reflections on the Gezi Park Protests in Turkey," Hot Spots series
            edited by Umut Yıldırım and Yael Navaro-Yashin, *Cultural Anthropology* website,
            October   31.   http://www.culanth.org/fieldsights/396-a-look-at-gezi-park-
            from-turkey-s-kurdistan.
Brink-Danan, Marcy
    2011   *Jewish Life in Twenty-First-Century Turkey: The Other Side of Tolerance*. Bloomington:
            Indiana University Press.
Brown, Wendy
    2006   *Regulating Aversion: Tolerance in the Age of Identity and Empire*. Princeton, N.J.:
            Princeton University Press.
Bryant, Rebecca
    2012   "Partitions of Memory: Wounds and Witnessing in Cyprus." *Comparative Studies
            in Society and History* 54, no. 2: 332–60. http://dx.doi.org/10.1017/
            S0010417512000060.
Butler, Judith
    2009   *Frames of War: When is Life Grievable?* New York: Verso.
Cody, Francis
    2011   "Publics and Politics." *Annual Review of Anthropology* 40: 37–52. http://dx.
            doi.org/10.1146/annurev-anthro-081309-145626.
Coronil, Fernando
    2011   "The Future in Question: History and Utopia in Latin America (1989–2010)."
            In *Business as Usual: The Roots of the Global Financial Meltdown*, edited by Craig
            Calhoun and Georgi Derlugian, 213–64. New York: New York University Press.
Demirtaş, Selahattin
    2013   "BDP Grup Toplantısı." June 18. https://youtu.be/6WXaA7yaNd8.
Ekmekçioğlu, Lerna
    2014   "Republic of Paradox: The League of Nations Minority Protection Regime and
            the New Turkey's Step-Citizens." *International Journal of Middle East Studies* 46,
            no. 4: 657–79. http://dx.doi.org/10.1017/S0020743814001007.
Faubion, James D.
    2011   *An Anthropology of Ethics*. Cambridge: Cambridge University Press.
Ferguson, James
    1999   *Expectations of Modernity: Myths and Meanings of Urban Life on the Zambian Copperbelt*.
            Berkeley: University of California Press.
Göker, Zeynep Gülru
    2011a   "The Politics of Silence: Discussing Deliberative and Agonistic Democracy vis-
            à-vis Gendered Responses to the Militarization of Everyday Life in Turkey." PhD
            dissertation, City University of New York.
    2011b   "Presence in Silence: Feminist and Democratic Implications of the Saturday Vigils
            in Turkey." In *Social Movements, Mobilization, and Contestation in the Middle East
            and North Africa*, edited by Joel Beinin and Frédéric Vairel, 107–24. Stanford,
            Calif.: Stanford University Press.
Haugerud, Angelique
    2012   "Satire and Dissent in the Age of Billionaires." *Social Research* 79, no. 1: 145–
            68. http://dx.doi.org/10.1353/sor.2012.0018.
Jakobson, Roman
    1960   "Closing Statement: Linguistics and Poetics." In *Style in Language*, edited by
            Thomas A. Sebeok, 350–77. Cambridge, Mass.: MIT Press.
Jamison, Kelda
    Forthcoming   "Hefty Dictionaries in Incomprehensible Tongues: Commensurating Code
            and Language Community in Turkey." *Anthropological Quarterly*.

Keane, Webb
    2014 "Affordances and Reflexivity in Ethical Life: An Ethnographic Stance."
          Anthropological Theory 14, no. 1: 3–26. http://dx.doi.org/10.1177/
          1463499614521721.
Koselleck, Reinhart
    2004 *Futures Past: On the Semantics of Historical Time.* Translated by Keith Tribe. New
          York: Columbia University Press.
Laclau, Ernesto
    2005 *On Populist Reason.* New York: Verso.
Laidlaw, James
    2014 *The Subject of Virtue: An Anthropology of Ethics and Freedom.* Cambridge: Cambridge
          University Press.
Mahmood, Saba
    2005 *Politics of Piety: The Islamic Revival and the Feminist Subject.* Princeton, N.J.:
          Princeton University Press.
    2012 "Religious Freedom, the Minority Question, and Geopolitics in the Middle East."
          Comparative Studies in Society and History 54, no. 2: 418–46. http://dx.doi.org/
          10.1017/S0010417512000096.
Makley, Charlene
    2015 "The Sociopolitical Lives of Dead Bodies: Tibetan Self-Immolation Protest as
          Mass Media." *Cultural Anthropology* 30, no. 3: 448–76. http://dx.doi.org/
          10.14506/ca30.3.05.
Mazower, Mark
    1997 "Minorities and the League of Nations in Interwar Europe." *Daedalus* 126, no.
          2: 47–63. http://www.jstor.org/stable/20027428.
Mazzarella, William
    2013 *Censorium: Cinema and the Open Edge of Mass Publicity.* Durham, N.C.: Duke
          University Press.
Muir, Sarah
    2015 "The Currency of Failure: Money and Middle-Class Critique in Post-Crisis
          Buenos Aires." *Cultural Anthropology* 30, no. 2: 310–35. http://dx.doi.org/
          10.14506/ca30.2.10.
Navaro-Yashin, Yael
    2002 *Faces of the State: Secularism and Public Life in Turkey.* Princeton, N.J.: Princeton
          University Press.
Özsoy, Hişyar
    2013 "Introduction: The Kurds' Ordeal with Turkey in a Transforming Middle East."
          Dialectical Anthropology 37, no. 1: 103–11. http://dx.doi.org/10.1007/s10624-
          013-9297-y.
Özyürek, Esra
    2009 "Christian and Turkish: Secularist Fears of a Converted Nation." *Comparative
          Studies of South Asia, Africa, and the Middle East* 29, no. 3: 398–412. http://dx.
          doi.org/10.1215/1089201X-2009-027.
Paker, Evren Balta
    2010 "Dış Tehditten İç Tehdide: Türkiye'de Doksanlarda Ulusal Güvenliğin Yeniden
          İnşası." In *Türkiye'de Ordu, Devlet ve Güvenlik Siyaseti,* edited by Evren Balta Paker
          and İsmet Akça, 407–31. Istanbul: Bilgi Üniversitesi Yayınları.
Pandey, Gyanendra
    1999 "Can a Muslim Be an Indian?" *Comparative Studies in Society and History* 41, no. 4:
          608–29. http://www.jstor.org/stable/179423.
Parla, Ayşe
    2011 "Labor Migration, Ethnic Kinship, and the Conundrum of Citizenship in Turkey."
          Citizenship Studies 15, nos. 3-4: 457–70. http://dx.doi.org/10.1080/
          13621025.2011.564809.

Piot, Charles
    2010   *Nostalgia for the Future: West Africa after the Cold War*. Chicago: University of Chicago Press.

Robbins, Joel
    2004   *Becoming Sinners: Christianity and Moral Torment in a Papua New Guinea Society*. Berkeley: University of California Press.

Robinson, Shira
    2013   *Citizen Strangers: Palestinians and the Birth of Israel's Liberal Settler State*. Stanford, Calif.: Stanford University Press.

Rodrigue, Aron
    2013   "Reflections on Millets and Minorities: Ottoman Legacies." In *Turkey Between Nationalism and Globalization*, edited by Riva Kastoryano, 36–46. New York: Routledge.

Sabah
    2013   "Başbakan Erdoğan Kazlıçeşme'de Konuştu." June 16. http://www.sabah.com.tr/gundem/2013/6/16/basbakan-erdogan-kazlicesmede-konusuyor.

Schafers, Marlene, and Çiçek İlengiz
    2013   "Improbable Encounters: Marching for Lice in Kadıköy." In "An Impromptu Uprising: Ethnographic Reflections on the Gezi Park Protests in Turkey." Hot Spots series edited by Umut Yıldırım and Yael Navaro-Yashin, *Cultural Anthropology* website, October 31. http://www.culanth.org/fieldsights/404-improbable-encounters-marching-for-lice-in-kadikoy.

Scott, Joan W.
    1996   *Only Paradoxes to Offer: French Feminists and the Rights of Man*. Cambridge, Mass.: Harvard University Press.

Tambar, Kabir
    2012   "Islamic Reflexivity and the Uncritical Subject." *Journal of the Royal Anthropological Institute* 18, no. 3: 652–72. http://dx.doi.org/10.1111/j.1467-9655.2012.01781.x.
    2014   *The Reckoning of Pluralism: Political Belonging and the Demands of History in Turkey*. Stanford, Calif.: Stanford University Press.

Tuğal, Cihan
    2013   "'Resistance Everywhere': The Gezi Revolt in Global Perspective." *New Perspectives on Turkey* 49: 157–72. http://dx.doi.org/10.1017/S0896634600002077.

Türk Tabipleri Birliği
    2013   "Göstericilerin sağlık durumları/The Health Status of the Demonstrators." August 1. http://www.ttb.org.tr/index.php/Haberler/veri-3944.html.

Weitz, Eric D.
    2008   "From the Vienna to the Paris System: International Politics and the Entangled Histories of Human Rights, Forced Deportations, and Civilizing Missions." *American Historical Review* 113, no. 5: 1313–43. http://dx.doi.org/10.1086/ahr.113.5.1313.

White, Jenny
    2013   *Muslim Nationalism and the New Turks*. Princeton, N.J.: Princeton University Press.

Yeğen, Mesut
    2007   "'Jewish-Kurds' or the New Frontiers of Turkishness." *Patterns of Prejudice* 41, no. 1: 1–20. http://dx.doi.org/10.1080/00313220601118736.

Yörük, Erdem, and Murat Yüksel
    2014   "Class and Politics in Turkey's Gezi Protests." *New Left Review* 89: 103–23. http://newleftreview.org/II/89/erdem-yoruk-murat-yuksel-class-and-politics-in-turkey-s-gezi-protests.

Yurchak, Alexei
    2008   "Necro-Utopia: The Politics of Indistinction and the Aesthetics of the Non-Soviet." *Current Anthropology* 49, no. 2: 199–224. http://dx.doi.org/10.1086/526098.

Zigon, Jarrett
    2007   "Moral Breakdown and the Ethical Demand: A Theoretical Framework for an Anthropology of Moralities." *Anthropological Theory* 7, no. 2: 131–50. http://dx.doi.org/10.1177/1463499607077295.

DECOMPOSITION AS LIFE POLITICS: Soils, *Selva*, and Small Farmers under the Gun of the U.S.-Colombian War on Drugs

KRISTINA LYONS
University of California, Santa Cruz
http://orcid.org/0000-0003-2832-9425

Having momentarily broken away from the group, I stood, waiting in silence, between rows of climbing plants, fruit trees, beds of tubers, and shrubs. The sunflowers by my side leaned forward only slightly. A nearly imperceptible breeze caused the vines to quiver. The scent of rotting fruit rinds rose up from the ground. There was a distant flap of wings. Much closer, I could hear larvae chewing on the granadilla leaves and insects humming from within knotty bundles and flower petals. It was cooler here, and the humming grew more intense. My only words for it, a hundred damp index fingers gliding around the rims of water glasses. Life as it pulsates, withers, draws at once a next and last breath. This was the distinct sound—better yet, force—permeating the air when I first stepped off the bus in San Miguel, Putumayo, at the Amazonian farm school La Hojarasca, which means "litter layer" or, more colloquially, decomposing leaves often used as compost. Groups of farmers were conversing next to a wooden table lined with seeds as big as fists, others as tiny as mites. Hens and wild turkeys roamed about trampling through the underbrush. A family of geese honked noisily as they descended on their lunch of minced sugarcane. There was the crunch of boots pressing down on layers of decaying leaves and stalks, a sound quite distinct from the squish of shoes sliding against bare mud. I heard the slice of a machete, the heavy thump of copoazú when the fruit hit the ground, laughter, buzzing, and the friction of scraped stone as bore leaves were ground into grain. The trees were lined with mochilero nests, and every so often I could make out the birds' call—the sound of water, the reverberation of a drop of water, that almost-electric sound it makes in the

CULTURAL ANTHROPOLOGY, Vol. 31, Issue 1, pp. 56–81, ISSN 0886-7356, online ISSN 1548-1360. © *by the American Anthropological Association. All rights reserved. DOI: 10.14506/ca31.1.04*

exact moment it hits a surface and morphs into disparate forms. I failed to sense Heraldo's presence until I heard a voice call out from behind. "Wouldn't you agree," he asked as he approached where I stood in the middle of the creeping plant garden, "life makes life happier?"

Figure 1. A small farm in the Andean-Amazonian foothills of Colombia.
Photo by Kristina Lyons.

From April 2008 to March 2011, and again between June 2013 and April 2014, I conducted fieldwork in and around the southwestern frontier state of Putumayo among small farming families, rural social movements, soil scientists, state officials, armed actors, and aid workers. Referred to as the gateway to Colombia's Amazon, Putumayo shares borders with Ecuador and Peru, and transitions from central Andean foothills into the extensive Amazonian plains that comprise 85 percent of its territory. With 66,022 hectares of commercial coca under cultivation in 2000, the year the bilateral U.S.-Colombian antinarcotics policy Plan Colombia commenced, Putumayo produced around 40 percent of the nation's illicit coca (UNODC 2005). The region quickly became the focus of militarized eradication, as well as state and U.S. Agency for International Development (USAID) crop-substitution efforts. The global militarization of the drug war in the 1980s became more explicitly intertwined after 9/11, with the hemispheric conflation of counternarcotic and counterterrorism wars. This merger resulted in a series of military surges into southern Colombia, where the oldest and largest leftist guerilla group in the country—the Revolutionary Armed Forces of Colombia (FARC-EP)—and right-wing paramilitary groups operating with the complicity of state military and police forces had battled over territory and control of the cocaine trade since the 1980s. After the official demobilization in 2006 of the umbrella paramilitary organization, the United Self-Defense Forces of Colombia (AUC), paramilitaries are said to no longer exist.[1] Yet overwhelming evidence suggests that mid-level commanders failed to demobilize or simply reorganized into countrywide narcocriminal structures, such as Los Rastrojos, Los Urabeños, or Los Constructores, which continue to operate in Putumayo. The Colombian government now refers to these groups as *bacrim* (emergent criminal bands).

Since 2000, Plan Colombia has provided around $9 billion in supply-side drug interdiction assistance. As much as 75 percent of aid has been invested in provisioning weapons, equipment, technical assistance, and training for Colombian military and police through contracts with U.S.-based multinationals like Monsanto, Sikorsky Aircraft, and Dyncorp International (Beittel 2012). For twenty years, forced eradication strategies relied on a controversial aerial fumigation program that remains a heated topic of science wars disputing its environmental and public health risks. The program consisted in deploying crop-duster planes to spray a concentrated formula of Monsanto's herbicide glyphosate over suspected illicit crops.[2] Aerial aspersion operations were coupled with manual eradication by contracted workers who were sent, accompanied by the military and police, to rip out whatever stubborn coca plants remained after crop dusters passed overhead. In Putumayo alone, 277,849 hectares have been aerially fumigated since 2000, and 82,780 hectares of coca have been manually eradicated since 2004.[3] Despite this, Putumayo continues to produce 20 percent of the country's illicit coca, exemplifying long-standing critiques of the effectiveness of repressive eradication strategies in achieving permanent national reductions in illicit crops (UNODC 2015). A long-awaited resolution to suspend aerial fumigation with glyphosate was issued by the Colombian government on May 29, 2015, in the wake of a report published by the World Health Organization's cancer research arm declaring the world's most widely used herbicide a probable carcinogen to humans. It is still unclear what policy will come to replace aerial spraying after the National Environmental Licensing Agency (ANLA) suspended the license to use glyphosate in aerial fumigation operations on October 1, 2015.

Colombia, up until that point, was the only country in the world to implement aerial fumigation as a counternarcotic strategy.

I began fieldwork in the Andean-Amazonian foothills in 2004, at the height of renewed critiques of Plan Colombia. Through the ensuing years, as I returned to Putumayo for further research, to film a popular education project, and to accompany farmers during the 2013 National Agrarian, Ethnic, and Popular Strike, I was struck not so much by the kinds of violence and ecological destruction produced by the War on Drugs, but rather by the tenacious vitality of life in the midst of war. Indeed, what most impacted me when I first arrived at La Hojarasca in 2007 was the pulsation the farm school was generating, literally resonating by its very existence in the midst of a criminalized ecology. It was bundles of life pulsating away—dense entanglements of diverse plants, decomposing leaves and rootlets, the buzz of insects, the sounds of small animals and birds cloaked by *selva* canopy—that allowed it to carve out a transformative space for itself, even if precariously so. This was not a space where life was simply enduring within social suffering and contamination, but rather one where other modes of eating, growing, seeing, exchanging, cultivating, and hence, decomposing were being set in motion—what the farmers I met refer to as *selva* or *agricultura amázonica* (Amazonian agriculture). While *selva* is often translated into English as "jungle"— a word imbued with a complex colonial history and civilizatory connotations—I continue to use the Spanish word *selva* throughout this article, because I learned from farmers to treat *selva* as a concept, analytic, and relation, rather than as an entity that can easily be divided into units or reduced to a representational land-scape descriptor. Furthermore, these farmers explained that the word *forest* does not necessarily convey biodiversity, since it may refer to a monocrop or arrange-ments of commercial timber. Indeed, my research questions and political com-mitments were deeply impacted by this pulsating farm, La Hojarasca, and I set out to explore the contrasting logics of life and death, the kinds of possibilities and foreclosures for both living and dying, in a tropical forest ecology under military duress. What I learned was that rather than on productivity—one of the central elements of modern capitalist growth—the regenerative potential of these ecologies relies on organic decay, impermanence, decomposition, and even a robust fragility that complicates modernist bifurcations of living and dying. This allows, I argue, for ecological imaginaries and life processes that do not depend on productivity or growth to strive into existence.

PEACE THROUGH POISON

"The general did not mince words. He said it like this: 'The only solution is to arm yourself, leave, die, or figure something out.'"

—Small farmer, Piñuña Blanco, Putumayo, August 2013

At times I heard farmers in Putumayo speculate that not only herbicides but also biological weapons had been released in covert experiments to attack coca crops. They described swarms of black butterflies descending on fields, and a pathogenic fungus—*Fusarium oxysporum*—infecting forest floors.[4] However, the butterflies' larval offspring seemed to munch on just about anything besides coca leaves, and suspiciously mirrored the way spray-drift from aerial fumigation most often kills staple foods, pasture grass, forest canopy, and even USAID alternative development crops rather than targeted illicit plants. Furthermore, alternative development programs have tended to follow the same market logic of commercial coca, largely failing to substitute illicit export-oriented crops with legal market-oriented varieties, such as pepper, coffee, vanilla, heart of palm, and cacao.[5] I clearly remember the day I accompanied a farmer as she pointed to a row of dying cacao plants that were part of a USAID crop substitution pact that local communities had signed, and that had been fumigated two weeks earlier. "There is no way to say this," the woman told me. We stood for a long while in her field in silence. A group of indignant neighbors gathered near the front of the house displaying deformed plantains, wilted husks, and more cacao and pepper leaves riddled with holes and spots. Others expressed growing uncertainties about the protracted life span of chemical agents in human bodies, soils, and watersheds. Antidrug policy "*está acabando con la vida* [is finishing off life]," they said. Toxicity seemed likely. One waited to be deprived of the resources that allow living beings to thrive—at any moment the sting of a droplet, a dampened leaf, inhibited enzyme, and the end to synthesis—a strangling of life from the inside out. It was not lost on this woman or any of her neighbors that their life staple had been excised so that life elsewhere, and in the wounded soil itself, could claim to be protected and flourish.

Cocaleros (coca growers) have argued since the first massive coca growers' protests in southwestern Colombia in 1996 that repressive antidrug policy produces a cocriminalization of "natures" and "subjects"—plants and people (Ramírez 2001). A criminalized nature is no longer the object of conservation or protection, and is perceived to be in cahoots with a criminal subject rendered ineligible for humanitarian aid even when public policies turn people into internally displaced populations and refugees. On the one hand, the Colombian government has been willing to aerially fumigate its national parks and the biodiverse Amazon Basin. On the other, Law 30, passed in 1986, criminalizes the cultivation of marijuana, coca, and opium poppies in excess of twenty plants. This places small growers, who account for around 70 percent of coca cultivation (UNODC 2005), and large-scale traffickers in the same legal category by ignoring the structural forces that lead individuals and families to settle in rural frontier zones and resort to illicit livelihoods in the first place.

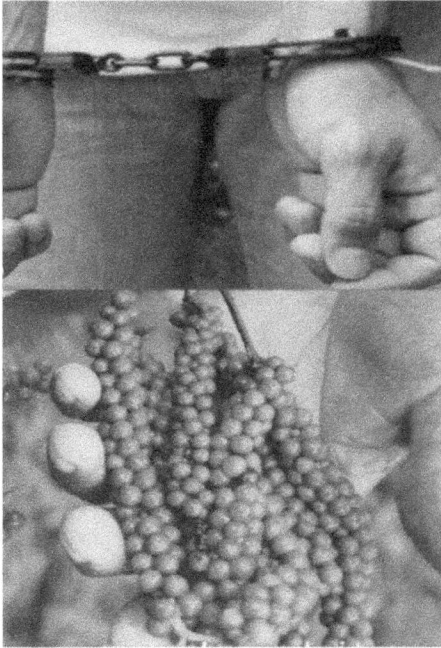

Figure 2. USAID postcard distributed during the 2009 *Volvamos a la Vida* campaign.

It is a liberal way of making and justifying the ongoing nature of war that wraps various kinds of killing within an imaginary of safeguarding and life-making narratives. Killing is posed within a "future perfect" tense (Povinelli 2011a, 167) as a necessary redemptive mode of birth that will bring new beings and domains of social life—in this case, the geopolitical intervention of liberal moralities, such as rule of law, culture of legality, public health, and licit capitalist-based economies—into existence. The capacity to make live rests on the necessity to make die, rendered evident in the dual meanings of the Colombian Spanish word *arrancar* (as in *arrancar la coca*). *Arrancar* means to start something—an engine, for example—and also to uproot or rip out, a violent cleansing or weeding out that pries open the space for regrowth. A 2009 *Volvamos a la Vida* (Back to Life) campaign organized by USAID in Putumayo posed what one government official called "reflective questions about the social drawbacks of cultivating illicit crops." Postcards distributed during the campaign starkly contrasted black-and-white images with images in color. They read: "Live or die? Smile or cry? What kind of life are we sowing?" and pose a moral choice between pepper harvests or handcuffs, saxophones or headstones, goalie kicks or toes tagged in a morgue. *La mata que mata* (the plant that kills, according to stigmatizing state campaigns) must be purged from soils and souls. A disavowal of criminal mentalities—crime blamed on a primitive form of individual propensity—becomes necessary for *cocaleros'* resuscitation not only back into the nation's productive citizenry but also back to what state and USAID officials sanction as a better and more dignified life than the social and literal death supposedly produced by an illicit livelihood.

At first glance, it seems possible to situate the chemical warfare and overall eradication component of antidrug policy within other biopolitical histories and formations of killing: in this case, one in which a future peace is actively pursued through present acts of poisoning.[6] However, at stake at the heart of antidrug policy is not only the taking of the biological life of a plant or the severing of illicit human-plant relations in the defense of security, territory, and population in the context of international pressures to wage a war against narcotic drugs. Rather, it is the increasingly evident association between eradication efforts and the expansion of a national development model euphemistically referred to as a *locomotora minero-energética*, which I roughly translate as "mining-energy locomotive" (Departamento Nacional de Planeación 2010). In 2011, more than half of Putumayo, along with several neighboring regions, was reclassified from Amazonian territory to Special Mining District, accelerating oil production from 8,000 barrels a day in 2000 to 48,000 in 2013 (Calle 2014). The biodiverse ecosystems of the Andean-Amazonian foothills have never been conceived of as anything other than a commodity frontier, beginning in the nineteenth century with the voracious extraction of quinine, rubber, and timber, and followed in the twentieth century by intensified oil exploitation and the boom-and-bust waves of monoculture coca (Aguilar 1999; Taussig 1984). These extractive activities violently dispossessed native indigenous populations and propelled the modern colonization of the region, as well as the sporadic extension of the nation's agricultural frontier. Waves of small farmers, urban dwellers, and indigenous peoples not originary to the western Amazon were driven to occupy the territory due to land concentration in the country's Andean interior, increasing urban poverty and ongoing political violence since the 1940s (Ariza, Ramírez, and Vega 1998).[7]

The prevailing analysis among rural communities living in coca-growing regions is that antidrug policy has allowed for an intensified and qualitatively different mode of transnational capitalist expansion, linking the role of foreign direct investment in war through the securitization of development. Antidrug policy has become a pretext not only to wage a war against the people (*guerra contra los pueblos*) (Paley 2014) but also to wage a war against life (*guerra contra la vida*). Or, similarly, a war waged in defense of growth at the expense of all forms of life. In the process, a variety of social values become reduced to one exchange value, and a diversity of ecologies, ethics, and practices said to produce death in life (that is, illicit coca cultivation), or that cannot be assimilated to or openly resist growth-oriented and extractive-based priorities, are actively dismissed or rendered impossible. Indeed, rural communities in Putumayo perceive militarized aerial fumigation as yet another violent attempt to weaken their will: one mode of destroying the material base and food crops of local sustenance, starving them out in an effort to force the abandonment of territory that facilitates industrial oil and mining concessions. Moreover, Colombia's Law 160, passed in 1997, prohibits the titling of land within a five-kilometer radius of oil or mining exploitation. Small farmers argue that this law contributes to the ongoing concentration of land and the precarity of property titles in a country that has never undergone a lasting history of agrarian reform.[8]

It is *life*, and not only human rights or land rights, that has come to the fore in rural struggles against extractivism, GMO seeds, biofuels, and other forms of industrialized agriculture, large-scale infrastructural projects, free-trade agreements, and all sorts of neoliberal reforms privatizing public goods and services and fomenting transnational capitalist growth throughout the hemisphere. Of course, development has always signaled more than just material progress and economic growth indicators: it has marked a historically specific model of judgment and control over life itself. Although modern capitalist principles such as growth, progress, better living, and their correlate—more development—have been thoroughly repudiated in theoretical debates emerging in the global South since the mid-twentieth century, these principles remain politically and economically dominant (Escobar 2011, 2014). A new set of struggles over the definitions of and relations between nature and resources has become one of the most salient features of contemporary Latin American political dynamics in both overtly neoliberal regimes and in self-declared post-neoliberal ones. Economic convergence around a growth-oriented development model—mostly a wave of neoextractivism—can be witnessed across ideologically opposed progressive leftist and conservative governments (Gudynas 2014; Veltmeyer and Petras 2014; Bebbington and Bury 2013). It becomes crucial, therefore, to ask: What kinds of radical politics or structural transformations can exist if socioenvironmental justice and sociopolitical inclusion tend to be fueled through the same modern, capitalist-based model of extraction? Indeed, what relations to life and death, place and territory will be potentiated and which others will continue to be criminalized, rendered obsolete, or sacrificed in the name of national growth and social(ist) good? These questions lie at the heart of Colombia's ongoing national peace process between FARC-EP guerrillas and the state as the country continues to debate its socioeconomic-environmental future, including the terms of a democratic reformulation of antidrug policy and integral agrarian reform in a possible post-conflict scenario of transitional justice.[9]

THE CULTIVATION OF COUNTERLIFE AND DEATH

Rather than ask what it means for rural communities to live in coca-growing regions that have been epicenters of Colombia's violence, I follow the practices that make life possible in a criminalized and poisoned ecology. How do people keep on cultivating a garden, caring for forest, or growing food when at any moment a crop-duster plane may pass overhead, dousing entire landscapes with herbicides? Beyond official policy imperatives to "uproot (coca) or be uprooted"—extract or be extracted from—what other potentialities and limits emerge among communities that are responding to war by cultivating life, which is not altogether separate from death? I came to these research questions from a shared conceptual ground built through my long-term relationships with a dispersed network of farmers whom I first met at La Hojarasca. These farmers did not tell me stories of social suffering and abandonment or the endurance against all odds of precarious life (Nouvet 2014; Allison 2013; Das 2006; Biehl 2005). Nor did they dwell on modern life rendered meaningful only by denouncing its finitude, and thus animating biopolitical logics that aim to optimize, regulate, and police all sorts of transgressors against proper human ways of living and dying (Stevenson 2014; Zeiderman 2013). Instead, they obliged me to depart from a biopolitical register that distinguishes between life and death, and between human life and the well-being of other entities to make an ethico-analytical move and pay careful attention to processes of human and nonhuman material composition and decomposition. The farmers did not describe a romantic relationship with the *selva*, but rather what and how they were learning from the recycling nature of *hojarasca*—rot, decay, and regeneration—which emerges along with the cultivation of experimental practices on farms and forests in the midst of war. The agrarian-based material practices and corresponding life philosophies they shared open up ways of thinking about the different kinds of political, economic, and ecological relationalities that emerge when life and death are no longer (or never could be) experienced as oppositional categories or morally dictated ultimates.

My work is influenced by scholarship at the interface of anthropology and feminist science studies that critically bypasses a modern nature/culture divide and a cascade of associated distinctions (such as objects/subjects, bio/geo, and organic/inorganic) to arrive at processual understandings of life that necessarily reconceive our notions of the human, and consequently of politics and ethics (Tsing 2011; de la Cadena 2010; Stengers 2010; Haraway 2008; Mol 2008; Barad 2007; Verran 2002). However, rather than concentrate on realized things or achieved political events, which has been the focus of much of the twentieth century's and, especially, the international left's political thinking, I build on scholarship that emphasizes everyday transformations in the ways people produce, reproduce, consume, and hence compost their material worlds (Puig de la Bellacasa 2013; Papadopoulos, Stephenson, and Tsianos 2008; Gibson-Graham 2006). In particular, I focus on what these processes of decomposition and renewal may tell us about the everyday practices through which not only people but entire ecologies—trees, soils, plants, seeds, insects, chickens, microbes, and farmers— strive to collectively change the conditions of their lives. They do so not by transcending these conditions, but rather by sinking into them, slowly turning them over, aerating, and breathing in new life that also potentiates different possibilities for and relations to death.

I draw on Elizabeth Povinelli's (2011a, 2011b, 2011c; Povinelli and Berlant 2014) and Kathleen Stewart's (2007) discussions of potentiality to open up ways of thinking about how alternative life processes—always at risk of disappearing and with no guarantees—come to shake loose, to whatever degree possible, from dominant definitions to set something else in motion. Not in the sense of denouncing the world in the name of an ideal world, or in the rush to push aside one set of object and subject positionalities to replace it with another, but rather in the ways that bodies, dreams, and socioecological relations of all kinds strive to pick up density and texture without necessarily being rooted in fixed conditions of possibility. I depart from Povinelli's work in that I am interested not only in potentiality but also in the actualizations germinating in the very thickness of the present. The creative emergences and actual work occurring in the present when cultivating different conditions for life and death also constitute a contestatory act motivated by what farmers in Putumayo describe as "propositional rage" (Mesa Regional de Organizaciones Sociales 2015). Propositional rage not only opposes or denounces current social conditions but also works to cultivate alternatives to the asymmetric forces that make certain ecologies thrive at the expense of forcing others to endure.

It was a dispersed group of farmers in Putumayo, including my closest farmer friend and intellectual colleague, Heraldo Vallejo, who rejected commercial coca since its arrival in the region in 1977, even though they respect coca leaves as medicine, sustenance, spiritual substance, and a constitutive element of local biodiversity. These farmers argue that both monoculture coca and its official alternatives force not only people, but all the life forms with whom they live and labor, into dependent relations with market-based goods, modes of exchange, and values. They critique this singular economic logic, in part, because it treats commodity exchange as a founding principle of agrosociality, assuming that small farmers are simply poor farmers lacking the proper technology, financial capital, alliances, and work ethic to become full-blown agroindustrial farmers. This kind of economic model dismisses small farming as an obsolete livelihood of the past. It has also turned Putumayo into a laboratory for public policies gone awry by denying the cultural particularities of small farming families and economies, as well as the ecological conditions of a particular Amazonian territory. Heraldo is an animal husbandry technician, and one of two students from his rural elementary school who finished high school and went on to study at the closest university in the neighboring Andean state of Nariño. Following graduation and imprisonment as a leftist student leader, he returned to Putumayo to, as he says, "unlearn" the dominant teachings of agricultural science. He uses the term *agricultura de la muerte* (agriculture of death) to refer to the extractive-based practices that result when farmers begin to perceive themselves as external to, rather than conforming relations within Andean-Amazonian ecologies. Concretely, *agriculture of death* refers to the use of chemical inputs, patented and transgenic seeds, monoculture and export-oriented crops, land-titling premised on deforestation, a singular notion of the market, and neoliberal reforms implemented during the past two decades—all of which strangle and attempt to render obsolete diverse small-farming practices and economies.[10]

For two years, I spent at least part of every day accompanying Heraldo and other farmers as they worked on their farms to turn them into collective spaces of *aprendizaje e intercambio* (learning and exchange). They conceive of their farms as spaces of learning rather than knowing, and contrasted them with the model farms that form part of conventional state agricultural extension. Rather than teach standardized technical models intended to be replicated from one farm to the next, these farmers strive to multiply biodiversity across farms by engaging in the production of what Heraldo calls *conocimiento vivo* (live or living knowledge). Living knowledge results from ongoing experimental processes in gardens, orchards, and forests precisely because seeds, soils, plants, and trees become entities through recursive relationalities that are always in the making, awaiting their next realization based on different socioecological conditions, human aptitudes, and imaginaries. Given the historic lack of agroecologically appropriate state-based technical assistance, the decades of breached political agreements on the part of the national government after previous civilian protests and mobilizations, and the ways both monocrop coca and repressive antidrug policy have largely eliminated local food production, these farmers have come to provide an informal regional network of alternative agricultural technical assistance. Thus I also joined them when they worked in solidarity with small-farming associations, unions, and indigenous communities interested in gradually transitioning from commercial coca, USAID development models, and other unsustainable agricultural systems to what they refer to as *selva* or Amazonian practices. This included attending popular education workshops with the Regional Working Group of Social Organizations of Putumayo, Baja Bota Caucana, and Cofanía, Jardines de Sucumbíos Nariño; Inga and Nasa indigenous reservations; guardians of seeds networks; and rural communities that form part of the environmental clinic in neighboring Sucumbíos, Ecuador.[11] My fieldwork also led me to collaborate with the Regional Working Group of Social Organizations in the design of an Andean-Amazonian Integral Development Plan (PLADIA). This plan aspires to provide a community-designed alternative to official rural development paradigms, and to address the structural conditions that lead to illicit coca production and the displacement and impoverishment of rural families in the region.[12]

The mere existence of these *selva* practices in gardens, orchards, and forests brings something into being. They express the capacious potential for life to strive to resist the polarizing and irreconcilable terms of life and death embedded in public policy. However, Amazonian or *selva* agricultural practices are not yet widespread beyond a dispersed network of small farming families. Alternative agricultural proposals form part of an ongoing twenty-year political struggle between the state and regional social movements as the latter oppose antidrug policy and extractive economic development, and reimagine how to build a different political, economic, and socioenvironmental future for the territory. The Amazonian-based agricultural practices I witnessed are a central component in the design of what PLADIA calls a transition to *fincas agroproductivas sostenibles* (sustainable agroproductive farms).

Inspired by what I came to think of as pulsations of cosustainability—these dispersed *selva* practices striving to resonate and multiply across the Andean-Amazonian foothills outside existing modes of agrarian regulation—I now focus on one family that forms part of this alternative agricultural network. What most compelled me is their everyday cultivated partnership with soils, and in particular, how this partnership enabled a sundry of organisms and elements, including humans, to resist violent modes of death by becoming into death rather than working against it in the pursuit of a better life. By *becoming into death*, I refer to a mode of dying that is an aspect of the transformation of being, an emerging into many other living and dying things much like the regenerative decay of *hojarasca* or decomposing leaves. This kind of death results from the recycling of *selva* life rather than the violence of war, or, what is the same, killing in the defense of growth.

***

The story of the family's forced return to Mocoa pivoted on a negotiated displacement between Don Nelso and members of the AUC who forcibly occupied the subregion known as Bajo Putumayo in 1998, where the majority of coca in Putumayo is still grown. The paramilitaries explained that they had no real reason to chase Nelso out of town, as they had been watching him for months and found no evidence that he was collaborating with FARC guerrillas. However, other people wanted him gone, and these families made use of a generalized context of violent displacement to wage personal vendettas.[13] Nelso had acquired enemies as a community leader encouraging cocaleros *to stop cultivating the crop before the state's threat of aerial fumigation honed in on the region. This was 2001, and visible seesaw trajectories between town and country drew immediate suspicion due to the strict territorial divide imposed by the FARC and the paramilitaries as they vied for control over land, local populations, coca production, and the cocaine trade. The death threat that paramilitaries nailed to Nelso's front door read: "WE WILL MOW YOU DOWN WHILE YOU WALK HOME!" Paramilitary violence was most gruesome in the dismembering of bodies and the public throwing of corpses into nearby rivers, a kind of ultimate deterritorialization of bodies from soils and souls. It was a quick decision. Nelso and his wife, María*

Elva, packed up a few belongings and headed north with their five children until they reached Putumayo's capital town of Mocoa.

What followed was a year, as they described it, of quedándonos quietos (lying low; staying still), a forced retreat from public life and the exposure inherent in too many social relations. They were lucky enough to receive a government housing subsidy for displaced families, but when the first opportunity arose, they traded the one-room apartment for half a hectare of land on the outskirts of Mocoa. The family has not yet been able to formalize the land title, and a handwritten note continues to serve as a deed. "We were getting sick living in a matchbox," Elva tells me. She is bent over a cafeteria tray full of seeds, varieties of beans we inspect for tiny holes, a literal worming-in of uninvited mouths. These are "beans for eating, not for commercial purposes," Nelso explains, but of course, not all mouths are the same, nor are they fed equally. These are beans to feed other beans, beans to feed microorganisms and cloak naked soils, to gift and trade; they are also for the family's lunch and dinner. Red, black, speckled, gray, maroon, shades of café and mustard. Not only seeds, then, but mouths as well. One by one these seed-mouths are turned over in the palms of hands and stored again, a laborious practice to cleanse rather than submerge them in chemical insecticides.

Figure 3. Thirty varieties of beans grown in Nelso and Elva's garden. Photo by Kristina Lyons.

Glancing over at their neighbor's plot, I begin to envision what the area looked like more than ten years ago when they first arrived. A stretch of rust-colored earth, compacted by hooves, burned out by herbicides, open faced and exhausted. "Seemingly left for dead," says Nelso, referring to a state of being which, as I explain later, can be conceived as refusal—a state of imperceptible playing-dead through which regenerative transformation may be achieved. In the case of their neighbors, like so many farmers following the Green Revolution technical advice of agronomists advocating for the use of chemical inputs—and to whom Nelso refers as ladrónomos (or "thiefgronomists")—the natural limitations of Amazonian soils have to be continuously struggled against and corrected.[14] Nelso's punning neologism for the agronomists speaks to the softer kinds of violence exerted through dominant technoscientific paradigms, and to how small farmers find their knowledges, ethics, and practices under the gun of capitalist productive imperatives. To combat the so-called poverty of the soils—their thinness, acidity, old age, and mineral deficiency—Nelso describes the conventionally prescribed technical treatment plan: drips of urea and Triple 15, a chemical pump strapped to the back of a farmer, the hissing sound it makes close to an ear like an old man's raspy breath. An entire life-support system is assembled not only to resuscitate the soil but also to force its betterment. It is treated not as a natural body with corporeal finitude, but rather as artificial strata whose mortality is not only cast as a weakness to be overcome but is all but denied.

In stark contrast to this kind of optimization of the soil's regenerative capacities, Doña Elva spoke about "creating conditions." These conditions do not forcibly supersede corporeal vulnerability to resuscitate soils, but allow for the kind of withdrawal that the family sees its own lives cyclically retreating into and slowly emerging back from: under-employment, displacement, landlessness, lying low, and the ongoingness of recovery. They were not in the business of imposing conditions to make productive soils or—in a broader sense—productive lives emerge. Rather, each day Nelso and Elva bring together seeds, manure, eggshells, husks, and vegetable and fruit skins to create conditions for their inter-mingling in anticipation of what might emerge. An example is the way decomposing bodies and elements—litter layer, ash, rinds, rootlet, manure, human urine, sugarcane mash— come to mutually constitute each other as they transform into hojarasca, which holds their traces while also constituting something new.

Nelso and Elva began by collecting the cans, tires, and plastic bags left behind by previous residents. They discussed which plants would be their allies in interrupting the life cycles of the domineering pasture grasses that flourish in open sunlight. They planted sunflowers, low-growing kisses, yams, beans, cowitch, cudzú shrubs, and wild clover: food and protective covering for others, mostly microbes that would nurture plant rootlets that would eventually come to shade soil. Then they waited, thinking, searching for building *materials to "create conditions" for the house itself. In this way their shared lives—soils, farmers, plants, worms, microbes—emerged out of a retreat as necessary as it was imposed. Many neighbors and agricultural extension experts looked on in bewilderment as they watched them sow what appeared to be roadside weeds.* "Los locos viviendo en medio del rastrojo," *they said—crazy people living in the midst of animal fodder, or the* selva *that returns when left unattended, and that most farmers clear in the act of occupying and working the land.*

Figure 4. Living in the midst of "animal fodder." Photo by Kristina Lyons.

Only after knotty bundles of diverse roots and organisms had, as Elva explained, "created a climate" was it acceptable for human hands to loosen up and turn the insides of soils out, allowing for the aeration that invites life and death—digestion, defecation, and decomposition—to proliferate. Later on they began to plant human food crops, most of which were noncommercial (or at least nontraditionally commercial) perennial varieties that do not require replanting after each harvest, purchased seeds, chemical inputs, or daily upkeep: for example, Amazonian wheat, medicinal plants, star nut, plantains, tubers, fruits, and greens for the hens, ducks, rabbits, and guinea pigs that provide manure for the farm (and that are also easily stolen by petty thieves). Nelso and Elva's children did not show initial interest in farming, and instead took minimum-wage jobs in town to support their own growing nuclear families. However, they continued to share the same house and eat from the gardens. Over time, they watched the farm convert into a dynamic space frequented by other farmers interested in trading seeds, produce, and recipes, and also town folks who came to buy fruits, vegetables, and medicinal plants unavailable at commercial markets in Mocoa. Elva now specializes in preparing more than three hundred Amazonian recipes that she shares with other women, especially those of Mocoa's network of displaced rural families who have lost their land, their food security, and their food autonomy.

DYING DECOMPOSITIONALLY: Creating Conditions and Living *en Medio del Rastrojo*

The different waves of structural and armed violence in the late-nineteenth and twentieth centuries that expelled families from the country's fertile Andean regions into frontier territories impacted by extractive economies, "poor" soils, and armed conflict necessarily transformed biopolitically informed attachments to life. For example, Nelso and Elva seek to create conditions to combat displacement in a context of ongoing uncertainty by working toward a future they may never see. They partake in material practices in the present that are overly inhabited by a future territory that does not yet exist, but that strives to materialize its collective affordances and capacities (for example, in grassroots struggles to fund PLADIA and transform the state's rural development model, and in everyday practices through which people attempt to figure something out without abandoning their farms). At the same time, a past territory can never be fully eradicated because it remains present in different modes of cultivating, and in the recovery of recipes, medicines, and seeds. In this way, the cultivation of a farm or garden strives to farm itself as a community of future human and nonhuman cultivators.[15] The network of farmers I accompanied engages in a recursive balance between creative innovation and the recovery of diverse popular, traditional, and ancestral practices. For example, they combine popular processes to low-tech their farms with elements from specific sciences they consider subversive, such as agroecology and soil microbiology, without granting science a unique authority over indigenous and popular knowledges and experimental practices.

There is no singular story to tell about how these farmers come to engage in *selva* practices. They read agroecology pamphlets and remember practices their grandparents and indigenous neighbors performed. They exchange experiences and seeds with other small-farming families. They take long walks in the forest to study plants and trees. Some have read Marx. Others explain that they are "apprentices of the *selva*" and have learned to cultivate *ojos para ella* (eyes for her [*la selva*]) (Lyons 2014). Farmers engaged in these *selva* life processes are becoming what Heraldo calls "Amazonian men and women" (Vallejo 1993). I argue this is less an environmental subjectivity than an ongoing relationality: learning to cultivate new modes of eating, walking, seeing, tasting, exchanging, growing, and inhabiting the Andean-Amazonian foothills that do not rely on the idea of a human who is somehow separate from and master over a selvatic nature. Heraldo contrasts Amazonian men and women with *líderes sociales* (social leaders) who constitute a newly organized generation of activists leading protests, denouncing human rights violations, and negotiating with government officials to demand the recognition of rural communities as legitimate political interlocutors. If they have time to carry on farming, many of these social leaders continue to be *cocaleros*, or have replaced coca with other monocrops such as pineapple, which has the ability to resist the acidity left behind by intensive coca production in naturally acidic soils. While they stand in solidarity with these social leaders and the ideological struggles they represent and provide regional social organizations with the kind of alternative technical assistance I have mentioned, Amazonian men and women do not necessarily have the time or disposition to attend every protest, sit through bureaucratic meetings, or negotiate with elected officials.[16] Their lives are deeply enmeshed with, and hence mutually obliged by, other beings and elements that share life and labor among gardens, orchards, and forests. The ecological temporalities of these kinds of relations are largely imperceptible within the official time of politics, such as government reports on competitive agricultural yields, the four-year development plans that accompany elected officials or news reports on popular uprisings.

After being violently dispossessed of five farms during the past twenty-five years, Heraldo now lives fifteen minutes down the road from Nelso and Elva. When we received news that his neighbor was gunned down at dawn, he explained to me: "I can die, but the farms will remain." He was not referring to the desire to demarcate private property inhabited by a self-interested household, deforested fields, and ordered rows of commercial crops. These kinds of farms that fall in line with conventional state-based forms of property acquisition can easily slip away, working against the continuation of rural life in the territory. Instead, he referred to cultivating conditions for life by "recolonizing the farm with *selva*." This recolonization of farms with forest materially and conceptually disrupts notions of private property. Farms are never only farms when they are also always regional watersheds, foothills, forests, biological corridors, and floodplains. It is farms *as more than farms* that multiplies what I have referred to as pulsations of cosustainability: the different birds and bees attracted to creeping plant gardens, the reawakening of microbial worlds as communities of plants return, the multiplication of diverse *selva* practices resonating throughout a territory in community seed banks, the bartering of food, the stimulation of small-farmer markets, the recovery of food autonomy, the multiplication of happiness one farm at a time, and the creation of conditions for the recycling of *hojarasca* itself. This layer of fallen and dying leaves eventually undergoes natural processes of decomposition, and when incorporated back into the germination of the earth, it is always already regenerative of *selva* life.

In an attempt to reflect carefully on the contingent potentiality of this kind of germinating withdrawal or decompositional mode of retreat, I take inspiration from discussions in feminist and disability studies (Davis 2013; Harrison 2008; Diprose 2002) on corporeal vulnerability, and such phenomena as susceptibility, indolence, and fatigue. Rather than conceive of these states as degraded ways of being in the world that must be set right or transcended by benevolent action, we can think of fatigue as an occurrence whose reality is made up of refusal or hesitancy. One of the most poignant lessons Nelso, Elva, Heraldo, and other farmers shared with me is that the region's soils—and by soils they were never referring to a stable entity, but to continuous relations of composure and decomposing that in fleeting, massifying moments produces a natural body scientists call "soil"—could never be colonized, but only destroyed. Amazonian soils could not be tamed by human-led productive fantasies, but they could be used up and abandoned. Furthermore, through this seeming destruction a vocation to live might resist violent modes of death by becoming into it, which is not necessarily death or dying, but a melding back into a transformative fatigue.

According to Nelso, what many agronomists and farmers describe as the "limiting fragility" of Amazonian soils is actually a mode of resistance that might allow—indeed oblige—farmers to slow down as well. It is not soils' intentional refusal in the same way that they express their own growing recalcitrance before the commodified notion of life underpinning growth-oriented economic imperatives. Rather, it may be an expression of a capacity for weariness and recoil from the impossibility of existing under the relentless strain of extractive conditions that exceed the soil's abilities to absorb, repose, and transform. Thus what appears dead is not; rather, for Nelso, this transformational period marks the soil's imperceptible and regenerative unworking and reworking. The reworking evades not only its own exploitation but also a continuum of exploitation linking farmers, microbes, plants, seeds, soils, and trees. Not simply a mechanical cause-and-effect interaction or biological breakdown, but the sheer physical force of fragility, the feeding loop of activity and withdrawal characterizing an ecological relationality. Relatedly, Heraldo and Nelso argue that when technicians and bureaucrats claim that one cannot sustain a productive agricultural livelihood in the Amazon, they are really suggesting that one cannot sustain a colonizing, extractive, and neoliberal agricultural livelihood.

In this article, I have not tried to tell a triumphant tale of small-scale agroecological farming as an improved agricultural model that should be singularly adopted throughout Colombia's western Amazon. Nor do I want to argue that technical decisions over crop choice and livelihood are always or simply a political choice. Rather, I have highlighted the built-in expectation of vulnerability present in an ecological sense of being in the world: farmers' necessary acceptance of decay, looping back to begin again, a cautionary lying low and a decompositional mode of regeneration. They remind us that transformative potentiality is not a human privilege, but rather a relational matter dispersed in the connections and labor among people as well as other kinds of beings and things. They urge us to take seriously the ways different human and nonhuman relations afford differential political and economic capacities. At stake in these farmers' struggle is not the right to idleness, but the right to another kind of work, another kind of dream, and a world that does not run only on the inevitable and structurally designed market-based time and velocity. What may be most inspiring is how their *selva* practices slow down the power of dominant reasoning: for example, planting "weeds," living "in the midst of animal fodder," preferring not to correct or resuscitate "poor soils," and rejecting the salvation offered by the eradication of illicit crops. Much as the feminist philosopher of science Isabelle Stengers (2005) does, their practices demand that we slow down the power of reasoning imbued in our own concepts to create a space for hesitation. This hesitation obliges us to ask what we claim to know when we say that we are constructing a good or common world, and how this knowledge comes to justify war while rendering unimaginable other kinds of political thought and action.

In the Andean-Amazonian foothills of Colombia a growing number of rural communities argue that there is something more important at stake than uprooting illicit crops or biopolitically improving the productive capacities of soils and souls, something more vital than producing enough exportable commodities to feed a far-off world whose moral standing is protected by continued assaults against the worlds that these farmers strive to build. They suggest that the wrong kinds of questions are being asked. Perhaps it is not a question of becoming better—more productive farmers, more legal and more responsible citizens, or more efficient capitalists. It is necessary to slow down and ask what kinds of questions emerge from an ecologically relational world that not only obliges different strategies for how to keep on enduring in the face of a war machine that proposes peace through poison, but that is also striving to cultivate a different socioecological, economic, and political reality. These struggles in southern Colombia articulate with larger contemporary political processes in the global North and South, including antiextractivism, anticapitalism, degrowth, and—throughout the Andes—heterogeneous practices of *buen vivir* (living well) that reject human-centered notions of growth and productivity tied to a universal *vivir mejor* (living better) (D'Alisa, DeMaria, and Kallis 2015; Gudynas and Acosta 2011). Living well is, of course, never separate from the question of the right to die well—of the right to modes of dying in which death is allowed to decompose into life, rather than being violently ripped from place, territory, soil, *selva*, and home. This is a death that decomposes into life, just as leaves spill from branch to ground, turn over and slowly rot to germinate from a pulsating layer of *hojarasca* again.

ABSTRACT

How is life in a criminalized ecology in the Andean-Amazonian foothills of southwestern Colombia? In what way does antinarcotics policy that aims to eradicate la mata que mata *(the plant that kills) pursue peace through poison? Relatedly, how do people keep on cultivating a garden, caring for forest, or growing food when at any moment a crop-duster plane may pass overhead, indiscriminately spraying herbicides over entire landscapes? Since 2000, the U.S.–Colombian War on Drugs has relied on the militarized aerial fumigation of coca plants, coupled with alternative development interventions that aim to forcibly eradicate illicit livelihoods. Through ethnographic engagement with small farmers in the frontier department of Putumayo, the gateway to the country's Amazon and a region that has been the focus of counternarcotic operations, this article explores the different possibilities and foreclosures for life and death that emerge in a tropical forest ecology under military duress. By following farmers, their material practices, and their life philosophies, I trace the ways in which human-soil relations come to potentiate forms of resistance to the violence and criminalization produced by militarized, growth-oriented development. Rather than productivity—one of the central elements of modern capitalist growth—the regenerative capacity of these ecologies relies on organic decay, impermanence, decomposition, and even fragility that complicates modernist bifurcations of living and dying, allowing, I argue, for ecological imaginaries and life processes that do not rely on productivity or growth to strive into existence. [violence; development; small farmers; soil; decomposition; War on Drugs; Colombian Amazon]*

NOTES

Acknowledgments   This article would not have been possible without the ongoing friendship of Heraldo Vallejo, Nelso Enríquez, María Elva Montenegro, and members of the Mesa Regional de Organizaciones Sociales del Putumayo, Baja Bota Caucana y Cofanía, Jardines de Sucumbíos, Nariño, among innumerable others in Colombia with whom I have learned to think and live. I am also very grateful for the careful readings that versions of this article received from Marisol de la Cadena, Andrew Mathews, Tanya Richardson, Jake Culbertson, Morten Pedersen, Brent Crosson, and Iván Vargas, as well as three anonymous readers. I received invaluable feedback from audiences at the Ethnographic Engagements workshop at the University of California, Santa Cruz, the Feminist Studies Department at the University of California, Santa Cruz, the Center for Studies on Political Ecology in Bogotá, and the biennial meeting of the Society for Cultural Anthropology—in particular, from Karen Barad, Donna Haraway, Mark Anderson, Don Brenneis, Judith Farquhar, Diana Ojeda, and Diana Bocarejo. My research was funded by the Wenner-Gren Foundation, the Social Science Research Council, and the University of California Pacific Rim Research Program.

1.   With roots in the 1980s, the AUC grew to about twenty thousand members, and was heavily financed through the drug trade, local landowners, cattle ranchers, mining and oil companies, agroindustry, and Colombia's traditional political class.

2.   Glyphosate, which Monsanto packages as Roundup Ultra, has been used to spray illicit crops in Colombia since 1986. The quantity of glyphosate used in fumigation operations was estimated to be 110% more concentrated than the commercially available version. Glyphosate was mixed with polyethoxylated tallow amine (POEA) and an additional surfactant, Cosmo Flux 411F, to make the herbicide stick to plants in humid tropical climates (Vargas Meza 1999).

3.   The Antinarcotics Directorate of the National Police provided these official statistics on August 18, 2015.

4.   Between 2000 and 2002, controversial debates over whether to introduce biological agents into coca eradication strategies resurfaced in the U.S. Congress, the European Parliament, and the Colombian Ministry of the Environment. While the U.S. government affirmed that it would only support biological eradication research in Colombia through a multilateral mechanism, rural communities claim that covert experiments have occurred.

5.   In interviews, USAID employees explained more than a decade and $80 million of failed development projects in Putumayo in terms of an "unfortunate, but instructive learning curve." The cost of production in remote areas was much higher than anticipated; market studies were not conducted to ensure a niche for newly introduced agroindustrial products; offering aid only to coca-growing families stimulated the planting of coca and failed to help individuals who did not grow coca, but were employed within its broader commodity chain; market-oriented crops were plagued by problems of "quality control" (that is, rampant fungus and tropical pests).

6.   In *"Society Must Be Defended,"* Michel Foucault (2003) outlined the complex entanglements of the sovereign, disciplinary, and biopolitical forms of power at play in the machinery of Nazi genocide. Achille Mbembe (2003) then situated this industrialized European savagery within a history of African colonization, where colonists experimented with the spectacular display of irrational and excessive killing.

7.   There are nine indigenous peoples that currently inhabit Putumayo, five of which are original to the territory. Margarita Chaves (2005) elucidates the everyday interactions, shifting identifications, and political alliances between indigenous communities and small farmers in Putumayo, despite classic representations of their supposed isolation and conflicting forms of conviviality.

8.   Colombia is currently the second-most unequal country in the world. Despite its reputation as one of Latin America's most stable democracies, the state has never experienced a period of full labor incorporation, widespread land reform, or a true populist

phase. Its democracy has traditionally been described as restrictive, elite, and violent (Carroll 2011).

9.   Since October 2012, the FARC-EP and the Colombian government have been engaged in what is now the country's fourth national peace process. Colombia's second-largest guerrilla group, the National Liberal Army, has expressed interest in entering into a similar negotiation process.

10.   Constitutional reforms since 2004 have steadily declared a variety of food production, commercialization, and seed-propagating practices used by small farmers to be illegal. For more information, see www.semillas.org.co.

11.   The Regional Working Group of Social Organizations is an umbrella network of rural social organizations that has inherited a history of political protest and organizational work on the part of rural laborers and farmers, workers in the oil industry, civic organizations, indigenous and Afro-Colombian communities, and youth and women's organizations dating back to the 1970s. Some 80 percent of organizations that belong to the Regional Working Group are *campesina*. The Environmental Clinic is an initiative supported by the Quito-based NGO Acción Ecológica.

12.   After the *Marchas Cocaleras*, right-wing paramilitary organizations occupied the majority of towns in Putumayo and persecuted community leaders. This forced the majority of rural social movements to suspend their organizational activities for almost a decade between 1996 and 2006. PLADIA is the current version of the community-based development plan that was proposed during strike negotiations in 1996. Despite verbal and written accords, the implementation of PLADIA has yet to be funded at the municipal, state, or national level.

13.   For more on the relationship between government forces and paramilitaries, the role of FARC-EP with respect to the profitability of drug trafficking, and local results of the demobilization of the AUC, see Jansson 2008.

14.   The dominant scientific representation of Amazonian soils is that they are "senile" (León 1999). That is, they are inhospitable to conventional market-driven agriculture without heavy corrective measures, such as lime, fertilizer, and other chemical inputs. For insight into soil scientists' stakes in these debates and their growing dissatisfaction with the modern soil classification systems they institutionalized in Colombia in the 1970s, see Lyons 2014.

15.   I am indebted to Alberto Corsín Jiménez's (2013) discussion of the urban cultivation table produced in Handmade Urbanism workshops in Madrid, as a means of imagining how a city or territory may jump ahead of itself.

16.   The Regional Working Group of Social Organizations has come to reject what Winifred Tate (2013) calls "proxy citizenship" by distancing itself from NGOs that interfere with their ability to make direct claims for redress from the state.

REFERENCES

Aguilar, J.C.
    1999   *Evangélico y colonización: Una aproximación a la historia del Putumayo desde la época prehispánica a la colonización agropecuaria.* Bogotá: Ecoe Editores.
Allison, Anne
    2013   *Precarious Japan.* Durham, N.C.: Duke University Press.
Ariza, Eduardo, María Clemencia Ramírez, and Leonardo Vega
    1998   *Atlas cultural de la Amazonia Colombiana: La construcción del territorio en el siglo XX.* Bogotá: ICANH.
Barad, Karen
    2007   *Meeting the Universe Halfway: Quantum Physics and the Entanglement of Matter and Meaning.* Durham, N.C.: Duke University Press.
Bebbington, Anthony and Jeffrey Bury, eds.
    2013   *Subterranean Struggles: New Dynamics of Mining, Oil, and Gas in Latin America.* Austin: University of Texas Press.

Beittel, June S.
  2012 "Colombia: Background, U.S. Relations, and Congressional Interest." Congressional Research Service, RL32250. https://www.fas.org/sgp/crs/row/RL32250.pdf.
Biehl, João
  2005 *Vita: Life in a Zone of Social Abandonment*. Berkeley: University of California Press.
Calle, Maria Clara
  2014 "Putumayo está en crisis." *Semana*, August 30. http://www.semana.com/nacion/multimedia/putumayo-tendra-paro-campesino-por-petroleo-coca/400937-3.
Carroll, Leah Anne
  2011 *Violent Democratization: Social Movements, Elites, and Politics in Colombia's Rural War Zones, 1984–2008*. Notre Dame, Ind.: University of Notre Dame Press.
Chaves, Margarita
  2005 "Qué va a pasar con los indios cuando todos seamos indios? Ethnic Rights and Reindianization in Southwestern Colombian Amazonia." PhD dissertation, University of Illinois at Urbana–Champaign.
Corsín Jiménez, Alberto
  2013 "Three Traps Many." Paper presented at the John E. Sawyer Seminar "Indigenous Cosmopolitics: Dialogues about the Reconstitution of Worlds," University of California, Davis, March 18.
D'Alisa, Giacomo, Frederico DeMaria, and Giorgos Kallis
  2015 *Degrowth: A Vocabulary For a New Era*. London: Routledge.
Das, Veena
  2006 *Life and Words: Violence and Descent into the Ordinary*. Berkeley: University of California Press.
Davis, Lennard J., ed.
  2013 *The Disability Studies Reader*. 4th edition. New York: Routledge.
de la Cadena, Marisol
  2010 "Indigenous Cosmopolitics in the Andes: Conceptual Reflections beyond 'Politics.'" *Cultural Anthropology* 25, no. 2: 334–70. http://dx.doi.org/10.1111/j.1548-1360.2010.01061.x.
Departamento Nacional de Planeación de Colombia
  2010 "Plan nacional de desarrollo, 2010–2014: prosperidad para todos." Bogotá. https://www.dnp.gov.co/Plan-Nacional-de-Desarrollo/PND-2010-2014/Paginas/Plan-Nacional-De-2010-2014.aspx.
Diprose, Rosalyn
  2002 *Corporeal Generosity: On Giving with Nietzsche, Merleau-Ponty, and Levinas*. Albany: State University of New York Press.
Escobar, Arturo
  2011 *Encountering Development: The Making and Unmaking of the Third World*. Princeton, N.J.: Princeton Universty Press.
  2014 *Sentipensar con la tierra: Nuevas lecturas sobre desarrollo, territorio y diferencia*. Medellín, Colombia: UNALUA.
Foucault, Michel
  2003 *"Society Must Be Defended": Lectures at the Collège of France, 1975–1976*. Translated by David Macey. London: Picador.
Gibson-Graham, J. K.
  2006 *The End of Capitalism (As We Knew It): A Feminist Critique of Political Economy*. Minneapolis: University of Minnesota Press.
Gudynas, Eduardo
  2014 "Sustentación, aceptación y legitimación de los extractivismos: múltiples expresiones pero un mismo basamento." *OPERA* 14: 137–59. http://revistas.uexternado.edu.co/index.php/opera/article/view/3844/4155.

Gudynas, Eduardo, and Alberto Acosta
    2011   "El buen vivir más allá que el desarrollo." *Quehacer* 181: 70–81. http://www. desco.org.pe/node/6808.

Haraway, Donna
    2008   *When Species Meet*. Minneapolis: University of Minnesota Press.

Harrison, Paul
    2008   "Corporeal Remains: Vulnerability, Proximity, and Living On after the End of the World." *Environment and Planning A* 40, no. 2: 423–45. http://dx.doi.org/ 10.1068/a391.

Jansson, Oscar
    2008   "The Cursed Leaf: An Anthropology of the Political Economy of Cocaine Production in Southern Colombia." PhD dissertation, Uppsala University.

León, Tomás
    1999   "Perspectivas de la investigación en los suelos de la Amazonia." In *Amazonia colombiana: diversidad y conflicto*, edited by German I. Andrade, Adriana Hurtado, and Ricardo Torres, 237–55. Bogotá: ÁGORA.

Lyons, Kristina Marie
    2014   "Soil Science, Development and the 'Elusive Nature' of Colombia's Amazonian Plains." *Journal of Latin American and Caribbean Anthropology* 19, no. 2: 212–36. http://dx.doi.org/10.1111/jlca.12097.

Mbembe, Achille
    2003   "Necropolitics." Translated by Libby Meintjes. *Public Culture* 15, no. 1: 11–40. http://dx.doi.org/10.1215/08992363-15-1-11.

Mesa Regional de Organizaciones Sociales del Putumayo, Baja Bota Caucana y Cofanía, Jardines de Sucumbíos
    2015   *Putumayo: sembrando vida y construyendo identidad. Historia de la Mesa Regional (2006–2014)*. Bogotá: Corcas Editores SAS.

Mol, Annemarie
    2008   "I Eat an Apple. On Theorizing Subjectivities." *Subjectivity* 22: 28–37. http:// dx.doi.org/10.1057/sub.2008.2.

Nouvet, Elysée
    2014   "Some Carry on, Some Stay in Bed: (In)convenient Affects and Agency in Neoliberal Nicaragua." *Cultural Anthropology* 29, no. 1: 80–102. http://dx.doi. org/10.14506/ca29.1.06.

Paley, Dawn
    2014   *Drug War Capitalism*. Oakland, Calif.: AK Press.

Papadopoulos, Dimitris, Niamh Stephenson, and Vassilis Tsianos
    2008   *Escape Routes: Control and Subversion in the Twenty-First Century*. London: Pluto Press.

Povinelli, Elizabeth A.
    2011a   *Economies of Abandonment: Social Belonging and Endurance in Late Liberalism*. Durham, N.C.: Duke University Press.
    2011b   "Woman on the Other Side of the Wall: Archiving the Otherwise in Postcolonial Digital Archive." *differences: A Journal of Feminist Cultural Studies* 22, no. 1: 146–71. http://dx.doi.org/10.1215/10407391-1218274.
    2011c   "Routes/Worlds." *e-flux*, no. 27. http://www.e-flux.com/journal/ routesworlds/.
    2014   "Holding Up the World, Part III: In the Event of Precarity . . . A Conversation." *e-flux*, no. 58. http://www.e-flux.com/journal/holding-up-the-world-part-iii-in-the-event-of-precarity-...-a-conversation-between-elizabeth-povinelli-and-lauren-berlant/.

Puig de la Bellacasa, María
    2013   "Encountering Bioinfrastructure: Ecological Struggles and the Sciences of Soil." *Social Epistemology: A Journal of Knowledge, Culture and Policy* 28, no. 1: 26–40. http://dx.doi.org/10.1080/02691728.2013.862879.

Ramírez, María Clemencia
    2001   *Entre el estado y la guerrilla: identidad y ciudadanía en el movimiento de los campesinos cocaleros del Putumayo*. Bogotá: ICANH.

Stengers, Isabelle
    2005   "The Cosmopolitical Proposal." In *Making Things Public: Atmospheres of Democracy*, edited by Bruno Latour and Peter Weibel, 994–1003. Cambridge, Mass.: MIT Press.
    2010   "Including Nonhumans in Political Theory: Opening Pandora's Box." In *Political Matter: Technoscience, Democracy and Public Life*, edited by Bruce Braun and Sarah J. Whatmore, 3–34. Minneapolis: University of Minnesota Press.

Stevenson, Lisa
    2014   *Life Beside Itself: Imagining Care In The Canadian Arctic*. Berkeley: University of California Press.

Stewart, Kathleen
    2007   *Ordinary Affects*. Durham, N.C.: Duke University Press.

Tate, Winifred
    2013   "Proxy Citizenship and Transnational Advocacy: Colombian Activists from Putumayo to Washington, DC." *American Ethnologist* 40, no. 1: 55–70. http://dx.doi.org/10.1111/amet.12005.

Taussig, Michael
    1984   *Shamanism, Colonialism, and the Wild Man: A Study in Terror and Healing*. Chicago: University of Chicago Press.

Tsing, Anna
    2011   "Arts of Inclusion, or, How to Love a Mushroom." *Australian Humanities Review*, no. 50. http://www.australianhumanitiesreview.org/archive/Issue-May-2011/tsing.html.

United Nations Office on Drugs and Crime (UNODC)
    2005   "Colombia: Coca Cultivation Survey for 2004." https://www.unodc.org/unodc/en/crop-monitoring/?tag=Colombia.
    2015   "Colombia: Monitoreo de Cultivos de Coca 2014." https://www.unodc.org/unodc/en/crop-monitoring/?tag=Colombia.

Vallejo, Heraldo
    1993   "El nuevo hombre amazónico: Una visión de desarrollo para el departamento del Putumayo." *Putumayo: Expresión de Identidad Regional* 1: 8–25.

Vargas Meza, Ricardo
    1999   *Fumigación y conflicto: Políticas antidrogas y deslegitimación del estado en Colombia*. Bogotá: TNI/Acción Andina.

Veltmeyer, Henry, and James Petras
    2014   *The New Extractivism: A Post-Neoliberal Development Model or Imperalism of the Twenty-First Century?* London: Zed Books.

Verran, Helen
    2002   "A Postcolonial Moment in Science Studies: Alternative Firing Regimes of Environmental Scientists and Aboriginal Landowners." *Social Studies of Science* 32, nos. 5–6: 729–67. http://dx.doi.org/10.1177/030631270203200506.

Zeiderman, Austin
    2013   "Living Dangerously: Biopolitics and Urban Citizenship in Bogotá, Colombia." *American Ethnologist* 40, no. 1: 71–87. http://dx.doi.org/10.1111/amet.12006.

#INDEBTED: Disciplining the Moral Valence of Mortgage Debt Online

NOELLE STOUT
New York University
http://orcid.org/0000-0002-8442-9087

Since 2007, 14 million homeowners in the United States have lost their homes to foreclosure, the highest rate of bank seizures in national history. This massive wave of dispossessions has spawned an acute rise in homelessness, bankrupted entire cities, and caused the irreparable loss of generations of family wealth. Given that homeownership has served as the foundation for American middle-class imaginaries since World War II, it is inevitable that these inordinate rates of default have transformed the meaning of mortgaging and indebtedness within the United States. Indebtedness, as David Graeber (2011, 390) suggests, has become ever more tied to moral personhood in modern times, in that what he terms "the governing classes in the United States" have linked the ability to repay debt to moral standing. Yet in a context in which financialization has disrupted the social contract implicit within debt ties, those carrying insurmountable mortgage debt have begun to question the meaning of indebtedness and the moral assumptions about mortgage default. These everyday debates about homeowners' duty to pay on underwater mortgages have played out largely in the virtual world of online forums and blogs.[1]

These disputes about the stigma of delinquent homeownership and mortgagors' moral obligation to repay mortgages depart radically from those that characterized previous American foreclosure crises. For example, Kathryn Dudley (2000) opens her ethnography of the 1980s U.S. farm foreclosure crisis with the

CULTURAL ANTHROPOLOGY, Vol. 31, Issue 1, pp. 82–106, ISSN 0886-7356, online ISSN 1548-1360. © by the American Anthropological Association. All rights reserved. DOI: 10.14506/ca31.1.05

story of Dewayne Berg, a farmer facing the loss of the family farm who disappeared from his Midwestern home, leaving his wife and sons to suffer months of
grief and speculation. Berg was eventually discovered hiding out in Canada, a
testament to the stigma and community judgment affecting farmers confronting
foreclosure. Dudley observes the animosity community members expressed toward families undergoing bank seizures; instead of questioning how lenders had
pushed cheap credit onto farmers, Berg's friends and neighbors concluded that
anyone who lost a farm had "done something to deserve it" (Dudley 2000, 5).
But had Berg faced foreclosure during the 2008 mortgage crash, might the image
of him driving his muddy pickup truck to Canada have been transformed into one
of him hunched over the glow of a laptop, deciding to abandon his debt rather
than his family?

I argue here that homeowners confronting foreclosure in lower-middle-class
and middle-class Northern California neighborhoods are reconfiguring longstanding American interpretations of indebtedness through forays online. I focus on
homeowners participating in interactive online forums arising in the aftermath of
the 2008 crash to show how mortgagors are moralizing debt nonpayment and
disciplining the politics of stigma. To map this terrain, I analyze user-generated,
national online foreclosure forums and sites including advice boards, posts on
social networking sites, and blogs emerging since 2008 in combination with ongoing ethnographic research among people confronting foreclosure in California's
Sacramento Valley. The predominantly white and Latino homeowners presented
here neither identified as activists nor were involved with debt-related social
movements such as Occupy Wall Street or Strike Debt, which emerged from the
financial crisis. Yet they produced and participated in what I describe as *online
publics of indebtedness* through which they joined a broader, ad hoc social discussion
in which Americans question the established moral dimensions of debt repayment
after the 2008 foreclosure epidemic. Applying a multiattentional approach (Boyer
2007, 87), which considers the technological effects of media and the ways media
shape relations between people, I show how the distinct experiences of participating in anonymous and semipublic online domains proved central to shifts in
homeowners' interpretations of debt and default. I argue that unlike political
activists, California mortgagors participating online reconsider the politics and
morality of mortgage default for certain, but not all, homeowners. They deem
specific mortgagors worthy of sympathy, offering them nonjudgmental support
when they walk away from underwater mortgages, yet ultimately they do not
abandon wholesale the moralization of debt.

In a context of widespread foreclosure, homeowners often reframe credit-debt bonds through moral narratives in ways that invite a reconsideration of longstanding anthropological inquiries into moral economies (e.g., Edelman 2005; Scott 1977; Thompson 1971).[2] By focusing on eighteenth-century contexts or modern peasant societies, canonical anthropological scholarship on moral economies risks perpetuating the notion that late-capitalist economies function as amoral spheres in which economic activity remains untouched by ideas of propriety (Griffith 2009). Whereas peasants working the land are often seen as articulating utopian visions of a world in which morals determine economic fairness, the moral narratives of American suburbanites struggling with financialized mortgage markets and venturing online for assistance often go unrecognized. By relocating these moral economic narratives, so often linked to pastoral ideals of land and belonging, to middle-class suburban homeownership and online collectives, I show how contemporary hypercapitalist debt ties are complexly linked to the disciplinary regimes of moral discourses. If the ethnographic record has typically portrayed moral discourses as the power of creditors over debtors, ethnographic exceptions emerging after the mortgage crash indicate the shifting contemporary terrain of credit-debt relations (Peebles 2010).

These moral counternarratives regarding indebtedness respond to the rise of a contemporary capitalist context that Andrew Ross (2013, 11) describes as a creditocracy, where financiers wrap debt around every possible asset and income stream, requiring basic goods to be debt-financed and making indebtedness the precondition for acquiring life's necessities. Ross (2013, 32) argues that breaking the promise to repay is taboo in a creditocracy and ponders what will happen when the public psychology around debt retreats from automatic compliance with the morality of payback. An examination of homeowners in the context of the financial crisis, in which debt is increasingly defined as the moral obligation to repay (High 2012, 2), is therefore critical to understanding a shift in Americans' perceptions of debt obligations. In her research on Michigan's foreclosure crisis, for example, Anna Jefferson (2013) found that homeowners produced narratives of walking away from mortgage debt as a moral critique of corporate greed and government ineptitude. Likewise, since the 2008 crash, many Northern California homeowners with distressed mortgage debt have harnessed the authority of moral narratives to question traditional credit-debt ties, articulating online counternarratives that recast debt nonpayment into a moral stance.

Online publics are easily overlooked, however, when evaluating the impact of the 2008 crash, because most users participate from the privacy of their homes—sitting at desks and kitchen tables, or perched on sofas and beds. Although a wealth of quantitative scholarship examines the national, familial, and neighborhood effects of unprecedented rates of foreclosure, few scholars have explored American homeowners' experiences (Jefferson 2013; Reid 2010), and none have examined the discourses and practices arising from online domains in the wake of the 2008 crash. During thirteen months in the Sacramento Valley, one of the fastest-growing and hardest-hit regions in the nation, I studied homeowners experiencing foreclosure in neighborhoods with distinct racial and economic demographics. Here, I focus on a subset of these seventy interlocutors: twenty homeowners in middle- and lower-middle-class neighborhoods who consistently turned to the Internet to navigate the profound daily impacts of the foreclosure crisis and who, through their online encounters, began to rethink the meaning and moral valence of indebtedness.[3] I met many of these homeowners through close family and friends who had experienced foreclosure in the region, and contacted others through foreclosure counselors at nonprofit organizations with which I worked.

Online publics proved especially appealing to homeowners who hesitated to identify as unable to repay their debts but needed advice on impending foreclosures and wanted to participate in a broader discussion of the precariousness of economic life in the wake of the Great Recession. The recent rise of interactive Web 2.0 media platforms, as anthropologists have shown, offers new opportunities for users to shape online dialogues and redefine public engagement (Boellstorff 2008; Ginsburg 2012; Miller and Horst 2012; Postill 2011). Ironically, the same speed, automation, and computer interconnectivity fundamental to the financialization of mortgage markets that spawned the recent crash (e.g., Langley 2007; Pinch and Swedberg 2008; Poon 2008) have enabled significant discussions of mortgage default among homeowners dispossessed by these trends. Through interactive online modalities, for example, participants question the shame of foreclosure, critique mortgage lenders, validate others' choice to abandon underwater loans, and advocate staying in homes without paying, forms of refusal previously considered unethical within normative models of American middle-class propriety. Yet even as homeowners protest the increasing unfeasibility of post–World War II American middle-class life projects, long defined by stable employment, homeownership, and higher education, participants in online forums redefine respectability rather than abandon the notion entirely.[4]

SHIFTING MORAL ECONOMIES OF MORTGAGE DEBT

Beginning in the late 1930s, debt became socially accepted within the middle class, as the moral dimension of owing money dissipated when consumer debt came to support but also discipline every facet of daily life for those who gained access to it (Calder 1999, 20). Before 1917, U.S. lenders were prohibited from charging profitable interest rates, reselling debts, or borrowing against them (Hyman 2011a, 1). Americans did borrow, industrial workers especially, but the stigma of debt meant that they borrowed privately from a subterranean world of loan sharks, pawnbrokers, and retailers (Calder 1999; Hyman 2011a). In the 1920s, consumer credit entered mainstream middle-class American social life, as business and government collaborated to enable Americans to purchase the goods of the developing manufacturing economy. Credit expanded further in the 1930s, with New Deal policies expanding consumer credit and federal mortgaging programs after the housing crash of the late 1920s. Consumer credit continued to fuel post–World War II suburban fantasies of the good life, as financial industries offered easy credit to white men and married white women, enabling them to purchase homes, automobiles, and consumer goods (Hyman 2011b). Americans borrowed unprecedented amounts on the assumption that their jobs were stable and their incomes would keep growing. Homeownership became central to blue-collar and middle-class class status, as those who carried so-called good debt were considered good citizens (Williams 2004). Whereas before the 1920s, it had been shameful to owe money, the expansion of consumer credit allowed long-term borrowing and debt repayment to become central to middle-class notions of stability and security.

As government mortgage programs expanded alongside consumer credit industries, society's disapproval shifted away from the usurious mortgage itself to the property owner who defaulted on a loan.[5] Failure to repay debt—rather than merely having debt—brought about social stigma and humiliation, as well as financial punishments such as bad credit, eviction, and repossession.[6] Hence, for post–World War II generations, so-called financial failures such as foreclosure and unemployment presented what Katherine Newman (1988) describes as the "fall from grace," the embodiment of American middle-class anxiety about downward mobility. In the case of mortgaging, government agencies and financial industries have intensified these tactics to cultivate borrowers' fear, shame, and guilt about foreclosures (White 2010a). Traditional forms of shameful publicity, such as publishing delinquent mortgagors' names in newspapers and posting foreclosure notices on the fronts of houses, have disgraced homeowners and led them to pay even against their own financial best interests.

Assumptions about the value of homeownership and debt repayments have been called into question following the recent housing market collapse. In Sacramento between 2007 and 2008, mortgage defaults increased sixfold, with foreclosures jumping 482 percent and one in every sixty-seven households filing for foreclosure. For the following five years, California's capital city would consistently rank in the top ten in foreclosures per capita in U.S. metro areas (Baker, Stein, and Eiseman 2008). Despite unprecedented rates of mortgage default, the stigma against default persisted in the early years of the epidemic. By 2009, seven out of ten mortgagors surveyed who had defaulted still believed it was unacceptable to stop payments on an underwater mortgage (Fannie Mae 2010). Local Sacramento culture heightened the stigma of nonpayment, as the dominant industries of farming, manufacturing, and government fueled blue-collar aspirations for middle-class status and linked homeownership to moral personhood.[7] After the crash, Sacramento Valley homeowners expressed fears that their friends, family, and coworkers would reject them or view them as incompetent or irresponsible for falling behind on mortgage payments. These were the sentiments they cited as leading them to make their initial forays online, where they could solicit advice anonymously.

Once online, many homeowners began to rethink their obligations to repay mortgage debts as they came to grasp the role of Wall Street investment firms in triggering the crash, a process that online participants often detailed in their posts. In the decade leading up to the collapse of mortgage markets, Wall Street investors took an interest in otherwise conservative mortgage markets, rapidly securitizing mortgage debt and trading debts as commodities on derivatives markets. Roping mortgage debts into complex financial transactions, as Karen Ho (2009, 2010) has argued, enabled Wall Street investment bankers and traders to leverage risk to turn quick and unprecedented profits, while also outsourcing risk to individual homeowners and the government, which many financial industry architects assumed would provide a bailout when the market collapsed.[8] Even as mortgage lenders such as Countrywide Financial, Lehman Brothers, Bank of America, and Wells Fargo were found guilty of illegal sales techniques and pushing through wrongful and illegal foreclosures, homeowners were still urged to honor financial obligations that often ran counter to their own financial interests (White 2010a, 972). These frustrations and resentments at lenders and the government constituted major distinctions between mortgagors who continued to pay on un-

derwater loans and those who chose to abandon mortgage debts after the crash
(White 2010a). In the wake of the foreclosure epidemic, many homeowners
participating in online collectivities came to recognize a double standard in the
morality of debt repayment and began reinterpreting the meaning of dispossession.

MEDIA CRITIQUE AND COUNTERPUBLICS

The collapse of U.S. mortgage markets inspired pundits and broadcast jour-
nalists to debate how best to regulate risk in financial markets and evaluate homeowners' responsibility to pay on underwater mortgages.[9] In the years immediately
following the 2008 crash, prominent news networks demonized mortgagors who
defaulted on home loans, often accusing them of immorality and a lack of patri-
otism (White 2010b, 999). Commentators, radio shows, and op-eds frequently
labeled defaulting mortgagors "unseemly," "offensive," and "unethical," and they
likened defaulters to "deadbeat dads who walk out on their children" or to ap-
peasers who would "give up" and hand over Europe to the Nazis (White 2010b,
999).[10] Black-oriented media, traditionally more politicized, performed no differently than the mainstream press in terms of blaming the crisis on mortgagors'
poor decision-making (Squires 2012). Local news reports in the Sacramento Valley proved more sympathetic to families facing eviction and default, as the scope
of the crisis appealed to the empathy of resident reporters and writers. Yet to
preserve the illusion of journalistic fairness, English- and Spanish-language networks such as Univision gave equal weight to the perspectives of lending executives at the expense of more in-depth analyses.[11] Generally, media discussions
failed to analyze how rampant financialization, the targeting of complex financial
products to unknowing consumers, and illegal lending practices contributed to
the crash. A majority of news networks ignored how racial and economic inequalities endemic to American late capitalism contributed to the foreclosure
epidemic (Chakravartty and Ferreira da Silva 2012; Roitman 2013; Shimpach
2012).

Online forums gave homeowners an opportunity to contest these media
representations, as users reposted and commented on articles and videos from
mainstream press outlets like the *New York Times*, *CNBC*, *CNN*, and the *Sacramento
Bee*. For example, one article in the online news aggregator *Huffington Post* (Goodman 2012), on the possibility of using eminent domain to fix Sacramento's mortgage meltdown, garnered more than three thousand comments in eight hours. In
another online forum, a participant using the online name Natomasucks (a riff on
the middle-class suburban development devastated by the housing crash) reposted

an article from the *Sacramento Bee* in which banking executives recommended loan modifications instead of mortgage default. The thread, entitled "To Walk Away or Not Walk Away?," inspired immediate commentary as another user named Coakl replied: "Loan executives are looking out for their interests; Don't play their game. . . . These loan executives are trying to pull one last sub-prime trick: persuading millions of upside-down homeowners to ignore the market collapse and make payments." Although the press heralded loan modifications as a source of much-needed assistance for homeowners, online posters often agreed that lenders misled homeowners by claiming that modifications would be in their interest. This discussion, suggesting that default was preferable to working with lenders to make payments, took place between 12:30 a.m. and 3:00 a.m. just days after the article's publication, showing the rapid-paced responses that online forums allowed. Online users whose days were filled with work and family responsibilities participated in public debate and critique even in the early morning hours.[12] Through online forums and the commentary sections of news articles, posters could anonymously and immediately challenge dominant media narratives of the crisis and debate alternatives to mortgage repayments.

By countering dominant media narratives, online homeowners could position themselves as media critics and producers without having to overcome the hurdles to mainstream media participation (cf. Boyer 2007, 78). In this way, online publics of indebtedness suggest an evolution of counterpublics, self-organized social spaces that depend on anonymity and an immediacy of response that empower stigmatized participants to formulate critiques (Berlant 2000; Fraser 1990; Negt and Kluge 1993; Warner 2002). The lack of editorial oversight and the ready access to Internet connections at all times of day or night helped online critics to circumvent the hurdles to audience participation erected by broadcast journalism. As Dominic Boyer (2013, 128, 136) points out in his ethnography of news production in a digital age, the technologies of digital communication associated with Web 2.0 developments fuse what he describes as "lateral and radial messaging potentials" to constitute interactive publics that sharply depart from twentieth-century models of Keynesian publics and broadcasting. The fragmented online collectives that erupted to critique and undermine the authority of broadcast media suggest more than a traditional public-counterpublic dialectic; they also show how digital media might be used to realize the promise of Jürgen Habermas's (1989) ideal democratic public sphere, through which alternative orientations toward debt could become viable.

DISEMBODIED AUTONOMY: ONLINE ANONYMITY AND DEFAULT

Consider Jack McGill, a thirty-three-year-old white computer programmer who had dropped out of high school and taught himself to code. McGill married his high-school sweetheart, a Latina preschool teacher, with whom he had four children and had purchased a house in a middle-class suburb of Sacramento. I sat with McGill on his sofa as he went online, guiding me to his favorite stops: Reddit and the Craigslist Housing forum.[13] After Bank of America denied his mortgage modification application, McGill discovered foreclosure-related discussion forums called subreddits, including categories such as "economy," "personal finance," "legal advice," and "WTF." According to Reddit, McGill fit the profile of their registered users, who tended to be socially liberal and interested in politics, with the slim majority of users being college-educated eighteen- to thirty-four-year-olds. McGill pointed to the Reddit posters who argued that speculators, not homeowners, drove most foreclosures. One user, Check-Please, argued that homeowners were "scammed into sub-prime [mortgages] by greedy brokers" and maintained, like many Reddit posters, that the mainstream press and the public unfairly scapegoated homeowners.

As McGill pointed out, both Craigslist and Reddit ensure a high level of anonymity, as users' identifying information remains private. In addition to criticizing lenders, posters on the forums recommended abandoning underwater mortgages as a response to personal hardships related to pending foreclosures, including mortgage troubles when contending with divorce, depression, suicidal thoughts, and chronic illness. Alongside these confessions, users provided detailed accounts of their mortgaging struggles, including concrete figures describing their loans, income, credit card balances, home prices, savings, and standing consumer debt. They freely exchanged financial information and opinions that would be considered taboo to share in face-to-face social settings, especially among Americans aspiring to middle-class status. That these novel forms of anonymous digital public-making arose in response to and shaped interpretations of indebtedness is not coincidental. Debt, as Janet Roitman (2005, 212) emphasizes, can offer a means to affirm or deny sociability, as it forces subjects to mark critical and, at times, strategic stances within social imaginaries. Rather than a negative social force, online indebtedness incites mediated forms of sociality.

In similar cases, many online participants encouraged homeowners to halt payments, often describing the relief and freedom they had felt when defaulting. When Renaldo Suarez, a fifty-six-year-old Latino veteran, faced foreclosure after his wife died from cancer, a friend guided him to online housing forums for advice. Suarez had moved to Sacramento from Los Angeles in the 1970s after securing a job as a factory manager, but he transitioned into educational services as the Sacramento Valley became deindustrialized in the 1980s. Now Suarez lived on a fixed income and owed nearly twice as much as his home was worth. After the loan counselor told him he would have to get a roommate to qualify for a modification, he posted his financial details on Craigslist in an attempt to solicit an alternative perspective. Many respondents suggested that he stop making payments but stay in his home:

> Jcasetnl: I bet he could just stay in it. Seriously. There's so many foreclosures in Sacramento . . .
>
> Whiskey_McSwiggens: I'm not sure how, but my neighbor [. . .] has been living in his house for over a year without paying mortgage payments and it's a bank-owned house. He's obviously going to lose the house at some point, but not until someone buys the house from the bank. OP [Original Poster] should look into how to do this.
>
> Chadcf: There is now [sic] 'how to do this'. It just involves not moving, until the Sherrif [sic] comes to kick you out. The bank isn't letting them stay there because they have some desire to not make people homeless, they do it because there are a ton of foreclosures and they have a huge backlog to deal with and if the house is upside down it's not like it's going to be any more profitable to move quickly.

Suarez eventually decided to stop payment on his mortgage, but he continued living in his home for two years until he was evicted. "As a man, I grew up knowing that you do the right thing. But this game is fixed. They [the banks] aren't doing the right thing, so why would I?"

In anonymous online domains, a diverse cross-section of homeowners similarly articulated the responsibility of lenders to assist homeowners and went further, even questioning the value of applying for loan modifications and encouraging mortgagors to default. While lenders shouldered no legal responsibility for modifying underwater mortgages, posters pointed to lenders' refusals to renegotiate mortgage contracts or to halt foreclosure proceedings for worthy candidates as evidence of the illegitimacy of some mortgage debt in the context of the crash. Walking away from underwater mortgages no longer suggested an unethical response to crushing debt, but a choice justified by the shifting landscape of credit-debt ties.

In the aftermath of the mortgage crash, anonymous online forums encouraged mortgagors to experience a sense of freedom in that they were protected by privacy and bolstered by the immediate responses of other posters. This sense of disembodied autonomy inspired them to question other forms of subjection, namely, what they identified as unfair debt servitude. In this way, anonymous online publics resonated with Northern Californians dispossessed by late liberal political economies. Anonymity protected participants from social stigma while allowing for a continued investment in the autological premises of late liberalism. Mortgagors could engage in frank and heated discussions about personal economic hardship that still remain taboo in many middle-class social circles throughout the Sacramento Valley, while permitting a heightened sense of individualism. Each poster could present his or her story as unique in its details but as one simultaneously linked with other participants' narratives. The pursuit of advice online also demanded that people become active consumers of knowledge, with the pursuit of financial competency as a normative ideal—a mark of late liberal regimes. As central as the content of forums, the form and medium of online publics of indebtedness generated experiential qualities of detachment and independence that inspired a reconsideration of the duty to repay underwater mortgage debts. If the anonymity and immediacy of Reddit and Craigslist online forums encouraged a detachment from the social contracts implicit in mortgage debt ties, the connectedness and performativity of social networking sites generated new ways of feeling about debt, though it de-emphasized strategies for outright debt refusal, as I show in the next section.

SEMIPUBLIC ONLINE NETWORKS AND DEBT AFFECT

"I didn't tell anyone what we were going through, not even my mom," Rachel Leibrock, a white journalist in her thirties, told me as we sat in a coffeehouse in Sacramento's midtown district and she described facing foreclosure after she lost her job at a local newspaper.[14] "I felt like I had failed as an adult." Leibrock eventually decided to tell her foreclosure story in a feature article she had written for the *Sacramento News & Review*, a weekly paper with a sizable online readership. She had been inspired to "go public" after reading a blog post in the *Huffington Post* about a homeowner who had fallen victim to dual-tracking, an illegal practice in which a homeowner pays into a trial modification program, but the loan servicer proceeds with foreclosure regardless.

In her article, Leibrock describes confronting a high-stakes Kafkaesque world of lost paperwork and endless phone calls with bureaucrats who monitored her monthly expenditures as she attempted to modify her mortgage. Ultimately, her loan administrator, Coldwell Banker, proceeded with foreclosure even though Leibrock actively participated in its government-sponsored modification program and had never missed a payment.[15] In the article, which features photos of Leibrock in her home, Leibrock describes how she and her husband had felt humiliated and depressed at the prospect of losing their home, but refused to "fall prey to the 'blame the victim' way of thinking." "We did nothing wrong," she wrote. "We refuse to feel ashamed." Within a week, Leibrock's article received nearly two hundred online comments, many from homeowners recounting their own struggles with lenders. After the article's publication, Leibrock heard from a government caseworker who offered to shepherd her case through Coldwell's modification process. Leibrock told me they chose to pursue a short sale instead.[16] "It's like a divorce," she said. "You go through so much that you eventually look around the house and it's like you can't even remember what you loved about someone."

Like Leibrock, not all homeowners sought the protection of online anonymity. Some participated in social networks such as Facebook and Twitter, which often link online and offline identities by making profiles visible in a semipublic arena populated by one's friends, relatives, and acquaintances in ways that indicate that the multivalent ability of online domains allowed them to become crucial publics in moments of upheaval. Among my interviewees, some homeowners in their late twenties through early forties confessed to financial hardships on social networking sites and posted images of their homes on Instagram and Tumblr. For example, Sara Jiménez, a Latina thirty-five-year-old unemployed kindergarten teacher and self-described "mom blogger," described chronicling her foreclosure experiences on Facebook as an important way to "emotionally process what was happening." Her posts often provided a sarcastic spin on her foreclosure trials. One post accompanied by a photograph showing her belongings in boxes on moving day read, "I hate moving . . . Living the american dream?" The fact that social media enabled homeowners to testify to the emotional toll of financial struggles considered taboo in offline interactions suggests that users can experience catharsis just from having Facebook followers to witness their suffering (Miller 2011, 172).

Despite the public tendency to conflate anonymous and semipublic digital forums under the rubric of Web 2.0 interactive media, these two modes created fundamentally distinct outlets for homeowners who faced financial hardship and underwater mortgages after the mortgage crash. The transformative potential of anonymous online publics such as Reddit and Craigslist allowed homeowners to abandon mortgage debt as a moral response to widespread foreclosures. Participants operating from behind anonymizing monikers advocated bankruptcy, mortgage default, and squatting without payment as mimetic responses to the unethical and immoral practices of financial institutions. The anonymity of these domains enabled users, detached from any requirement to reveal their identities, to experience a freedom of collective participation and to question the dispossessions resulting from neoliberal financial regimes.

Unlike participants in anonymous forums, homeowners who publicly linked their online and offline identities—either through sharing their narratives and photos, like Leibrock, or by posting in online social networks—focused more on the individual, affective, and sentimental qualities of debt obligations. Leibrock, for example, focused on her shame, humiliation, and frustration; she compared the process to the dissolution of a marriage and found sharing her feelings cathartic. Her decision to pursue a short sale held a marginal role in her story, whereas the great emotional toll of the process motivated her to go public. By publicizing personal experience, semipublic online domains appropriate the technologies of speed and automation to present an affective universe that undercuts the supposedly rational and objective domain of financial decision-making. Indeed, despair becomes a central force in the formation of an alternative affective public sphere (Cvetkovich 2007).

While anger, frustration, and outrage are present in both anonymous and semipublic online communities, the distinct forms of publicity of each generate specific forms of contestation. We might liken semipublic online publics to the "communities of sentiment" that Arjun Appadurai (1996, 8) describes in his post-electronic expansion of imagined communities (Anderson 1983), which, he argues, have the potential to move from "shared imagination to collective action." Whereas Appadurai focuses on transnational flows of film and media as forms of electronic capitalism that create the possibility for otherwise unimaginable forms of social action, interactive web-based social networks intensify these feelings of communal belonging. The distinct forms of circulation and publicity provided by social networking sites led participants to focus on sentiment as a form of action, as participants rarely placed the same emphasis on the moral valence of canceling debts found in anonymous forums. The experience of participating within an online public that saw itself as social and connected offered novel affective orientations toward debt, but it still tethered mortgagors to expectations of debt repayment that did not directly challenge the social contract implicit in postwar mortgage obligations. When posting on social networks like Facebook, home-owners remained connected to each other and upheld their duty to repay debts or, if unable to repay, felt obliged to justify themselves.

One important exception to the affective dimensions and politically circum-scribed nature of semipublic forums emerged on housing-activist blogs, in which participants also linked offline and online forms of identity by posting their images, but frequently advocated mortgage default as they criticized the banks and the government. For example, *America Underwater*, an activist blog launched jointly by nonprofits Rebuild the Dream and The New Bottom Line, encouraged home-owners with underwater loans to upload images of themselves holding signs show-ing how much they owed, accompanied by their personal stories.[17] On this blog, a diverse group of homeowners—men and women of white, African American, and Latino descent, teens whose families were going through foreclosure, baby boomers, seniors, and retirees—offered their individual stories, some even sign-ing their names, to create a collective narrative that linked their individual sen-timents of despair to mishandling by the mortgage industry and government officials, to whom they ascribed responsibility for foreclosures. Yet in many ways,

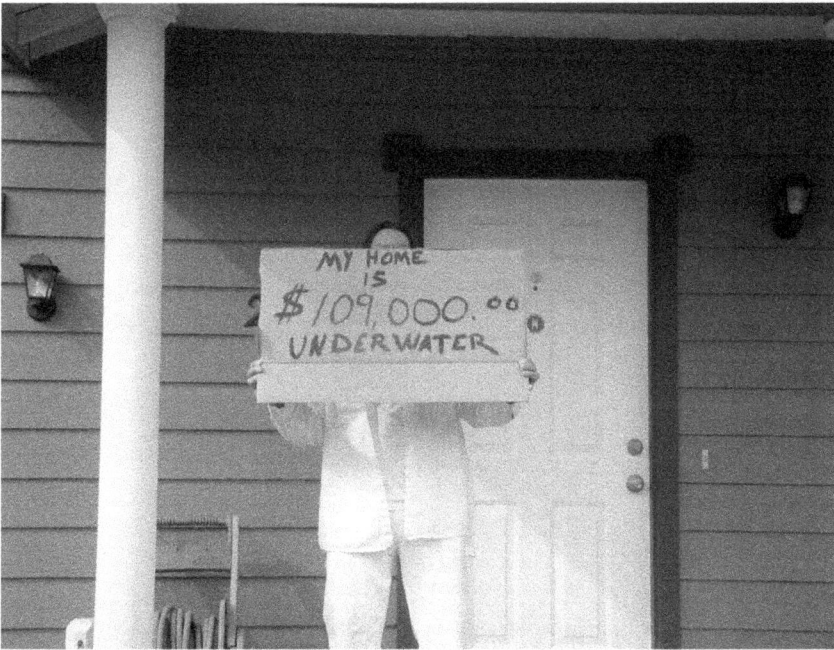

Figure 1. An anonymous homeowner holds up a sign indicating the amount by which her mortgage is underwater. Uncredited photo, http://america-underwater.tumblr.com/page/8.

the general principle that anonymity fostered more radical stances on debt refusal held true in these activist blogs. In their photographic posts on *America Underwater*, for example, many homeowners used their signs to obscure their faces and left their narratives unidentifiable, indicating a desire to maintain anonymity.

Even those who participated in online activist publics found anonymity, rather than semipublicity, a more acceptable stance from which they could advocate for the abandonment of mortgage debts.

DISCIPLINING THE POLITICS OF DEFAULT

Anonymous online users encouraged each other to default, declare bankruptcy, and squat in their homes while the banks dealt with backlogs of foreclosures. But not all posters on anonymous forums bought wholeheartedly into reformulated views arising from economic hardship. Instead, many posters resisted the indiscriminate democratization of acts of debt refusal. Even as anonymous online exchanges generated counternarratives of mortgage default, in many discussion threads posters suggested new forms of discipline to determine which homeowners qualified for respectable forms of default. By reframing only some forms of mortgage default as moral and ethically sound, users marked others as ethically suspect.

Anonymous online forums often erupted in impassioned debates and outright attacks on posters who advocated strategic mortgage default, which occurs when a homeowner can afford to pay his or her mortgage but nonetheless walks away. In one case, a Reddit user called Tvisforbabyboomers set off a firestorm when he described not feeling humiliated as he initiated strategic mortgage default:

> My wife and I are foreclosing **on purpose**. We live a middle class lifestyle and *can* afford our house, but our mortgage is "no longer sustainable." . . . Our house is $150,000 underwater. . . . We *do not* feel guilty about not paying our mortgage to our bank because when we asked for refinance assistance months ago, they said "google it" (seriously, they did). Furthermore, our mortgage is probably insured, so they will end up getting money anyway. Besides, it is business . . . the banks got bailed out, wall street got bailed out . . . and I'm middle class, this is *my* bail out. . . . **De-Occupy your home.**[18]

While most users, like McGill and Suarez, justified nonpayment by criticizing lenders' dishonesty, they stopped short of promoting wide-scale debt refusal. In contrast, Tvisforbabyboomers politicized his decision by drawing on an Occupy

Wall Street discourse that blamed the government and banks for the crisis while, paradoxically, drawing on a financial discourse to assert that mortgage default is a business decision, not an ethical one. Other commentators, however, attacked Tvisforbabyboomers and others like him, accusing them of adopting an "entitlement mentality." They derided borrowers' unwillingness to pay despite lack of hardship, such as unemployment or health crises, suggesting that these unscrupulous homeowners were unlike themselves, who were "hit hard by the crisis" and only forced into mortgage default by uncooperative lenders.

Unlike mainstream media representations, which did not suggest mortgage default as a viable option, these online discourses distinguished between a universe of morally appropriate mortgage default—in which bad things happened to good people despite their best efforts to uphold their end of the bargain—and one of selfish greed and irresponsible borrowing. Arguments strikingly similar to those in the Reddit thread, which sought to parse deserving victims from irresponsible overspenders, were deployed across online housing forums. In another Reddit thread, a homeowner who had bought a condo for $135,000 and owed $155,000 at the time of posting solicited advice on how to walk away. UnamusedPunk responded, "Your biggest problem is blaming everyone else for your problems, it is no one elses fault but your own that you didnt have a job for two years. IT IS ALL YOUR FAULT, ALL OF IT."[19]

Although online forums ostensibly presented a color- and class-blind public sphere, given the anonymity of participants, the discourses produced online frequently included biting expressions of racial and class discrimination. A recurring claim in various threads was that homeowners had bought homes they could not afford, blindly agreed to subprime loans, or were already chronically unemployed before the Great Recession. The racialized and class-based implications of the comments become clearer when we consider that African American and Latino homeowners were twice as likely as whites to be targeted by subprime lenders, even when they qualified for traditional, fixed-rate mortgages (Bocian et al. 2011). Likewise, working-class African American, Latino, and white homeowners often needed to borrow more to cover a mortgage on a basic, modest home, given the real decrease in income and rising costs of living since the 1980s.[20] On forums, as in the mainstream media, working-class homebuyers were accused of leveraging mortgages to purchase McMansions, boats, RVs, and luxury vacations. In reality, they typically used these loans to purchase modest homes, pay for their children's educations, and meet daily living expenses. Yet when identifiably non-middle-class homeowners proposed defaulting on their loans, they were rarely supported, suggesting the re-emergence of the pre–World War II stigma against working-class people who borrow and owe money. Nonpayment was given a positive moral valence for middle-class homeowners, but debt and default were still shameful for those with the greatest need.[21]

The anonymity of these forums enabled commenters to express great fervor and disdain. One popular Reddit user, for example, read through the archives of a New Jersey poster named Djspacebunny to attack her pleas for advice on an impending foreclosure. Citing her earlier posts with links, he accused her of being a lazy opiate addict who was trying to scam the system through malpractice lawsuits and bankruptcy, rather than a deserving, hardworking homeowner trying to do the right thing. He implored his fellow Reddit users to refuse to give her advice.[22] When other Reddit users criticized his rampage against Djspacebunny, he eventually removed his posts, but his impulse to police which posters were respectable enough to deserve guidance speaks to a recurring theme throughout the threads. If online privacy allows homeowners to participate in public dialogue, it also emboldens attacks on users who challenge longstanding notions of middle-class propriety. Through anonymous comments, online participants recalibrated the moral meanings of abandoning debts—but only to a point.[23]

THE MORAL VALENCE OF DEBT ABANDONMENT

Since the start of the Great Recession, analysts have revisited enduring questions about the moral valence of debt, the calculation of financial risk, and the necessity of regulating against unbridled greed within American capitalism. Yet many have suggested that these discussions have not gone far enough. They point out that Wall Street firms, bolstered by billion-dollar bailouts, have returned to business as usual, while any significant signs of social change have dissipated as Occupy protesters have packed up their tents. In his recent opus on debt, David Graeber (2011, 17), for example, suggests that these public debates initially promised to reveal the moral basis of market exchange, but then "sputtered into incoherence." The online forays of California homeowners caught in the grips of the 2008 crash and its protracted aftermath suggest otherwise: the longstanding social contract implicit within mortgage debt ties is losing its hold.

In the Sacramento Valley, homeowners who participated in online publics were influenced by others' decisions to reconfigure the morality of default in ways that challenge established interpretations of mortgage debt as the responsibility of the borrower alone. These significant shifts occur even as mainstream media narratives deride homeowners defaulting on mortgages and frame the absence of foreclosure stigma as a "contagion" that spreads the likelihood of default through neighborhoods (Chan et al. 2013, 101). Homeowners turning to online collectivities likewise changed their thinking about mortgage debt as they received advice from others in similar situations. They realized how many Americans struggled with unemployment, a rapid decline in home equity, and rising health-care costs, and they found the accessibility and privacy of online forums a particularly appealing means to navigate this foreboding landscape. Based on this evidence, I argue that anonymous participation in online domains such as Reddit and Craigslist housing forums presents opportunities to attach a positive moral valence to the abandonment of debt obligations for specific homeowners, whereas semipublic participation on social networking sites and public writing on blogs create new avenues for questioning the shame and humiliation that have accompanied postwar moral judgments about default.

The forms and mediums of both semipublic and anonymous online publics of indebtedness, not just their content, generated experiential qualities that inspired participants to reconsider, in different ways, the meaning of underwater mortgage debts. For my respondents, anonymous participation in online publics produced an experience of untethered freedom while still linking participants' experiences to broader collectivities. For example, participants in anonymous Reddit and Craigslist housing forums could challenge the authority of broadcast news narratives, formulating alternative moral economies that included abandoning insurmountable debts. Participation on semipublic domains such as Facebook and blogs encouraged participants to rethink the affective meaning of mortgage debts, moving from shame and stigma to outrage. These trends suggest a complex and unexpected convergence between digital media and neoliberalism, as interactive web platforms reinforce the autological premises of late liberalism while, simultaneously, leading those dispossessed by neoliberal financial regimes to question those institutions' role in perpetuating omnipresent debt economies.[24]

How do we classify the influence of homeowners experiencing foreclosure in lower-middle- and middle-class neighborhoods who, online, advocate new moral and affective stances in relation to debt but do not recognize these orientations as political?[25] Anthropologists have shown how digital technologies have been used for traditional political aims, such as mobilizing support for the indigenous Zapatista movement in Mexico (Castells 2001) and coordinating protests across national borders (Juris 2008; Shirky 2008), as was the case during the Arab Spring, but the transformations in perspective I am studying operate more clandestinely, making them more difficult to detect and analyze. Within anonymous and semipublic online domains, homeowners generated new affective orientations toward indebtedness and revised cultural conceptions of the morality of abandoning overwhelming debts; some then carried these conceptions into other social spheres by walking away from their mortgages. While resistant to collective political mobilization in a traditional sense, mortgagors with opposing political affiliations and worldviews often joined in online dialogue in a populist-inflected counterpoint to dominant narratives of immoral defaulters that is significant in its own right.

Across both anonymous and semipublic domains, online publics represent a significant expansion of American middle-class milieus and narrative resources to include diverse forms of digital sociality. Specifically, online publics shaped the expression and interpretation of indebtedness as a distinct part of an American lower-middle- and middle-class habitus, at a moment when these social positions were increasingly precarious. Participants within anonymous online publics drew on cultural capital to sort through uncensored and nonexpert online advice and to incorporate that guidance into their preexisting knowledge about debt, finance, and the moral valence of repayment. Those posting in semipublic online social networks described a sense of security that allowed them to share their hardships with their friends and family members online. These forms of online connectivity not only revised middle-class ideas about the moral underpinnings of indebtedness but also reflected and reproduced forms of social inequality by extending socioeconomic disparities into a new, virtual terrain.

Just as the technological apparatus of subprime lending, such as risk algorithms and automated debt-to-income ratios, disproportionately affected African American and Latino homeowners in low-income neighborhoods, participants managing indebtedness through these online technologies also excluded the most marginalized homeowners. Indeed, more in-depth research is needed to analyze how the intersections of class, ethnicity, and race influence the appeal and efficacy of online publics. As Margaret Atwood (2008, 41) points out in *Payback*, debt, like smoking cigarettes and drinking alcohol, has gone out of fashion—what was once considered harmless is now considered a sin to be avoided at all costs. Those Americans who are forced to rely on debt to finance the necessities of daily life, therefore, are once again seen as suffering a lapse in discipline and moral personhood that needs to be rectified.

My examination here of the "prosaics of the digital," or how digital media reflect and shape social practices (Coleman 2010), indicates a significant reorganization of debt imaginaries that reflects and extends a nationwide kitchen-table discussion about the culpability of mortgage lenders and the morality of abandoning unfair debt burdens. Although these online publics might seem fleeting, coalescing around crises and eventually succumbing to broken links and obsolete Internet browsers, the ways in which they participate in a larger restructuring of debt refusal promise to endure. While online forums emboldened middle-class homeowners to resist moral responsibility for distressed mortgage debt, these homeowners also sought to rediscipline the significance and virtue of mortgage default by determining who may respectably abandon underwater loans. Ultimately, the rise of such publics suggests how narratives that question the repayment of debt as central to moral personhood might gain traction through emerging technological forms of sociality and self-expression, virtual encounters that highlight the disorder of contemporary capitalism and play a significant role in redefining how Americans understand the debts they owe one another.

ABSTRACT

The 2008 mortgage crash and the online publics that have emerged in its aftermath have reshaped American interpretations of indebtedness. Combining research among homeowners facing foreclosure in California's Sacramento Valley with an analysis of the national online forums they frequent, I show how participants rethink the moral scaffolding of debt relations within what I describe as online publics of indebtedness. *Anonymous online publics foster experiences of disembodied autonomy that encourage debt refusal and discipline the middle-class ethics of debt abandonment, as participants distinguish between mortgagors who deserve not to pay their debts and those they deem irresponsible for defaulting on their loans. In contrast, participation in semipublic social networks and online forms of publicity emphasizes new affective orientations toward debt obligations. My analysis contributes to an anthropological scholarship on moral economies by exploring the role of distinct forms of new media in shaping everyday experiences of indebtedness in late-capitalist financial markets.* [online; publics; debt; moral economies; mortgage default; United States]

NOTES

1. An underwater mortgage is one in which the amount owed exceeds the property's current value.
2. For an overview of the valuation of credit and the morally suspect nature of debt within anthropological discussions, see Peebles 2010 and Gregory 2012.
3. As Tom Boellstorff (2012) emphasizes, ethnographies of online communities require deeper involvement than isolated interviews and textual readings.
4. As scholars have recently shown, online domains hold the same social potential and problems as any arena of offline life (Boellstorff 2008; Ginsburg 2008; Miller and Horst 2012).
5. Mortgaging and foreclosure reflect culturally specific and historically shifting ideas about homeownership, debt, and seizure (Graeber 2011; Maurer 2006; Shipton 2009).
6. Although the repossession of goods has long been reserved for the working poor rather

than middle-class households that fail to pay debts (Hyman 2011b, 204), foreclosure is a key exception to this trend.

7. This belief is found among those living in middle-class neighborhoods across the nation (Heiman, Freeman, and Liechty 2012, 8).

8. Unlike the government buyout of homeowners' bad loans during the mortgage crash that preceded the Great Depression, legislators passed policies that privatized assistance programs, leaving lenders to adjudicate homeowners' appeals and to refuse to modify distressed mortgages.

9. While there are literally thousands of examples of these media discussions, a few illustrations include Lowenstein 2010, Armour 2009, and Harney 2009.

10. Brent White (2010b) references specific shows such as Fox's *Your World with Cavuto*, "The Deal: Walk Away from Your Home"; *The Mike Gallagher Show*, "YouWalk-Away.com"; and *60 Minutes*, "The U.S. Mortgage Meltdown."

11. As Janet Roitman (2013) attests, a range of pundits trace a chain of events by which the "housing market fell" and homeowners lost equity and defaulted on their mortgages. The critical question of *why* housing prices began to fall, Roitman (2013, 57) suggests, is preemptively excluded.

12. For professionals working in office jobs, these online sessions proved appealing because they could take place surreptitiously during work hours. For homeowners with jobs in the service industries, online searches and participation were unrestricted to business hours and could commence after long workdays.

13. Craigslist discussion forums also harbor a robust community, with more than 200 million users and one hundred topical forums. As of 2012, Reddit, a site with over 1 million registered users, was divided into more than 100,000 "subreddits," or topic threads, and garnered 34.9 million unique views each month.

14. Due to the public nature of Leibrock's article, I have used her real name with her permission. All other names of homeowners are pseudonyms.

15. A representative from Coldwell told Leibrock that she should have been making her regular payments in addition to the trial modification payments to prevent default.

16. In a short sale, the proceeds from the sale will not cover the amount owed on the mortgage. Sometimes, though not always, the lender might prefer to absorb a moderate loss on the sale than have a homeowner default on a loan. The homeowner's credit is still damaged.

17. A progressive organization founded by the Obama advisor Van Jones, Rebuild the Dream, draws on digital technologies to campaign for social issues. See http://www.rebuildthedream.com/support_for_homeowners.

18. The thread can be viewed at http://www.reddit.com/r/Frugal/comments/sm8kr/i_got_hit_hard_by_the_crash_and_im_going_through_a_foreclosure.

19. The thread can be viewed at http://www.reddit.com/r/AskReddit/comments/11dzxs/my_condo_i_bought_when_i_was_22_has_been_in.

20. By the 1980s, many Americans faced a landscape less similar to the postwar era than to the 1920s, when consumer credit was used to shore up shortcomings from short-term unemployment and decreased income (Hyman 2011a, 99).

21. This dynamic is apparent in the rise of what Brett Williams (2004) describes as "debt porn," reality television shows in which Americans are shamed for their debts, repent, and promise to change their ways.

22. The thread can be viewed at http://www.reddit.com/r/newjersey/comments/10ycis/nj_help_a_sister_out_im_going_to_lose_my_house.

23. The anonymity of the sites is not absolute, as users might post otherwise private financial information in ways that raise pressing questions about the use of these data. Joe Deville (2013), for example, shows how an online loan company uses "leaky data," such as the browser and the device with which users access the site, as well as their Facebook activity, to determine the risk of a borrower and the interest rate a borrower is charged.

24. My findings offer a starting point for understanding what Dominic Boyer (2013, 135) sees as the phenomenological juncture between digital media and neoliberalism, through

which mobile media make late liberal discourse seem intuitive, while the interfaces promise to give the experience of autological freedom.

25. My findings advance Hannah Appel's (2014) claim that experiences of the 2008 crash and its aftermath have inspired a reimagining of capitalism. Analyzing the stories of individuals working in Wall Street banks who eventually joined Occupy Wall Street, Appel shows how her collaborators were radicalized after witnessing the unethical maneuvers of their colleagues and institutions leading up to the crash.

REFERENCES

Appadurai, Arjun
    1996   *Modernity at Large: Cultural Dimensions of Globalization.* Minneapolis: University of Minnesota Press.

Appel, Hannah
    2014   "Occupy Wall Street and the Economic Imagination." *Cultural Anthropology* 29, no. 4: 602–25. http://dx.doi.org/10.14506/ca29.4.02.

Anderson, Benedict
    1983   *Imagined Communities: Reflections on the Origins and Spread of Nationalism.* London: Verso.

Armour, Stephanie
    2009   "More Walk Away from Homes, Mortgages." *USA Today*, November 3. http://usatoday30.usatoday.com/money/economy/housing/2009-11-02-voluntary-foreclosure_N.htm.

Atwood, Margaret
    2008   *Payback: Debt and the Shadow Side of Wealth.* Toronto: House of Anansi Press.

Baker, Christi, Kevin Stein, and Mike Eiseman
    2008   "Foreclosure Trends in Sacramento and Recommended Policy Options." Report for the Sacramento Housing and Redevelopment Agency by the California Reinvestment Coalition. http://www.shra.org/LinkClick.aspx?fileticket=WaDLuiUot5s%3D&tabid=103&mid=454.

Berlant, Lauren, ed.
    2000   *Intimacy.* Chicago: University of Chicago Press.

Bocian, Debbie Gruenstein, Carolina Reid, Roberto G. Quercia, and Wei Li
    2011   "Lost Ground, 2011: Disparities in Mortgage Lending and Foreclosures." Durham, N.C.: Center for Responsible Lending. http://www.responsiblelending.org/research-publication/lost-ground-2011.

Boellstorff, Tom
    2008   *Coming of Age in Second Life.* Princeton, N.J.: Princeton University Press.
    2012   *Ethnography and Virtual Worlds: A Handbook of Method.* Princeton, N.J.: Princeton University Press.

Boyer, Dominic
    2007   *Understanding Media: A Popular Philosophy.* Chicago: Prickly Paradigm Press.
    2013   *The Life Informatic: Newsmaking in the Digital Era.* Ithaca, N.Y.: Cornell University Press.

Calder, Lendol
    1999   *Financing the American Dream: A Cultural History of Consumer Credit.* Princeton, N.J.: Princeton University Press.

Castells, Manuel
    2001   *The Internet Galaxy: Reflections on the Internet, Business, and Society.* Oxford: Oxford University Press.

Chakravartty, Paula, and Denise Ferreira da Silva
    2012   "Accumulation, Dispossession, and Debt: The Racial Logic of Global Capitalism—An Introduction." *American Quarterly* 64, no. 3: 361–85. http://dx.doi.org/10.1353/aq.2012.0033.

Chan, Sewin, Michael Gedal, Vicki Been, and Andrew Haughwout
2013   "The Role of Neighborhood Characteristics in Mortgage Default Risk: Evidence from New York City." *Journal of Housing Economics* 22, no. 2: 100–18. http://dx.doi.org/10.1016/j.jhe.2013.03.003.

Coleman, E. Gabriella
2010   "Ethnographic Approaches to Digital Media." *Annual Review of Anthropology* 39: 487–505. http://dx.doi.org/10.1146/annurev.anthro.012809.104945.

Cvetkovich, Ann
2007   "Public Feelings." *South Atlantic Quarterly* 106, no. 3: 459–68. http://dx.doi.org/10.1215/00382876-2007-004.

Deville, Joe
2013   "Wonga is Watching You . . . How Payday Lenders Follow Your Online Trail." *The Conversation*, May 21. http://theconversation.com/wonga-is-watching-you-how-payday-lenders-follow-your-online-trail-14541.

Dudley, Kathryn Marie
2000   *Debt and Dispossession: Farm Loss in America's Heartland*. Chicago: University of Chicago Press.

Edelman, Marc
2005   "Bringing the Moral Economy back in . . . to the Study of Twenty-First-Century Transnational Social Movements." *American Anthropologist* 107, no. 3: 331–45. http://dx.doi.org/10.1525/aa.2005.107.3.331.

Fannie Mae
2010   "New Nationwide Survey Provides Comprehensive Look at Sentiment toward Housing." Press release, April 6. http://www.fanniemae.com/portal/about-us/media/corporate-news/2010/4989.html.

Fraser, Nancy
1990   "Rethinking the Public Sphere: A Contribution to the Critique of Actually Existing Democracy." *Social Text*, nos. 25–26: 56–80. http://dx.doi.org/10.2307/466240.

Ginsburg, Faye
2008   "Rethinking the Digital Age." In *The Media and Social Theory*, edited by David Hesmondhalgh and Jason Toynbee, 127–44. New York: Routledge.
2012   "Disability in the Digital Age." In *Digital Anthropology*, edited by Heather A. Horst and Daniel Miller, 101–26. London: Berg.

Goodman, Peter S.
2012   "Eminent Domain as Underwater Mortgages Fix: Why Some Cities are Considering Unorthodox Measure." *Huffington Post*, October 1. http://www.huffingtonpost.com/2012/10/01/eminent-domain-mortgages_n_1917391.html.

Graeber, David
2011   *Debt: The First 5,000 Years*. New York: Melville House.

Gregory, Chris A.
2012   "On Money Debt and Morality: Some Reflections on the Contribution of Economic Anthropology." *Social Anthropology* 20, no. 4: 380–96. http://dx.doi.org/10.1111/j.1469-8676.2012.00225.x.

Griffith, David
2009   "The Moral Economy of Tobacco." *American Anthropologist* 111, no. 4: 432–42. http://dx.doi.org/10.1111/j.1548-1433.2009.01153.x.

Habermas, Jürgen
1989   *Structural Transformation of the Public Sphere: An Inquiry into a Category of Bourgeois Society*. Translated by Thomas Burger, with the assistance of Frederick Lawrence. Cambridge, Mass.: MIT Press. Originally published in 1962.

Harney, Kenneth R.

    2009   "Good Credit Scores, Deadbeat Choices." *Washington Post*, November 19. http://www.washingtonpost.com/wp-dyn/content/article/2009/09/18/ AR2009091800071.html.

Heiman, Rachel, Carla Freeman, and Mark Liechty

    2012   "Introduction: Charting an Anthropology of the Middle Classes." In *The Global Middle Classes: Theorizing Through Ethnography*, 3–29. Santa Fe, N.M.: School for Advanced Research.

High, Holly

    2012   "Re-Reading the Potlatch in a Time of Crisis: Debt and the Distinctions that Matter." *Social Anthropology* 20, no. 4: 363–79. http://dx.doi.org/10.1111/ j.1469-8676.2012.00218.x.

Ho, Karen Z.

    2009   *Liquidated: An Ethnography of Wall Street*. Durham, N.C.: Duke University Press.

    2010   "Outsmarting Risk: From Bonuses to Bailouts." *Anthropology Now*, May 14. http://anthronow.com/online-articles/outsmarting-risk-from-bonuses-to- bailouts.

Hyman, Louis

    2011a *Debtor Nation: The History of America in Red Ink*. Princeton, N.J.: Princeton University Press.

    2011b "Ending Discrimination, Legitimating Debt: The Political Economy of Race, Gender, and Credit Access in the 1960s and 1970s." *Enterprise and Society* 12, no. 1: 200–32. http://dx.doi.org/10.1017/S1467222700009770.

Jefferson, Anna

    2013   "Narratives of Moral Order in Michigan's Foreclosure Crisis." *City and Society* 25, no. 1: 92–112. http://dx.doi.org/10.1111/ciso.12006.

Juris, Jeffrey S.

    2008   *Networking Futures: The Movements against Corporate Globalization*. Durham, N.C.: Duke University Press.

Langley, Paul

    2007   "The Uncertain Subjects of Anglo-American Financialization." *Cultural Critique*, no. 65: 66–91. http://dx.doi.org/10.1353/cul.2007.0009.

Lowenstein, Roger

    2010   "Walk Away from Your Mortgage!" *New York Times Magazine*, January 7. http:// www.nytimes.com/2010/01/10/magazine/10FOB-wwln-t.html.

Maurer, Bill

    2006   *Pious Property: Islamic Mortgages in the United States*. New York: Russell Sage.

Miller, Daniel

    2011   *Tales from Facebook*. Cambridge: Polity.

Miller, Daniel, and Heather A. Horst

    2012   "The Digital and the Human: A Prospectus for Digital Anthropology." In *Digital Anthropology*, edited by Heather A. Horst and Daniel Miller, 3–35. London: Berg.

Negt, Oskar, and Alexander Kluge

    1993   *Public Sphere and Experience: Toward an Analysis of the Bourgeois and Proletarian Public Sphere*. Translated by Peter Labanyi, Jamie Owen Daniel, and Assenka Oksiloff. Minneapolis: University of Minnesota Press. Originally published in 1972.

Newman, Katherine S.

    1988   *Falling from Grace: Downward Mobility in the Age of Affluence*. Berkeley: University of California Press.

Peebles, Gustav

    2010   "The Anthropology of Credit and Debt." *Annual Review of Anthropology* 39: 225– 40. http://dx.doi.org/10.1146/annurev-anthro-090109-133856.

Pinch, Trevor, and Richard Swedberg, eds.
  2008   *Living in a Material World: Economic Sociology Meets Science and Technology Studies.*
          Cambridge, Mass.: MIT Press.
Poon, Martha
  2008   "From New Deal Institutions to Capital Markets: Commercial Consumer Risk
          Scores and the Making of Subprime Mortgage Finance." *Accounting, Organizations,
          and Society* 34, no. 5: 654–74. http://dx.doi.org/10.1016/j.aos.2009.02.003.
Postill, John
  2012   "Digital Politics and Political Engagement." In *Digital Anthropology*, edited by
          Heather A. Horst and Daniel Miller, 165–84. London: Berg.
Reid, Carolina
  2010   "Sought or Sold? Social Embeddedness and Consumer Decisions in the Mortgage
          Market." Federal Reserve Bank of San Francisco Working Paper. http://
          www.frbsf.org/community-development/publications/working-papers/2010/
          december/mortgage-market-social-networks-consumer-decision/.
Roitman, Janet
  2005   *Fiscal Disobedience: An Anthropology of Economic Regulation in Central Africa.*
          Princeton, N.J.: Princeton University Press
  2013   *Anti-Crisis.* Durham, N.C.: Duke University Press.
Ross, Andrew
  2013   *Creditocracy and the Case for Debt Refusal.* New York: OR Books.
Scott, James C.
  1977   *The Moral Economy of the Peasant: Rebellion and Subsistence in Southeast Asia.* New
          Haven, Conn.: Yale University Press.
Shimpach, Shawn
  2012   "Realty Reality: HGTV and the Subprime Crisis." *American Quarterly* 64, no. 3:
          515–42. http://dx.doi.org/10.1353/aq.2012.0032.
Shipton, Parker
  2009   *Mortgaging the Ancestors: Ideologies of Attachment in Africa.* New Haven, Conn.: Yale
          University Press.
Shirky, Clay
  2008   *Here Comes Everybody: The Power of Organizing Without Organizations.* New York:
          Penguin.
Squires, Catherine R.
  2012   "Coloring in the Bubble: Perspectives on Black-Oriented Media on the (Latest)
          Economic Disaster." *American Quarterly* 64, no. 3: 543–70. http://dx.doi.org/
          10.1353/aq.2012.0034.
Thompson, E.P.
  1971   "The Moral Economy of the English Crowd in the Eighteenth Century." *Past &
          Present*, no. 50: 76–136. http://www.jstor.org/stable/650244.
Warner, Michael
  2002   *Publics and Counterpublics.* New York: Zone.
White, Brent T.
  2010a   "The Morality of Strategic Default." *UCLA Law Review Discourse* 58, 155–64.
          http://www.uclalawreview.org/the-morality-of-strategic-default/.
  2010b   "Underwater and Not Walking Away: Shame, Fear and the Social Management
          of the Housing Crisis." *Wake Forest Law Review* 45: 971.
Williams, Brett
  2004   *Debt for Sale: A Social History of the Credit Trap.* Philadelphia: University of
          Pennsylvania Press.

RULE BY GOOD PEOPLE: Health Governance and the Violence of Moral Authority in Thailand

DAENA AKI FUNAHASHI
Aarhus University
http://orcid.org/0000-0002-3015-5391

Yok made no effort to hide her look of disapproval. She had arranged to pick me up in front of my apartment in eastern Bangkok, but had caught me outside the shrine of the neighborhood's tree spirit, deep in conversation with Praew, a street vendor who sold chilled drinks to the spirit's devotees. As Praew described her dream to me, one in which she saw this week's winning lottery numbers in the folds of the spirit's tangled hair, Yok urged me into her sedan. The minute I closed the door, she could hold back no longer: "What idiots [*man ngom ngai*]! . . . What do they know?"

In the privacy of the car, Yok chided me for encouraging what she called "primitive country beliefs." As we drove past the corrugated metal walls of Praew's alley, adorned with faded political campaign stickers, Yok became even more visibly irritated. The stickers featured the face of Thaksin Shinawatra, ousted by a military coup in 2006, and his sister Yingluck, prime minister at the time of my research in 2012 but soon to be deposed in another coup in 2014. "*This* is the problem," said Yok, pointing her finger and catching in its sweep the political stickers, the tree spirit's shrine, and Praew all at once.

Yok worked as a health expert for Thai Campaign for Health (TCH), a state-funded organization that had gained an expanded role in public policymaking under the military junta of 2006.[1] Yok and other conservative health experts at TCH claimed that, in the face of increasing political polarization and the loss of

CULTURAL ANTHROPOLOGY, Vol. 31, Issue 1, pp. 107–130, ISSN 0886-7356, online ISSN 1548-1360. © *by the American Anthropological Association. All rights reserved. DOI: 10.14506/ca31.1.06*

confidence in national juridical and legal mechanisms to implement necessary reforms, independent and apolitical bodies such as health organizations ought to intervene in the name of the common good. As Yok continued her tirade, she drew a clear link between the "idiocy" she saw in believing in the dreams sent by tree spirits and the "idiocy" of believing in the dreams of capitalist self-advancement spread by the Shinawatras. According to Yok:

> Many Thai people . . . still believe in spirits and don't have wisdom [*panya*]. [They believe that] you can be that person you see in the movie . . . [and that] all you have to do [to become that person] is to buy the same iPhone, the same car, the same whatever it is. If you don't have mental immunity [*phumikhumkanjit*][2] to want . . . you are just like a buffalo [*khwai*] who lives only to gratify its senses. . . . At TCH, we try to educate the masses, but they don't listen!

Yok and other conservative health experts in the larger realm of public health blamed Thaksin and Yingluck's reinvention of the nation as "Thailand, Inc." for having caused negative environmental, social, and health-related consequences. For these health experts, the repeated electoral victories of the Shinawatras despite these self-evident (at least to some) flaws proved that the voting majority lacked what they termed "mental immunity" to the cunning of politicians, and that, like "buffalo," they were incapable of voting for the greater good. Together with the anti-Shinawatra street movements of 2013 and 2014,[3] many health experts saw the military intervention as a necessary evil and demanded that the task of governance fall to "good people" (*khon di*). By good people, they meant those with a mental immunity to economic interests or party politics, those who could guarantee good governance from the basis of scientific, technical, and medical knowledge (or what the junta claimed as "moral truths"). More specifically, people like themselves.

The junta-written constitution of 2007 gave such claims legal legitimacy. The junta, having just wrested power from Thaksin, appealed to the apolitical basis of their intervention by enshrining in the new constitution the World Health Organization's (WHO) Health in All Policies (HiAP) initiative. The initiative redefined negative health outcomes as a natural limit to political ambition and capitalist expansion. According to the WHO, HiAP was intended to promote good governance and social equity by making population health "an overarching goal shared by everyone" (Kickbusch and Gleicher 2012, vi). Audit tools, such as the Health Impact Assessment (HIA), were to open new opportunities for concerned citizens to advocate for the making of "healthy public policy" (Kickbusch and Gleicher 2012, ix)—public policy driven by concerns for the common good, rather than by party politics or economic interests. Especially significant in light of the junta's attempts to depoliticize the political nature of their rule was the WHO's advocacy of a "knowledge society [where] power and authority are no longer concentrated in government" (Kickbusch and Gleicher 2012, vi).

In Thailand, the HiAP initiative as a legal mandate gave health experts jurisdiction over all aspects of public policymaking that affected national well-being. The mandate was intentionally broad, allowing for interventions in a wide variety of contexts, including anti-tobacco and alcohol campaigns, opposition to industrial development along Thailand's coast, and pressure to keep youth from violent or inappropriate television programming. Yet while the WHO sees HiAP as a globally applicable initiative that can be deployed in locally meaningful ways (Kickbusch and Buckett 2010), the way in which the Thai junta adapted HiAP into a monarchical and Buddhist framework of righteous rule,[4] as I demonstrate below, reveals an inherent problem in assuming that the particular local capture of a global initiative successfully preserves the supposedly global aspirations in the original. Health reframed within dharmic notions of wisdom (*panya*) and enlightenment holds within it political implications unrepresentable in nondharmic political worlds.

However, seeing the Thai adaptation of HiAP as an idiosyncratic diversion from an otherwise universal convergence would be to replicate Yok's dismissal of Praew's world (that is, to say that Yok simply does not understand health). As Akhil Gupta (1998, 216) argues in his now-seminal piece on the status of indigenous knowledge, there ought to be other ways of talking about how local knowledge is imagined against the presumed universality of Western science, rather than as a mere mistranslation or cultural alternative.

Isabelle Stengers's (2005) cosmopolitical proposal opens another frame through which to approach this problem. Rather than probing into the emergence of new knowledge that forms at the interface of the modern/rational/universal and the traditional/cultural/particular as a hybrid that destabilizes these dichotomies, Stengers invites us to turn our attention instead to what remains incommensurable. Inasmuch as we all occupy particular ontological horizons, the problem lies not so much in pitting one perspective against another, but in opening ourselves to the possibility of a radically other idea of politics, economics, and ethics. This includes having to consider, as Marisol de la Cadena (2010) does, entities such as "earth beings" as having a legitimate claim to modern politics, as well as to take seriously the idea that cotton cries and beans kill (Hetherington 2013). In this sense, Stengers allows us to question the assumption that we can speak for a common world.

Finding inspiration in this approach, I take the Thai adaptation of HiAP as a challenge to the notion that modern science can, from a universally valid standpoint, answer "the political question par excellence: Who can talk of what, be the spokesperson of what, represent what?" (Stengers 2005, 995). For the WHO, which sees health as a global common good, health represented an apolitical basis on which to evaluate local governments. While the WHO makes HiAP as it is mobilized by TCH experts equivalent to its own initiative, the ways in which HiAP is reframed within monarchical and Buddhist terms by the TCH manifest the radical incommensurability of these two notions of health. The disjuncture between these two different worlds, one in which health is biomedically determined and the other in which health is dharmically determined, thus opens an interstice through which we can question the basis of what we mean by "global" health and the promotion of "good governance."

Based on ethnographic fieldwork conducted between the years 2011 to 2014 at the TCH headquarters in downtown Bangkok, as well as at associated organizations, I examine the unintended consequences of assuming that positive knowledge can guarantee good governance. Specifically, I examine how the notion of the good as something that exists separately from public referendum mobilizes a conservative politics that justifies the rendering of citizens into "buffalo," as well as the use of military violence.

With health as the standard measure of one's ability to choose wisely (or healthily), experts such as Yok, along with conservative political forces, leave no room for individuals like Praew to speak except as those in need of care. Here, contra Stengers, who finds potential for radical democracy through engagement with divergent ontological horizons, the TCH's take on health as a way to define its legitimacy as "good people" in the eyes of those its members call "idiots" does not support such optimism. Taking conservative health experts like Yok seriously, then, means to see them as not just putting into motion health-based governance that challenges the biomedical hegemony inherent within WHO discourse, but also as individuals equally equipped with hegemonic powers of their own. An analysis of the Thai translation of HiAP within a Buddhist genealogy of ethics thus reveals how the antipolitics (Redfield 2012) of a global health movement unintentionally sustains the fantasies of an authoritarian regime.

At the same time, the TCH's claim to be an apolitical advocate of the common good places it in a double bind. In the eyes of an increasingly skeptical public, the activities of conservative health experts who benefited from the military intervention against a democratically elected government appeared political and in the service of the ancien régime. In the face of such opposition, I see the use of slurs by Yok and her colleagues to refer to individuals like Praew as "idiots" with the mental capacity of a "buffalo" (a mere beast of burden to whom political agency should not be granted) as a symptom of their inability to justify their claim to goodness without appearing too self-interested or lacking the very mental immunity to politics that they espoused. In this way, the double bind points to the problem of defining what counts as legitimacy when what counts as legitimate must emerge from a strictly antipolitical register.

BIOMEDICAL UNIVERSALISM AND ITS ANTIPOLITICS

In looking at how HiAP as a global movement enabled Thai conservative health experts to position themselves as good people unmoved by national party politics, I build on anthropological examinations of how interventions made in the name of humanitarian and/or biomedical necessity nonetheless deploy their own political and moral reasoning (Fassin 2011; Pandolfi 2003; Ticktin 2011). Whether in the form of bearing witness to psychic scars as recordable evidence of oppression (Fassin 2008), diagnosing symptoms in ways that entitle individuals to new forms of biological citizenship (Petryna 2002), or determining who will receive life-sustaining treatment in the face of limited medical supplies (Nguyen 2010), medical anthropologists have shown how health experts claim to act in the name of a good conceived as universally applicable, but which in fact stems from a specific (i.e., liberal, Western) lineage of morality (cf. Redfield 2005). The explicitly antipolitical drive behind these medical interventions offers, in Peter Redfield's (2012, 452) terms, a glimpse into politics "'beyond' politics," an increasingly relevant form of antipolitics in the face of emergent biosecurity concerns that require global responses.

We can examine HiAP as one point of entry through which international organizations such as the WHO connect local health experts, nongovernmental organizations, and community activists in what Andrew Lakoff (2010, 60) calls "'apolitical' linkages" that allow experts to reach individuals in need across national boundaries. The creation of such links based on bioscientific authority has opened new pathways for health experts to work with different sectors of society and to take on responsibilities formerly belonging to national governments, responsibilities now recast within a global framework. Bioscientific knowledge and medical expertise thus make possible an imagined community of experts united as one against the political limitations and particularisms of nationally bound public health.

The WHO defines HiAP as a framework conducive to the creation of such apolitical links, and as an approach that allows experts and concerned citizens to have a say in policy decisions in a way that "systematically takes into account the health implications of decisions, seeks synergies, and avoids harmful health impacts, in order to improve population health and health equity" (WHO and the Ministry of Social Affairs and Health, Finland, 2013). Against national governments with eyes fixed on growing GDP and local politics operating to the detriment of the population's well-being, HiAP aimed to open up a space for monitory democracy by making health outcomes the key "factor[s] defining good governance" (Kickbusch and Gleicher 2012, 1). Moreover, the WHO has come to promote health as a "global public good" (Kickbusch and Gleicher 2012, 46), and, on the basis of this public good, health experts called on governments to review the health consequences of their goals and policies (e.g., fiscal, environmental, educational). Key to providing experts with the necessary concrete data was the Health Impact Assessment (HIA), an audit tool that linked negative health consequences to specific public policy. Using it, experts were expected to collaborate with other concerned actors to intervene in local decision-making processes. Significantly, by making good or bad governance determinable by the assessment of health outcomes, the HIA allowed such interventions to be made in the idioms of biomedical necessity.

But such a notion of health carries with it certain assumptions. For one, the treatment of health as part of a universal objective truth divorced from cultural, social, and political realities belies what Philippe Descola (2013, xv) calls a Western "naturalist" tradition, a tradition that categorizes human biology on the side of nature, the "domain of objects" against which human subjects exert their divergent influence. It is this treatment of health as a natural condition accessible via biomedicine, albeit through different institutional and national contexts, that gives purchase to the WHO's idea of health as a global public good.

It is, however, just when we rush into believing that our positive knowledge of the world can guarantee a definition of the common good that Stengers (2005, 994) insists we "slow down." Thailand's efforts to implement the HiAP and the HIA as a governance tool, while recognized by the WHO as part of the global movement for health governance (cf. Evans 2010), promotes fundamentally different notions of health and the public good. Where the WHO, in the naturalist tradition, treats health as a shared biological condition that bears the mark of human influence, under Buddhist and monarchical readings, health outcomes matter not as mere effects, but as conditions indicative of the differential, innate capacities of individuals for political, moral, and social life. From this perspective, respective individual organs of the body politic speak through symptoms, such as the floods of 2011, environmental pollution, and farmer suicides, all of which gain social meaning as the failure of Yingluck Shinawatra's administration to make healthy public policy enabling the nation to thrive. The body, rather than a mute object and effect of individual agency, takes the position of a subject that reveals to the individual person his or her own lack of wisdom necessary to make healthy/ good choices.

Yet despite this incommensurable difference between the two frameworks of HiAP, the antipolitical emphasis at the core of this initiative resonated with attempts by anti-Thaksin forces in Thailand to intervene in the name of the people. Since the 1990s, King Bhumibol Adulyadej, or at least the large bureaucracy centered on promoting the Thai monarchy (see McCargo 2005), has attempted to curb an ethos of reckless consumerism (associated, at least since 2000, with Thaksin) by encouraging Thais to rein in aspirations for self-transformation via capital accumulation and to maintain goals appropriate to their station (Walker 2010). This push, officially known as the king's sufficiency economy theory (*se-thakit pho phiang*), demands that one be mindful of what one has in everyday life, and explicitly targeted Thaksin's attempts to run the country as Thailand, Inc. (with Thaksin himself cast as the self-professed "CEO Prime Minister"). Those who espoused the king's theory framed Thaksin as a self-interested plutocrat who had bought the people's vote by sweet promises of wealth, and as an exploitative "lackey of foreign capital" (Surin 2007, 349). Many at the TCH who saw Thaksin's policies as having increased domestic indebtedness and health problems associated with the breakdown of traditional communal ties saw the monarchy as a necessary force against the moral overreach of profit-minded politicians. And, in the logic of the king's sufficiency theory, street protests and political demands made by Thaksin supporters thus became mobs incapable of simply being happy with their lot in life. When, in 2007, the military junta rewrote the constitution, these Buddhist-informed ideas of mindfulness and the ills of over-desirousness became firmly anchored to the notion of health governance as per HiAP.

The Thai Health Act of 2007, a key document that articulates the junta's elevation of health as the guarantor of good governance, clearly shows this fusion of the biological, moral, and political. The act places *panya,* wisdom, as a pre-requisite for the attainment of health (*sukhaphab*; literally, "image of happiness"). The choice of the term *panya* is not accidental, as, unlike other terms for knowledge (e.g., *khwam ru*), *panya* is loaded with Buddhist significance.[5] The act defines *panya* as "knowing in total," a totality here specified as a knowledge of "perfection," a state of always already knowing what will bring "evil" before seeing ill effects. Health, then, is the manifestation of one's "knowledge of falsehood and trickery, the ability to distinguish between good and evil, [to distinguish] what will have benefit and what will cause harm, [and one's ability to bring] this knowledge into consciousness in order to make oneself bountiful, beautiful, and good" (Thailand National Health Commission Office 2007, 1–2; my translation). In this way, the act pulls together wisdom, health, and morality as three aspects of human perfectibility.

The blurring of the division between these categories has a long history in Thailand. As Stanley Tambiah (1977, 98) argues in his now-classic work on the idea of healing, the Thai Buddhist cosmology makes "no separation between the workings of 'moral laws' and 'physical' or 'natural laws'; the concept of *dhamma* encompasses both."[6] The power of those with *panya* is the capacity to act in tune with dharma, the "law of the universe, immanent, eternal, uncreated" (Gethin 2004, 519), a capacity, in other words, to make good decisions that precede all constructed notions of what constitutes goodness. In the *Dhammacakkappavattana Sutta,* for instance, the Buddha convinces critics doubtful of his enlightenment not through sermons, but through attaining a perfect state of well-being (Crosby 2014, 36). Those who can see his perfection move one step closer to understanding dharma, of how to be in line with and to think in terms of the quality of the entity that we are. Attaining health, the perfection of biological life, in this sense becomes the self-evident proof of one's all-knowing state.

Implicit in the explicit link between health and wisdom drawn by the act is a temporal element that sets the attainment of both on a karmic timeline. One's past moral behavior (one's *kam* [Sanskrit: *karma*]) determines access to *panya* and to resources in the present. As this moral account includes the balance of one's merits and demerits from another lifetime, health encompasses a condition that is not only the effect of one's immediate present but of events that took place beyond the knowledge of the individual. Thus, in the dharmic reading of health, human biology is not pitted against human action, but at that which lies at the core of why and how individuals have differential levels of *panya,* fortune, and the like. Poor health, then, reveals the limited capacity of those who imperfectly follow dharmic law, the law that would, for those who could comprehend its demands, allow one to prosper.

Andrew Alan Johnson (2014, 13) describes how, in Thai cosmological interpretations, these notions of karma and dharma order entities on earth, including gods and spirits, within a hierarchy of *panya* and enlightenment. Those occupying higher levels within this stratified order of entities have, owing to their lofty position, a panoramic vision of the world that begets them more *panya*. For instance, the *dhammaraja*, the divine king—a status often attributed to the Thai king Bhumibol (Jackson 2010) —is given a seat near the top from where he may see almost everything. Thus, while those with complete access to *panya* know "in total," those at lower levels have access to only limited visions of *panya*—that is, specialized knowledge—with those in even lower levels of the hierarchy (in with domesticated animals, recalling Yok's accusation of Praew as a "buffalo") have close to no *panya*.

In terms of governance, nothing good can thus come from rule under individuals lacking *panya*. Occupying lower levels of this cosmic hierarchy, they cannot see the consequences of their actions and can only cause more suffering. On the other hand, good governance comes from those with perfect health, those with mental immunity and total knowledge. Their knowledge of how to be within the cosmic order of things wards off sickness, strife, and social disorder. Health as a perfectible condition, albeit within the limits of one's karmic status, thus reveals the individual as a specific cosmological entity set on a path of reincarnation that is shaped by the moral choices made in past lives.

Experts like Yok at the TCH do not necessarily consider themselves on the top of the hierarchy of *panya*, but rather as those knowledgeable enough to mediate between beings and people on the higher rungs of dharmic wisdom and those situated below. For instance, Yok sees herself as a "coordinator," someone who relays information between community leaders, physicians, monks, public intellectuals, and royalty to bring diverse sectors of society together to make all more mindful of how health sits at the intersection of governance, policies, and individual life choices (see also Prawase 2000; Rasanathan et al. 2012, 3).

The implementation of HiAP in Thailand points to a fundamental problem inherent in the act of translation. In contrast to the WHO's intention of promoting monitory democracy around the world via HiAP, the translation and adaptation of HiAP in the Thai institutional context through the Thai Health Act of 2007 grants legitimacy to military rule. Health as it is translated within the frameworks of *panya* in the act reveals how divergent boundaries can be drawn in between matters of health, politics, and religion. As Talal Asad (2003) argues, such differences force us to rethink the secular-sacred divide built around Western assumptions, and to pay attention to what the irresolvable differences between worlds express. The TCH and the WHO meet in their reliance on the language of moral and biological necessity, reminiscent of age-old claims by health experts that "the struggle against disease must begin with a war against bad government" (Foucault 1994, 33). It is, as I expand here, a claim that mobilizes a certain fundamentalism foreclosing the possibility of politics. Where, as Claude Lefort (1986) argues, politics and those who speak in its register cannot self-authorize, those who speak for biology, health, and nature can. In the next section, I explore what shape good governance takes under the fundamentalism of HiAP in Thailand.

GOOD GOVERNANCE

The TCH is representative of many nongovernmental, semigovernmental, and royally funded organizations that formed around the turn of the millennium following a new wave in Thai politics that sought to improve mechanisms for participatory democracy through decentralization (Rasanathan et al. 2012). Key to this new movement was the People's Constitution of 1997, one of Thailand's most liberal, and, owing to the increased role of electoral democracy in it, a central reason for the rise to power of the populist Thaksin administration. Many senior workers at the TCH and in the larger NGO community embraced Thaksin's rise—but not for long. Shortly after his first election, Thaksin took an increasingly combative stance toward NGO networks, closed down media outlets, and butted heads with long-established royal patronage networks—exactly those networks that lay behind much of the NGO community. By the middle of the 2000s, many former supporters of the 1997 constitution and, indeed, of Thaksin himself, backed his ouster (Pasuk and Baker 2009, 228). Key among this group was Prawase Wasi, royal physician to the king, one of the 1997 constitution's architects, public intellectual, and advisor to the TCH.

Prawase articulated an increasingly popular perspective in the NGO community that the liberal reforms introduced by the People's Constitution allowed politicians like Thaksin to abuse the system for his own political benefit (cf. Tejapira 2006). Pointing to how Thaksin promoted family members and those under his patronage into positions of power, Prawase argued that politicians "neither have the knowledge nor the competency [to rule]. . . . It is more suitable to call them election winners" (Walker 2006). Against politicians, he pitted independent expert bodies as those capable of returning competence to Thailand's legal, political, and juridical system.

It is with this backdrop in mind that I return to Yok and her open frustration at Praew and the residents of her alley for proudly displaying election stickers from Thaksin's campaign. Yok, like many in the health community, idolized Prawase and argued that, after seeing firsthand the vulnerability of the electoral system to the tyranny of "election winners," respect for the common good can only come from those with mental immunity against moral overreach. For Yok and others like her, the problem of election winners like Thaksin amounted to the fact that, when cunning and the manipulation of the public allow individuals into positions of power, nothing but the will of the politician gains representation. The voice of the people becomes merely an echo of this will.

Yok's support of HiAP stems from her perspective that something other than the wile of politicians ought to ground authoritative power. She often stressed to me that elections proved nothing, and that good governance could only come from those with mental immunity to self-interest, those "good people." Faced with volumes of domestic and international press that critiqued the support of such a notion by individuals like Yok as "fascist," Yok characterized them all as "the point of view of those with no *panya*." Even as I showed up to her office armed with new clips from the media that described positions like Yok's as "authoritarian," Yok waved a hand, dismissing critical foreign press and Thai voices alike:

> They don't understand. They see elections and think that, 'OK, [leaders that] come from [an] election are good.' They are 'demo-*crazy*' [in English]. But goodness for Thai people refers to something deeper than what for-eigners [*farang*] can understand, and the evil, the corruption of Thaksin is deeper [than what they think they know].

"Demo-crazy" foreigners (here explicitly named by Yok as *farang*,[7] a general term for Caucasians or Westerners) and the Thai academics who, in Yok's terms, "just follow the asses of the foreigners [*tam kon farang*]),[8] fail to see that some votes are worth more than others. Good governance, that is, good in the dharmic sense, emerges neither from the democratic rule of numbers nor from legal, social, or political definitions of what is good, but through the capacity of those who can access a notion of the good existing independently from human machination.

Good governance, *thammaphibaan* in Thai, has as its root word dharma (*thamma*) and points to rule emerging from those cosmic laws. Vibrant life, timely assurances of rain and fertility, and a peaceful public are all manifestations of a ruler consubstantial with dharma. In contrast, what characterizes bad governance is the use of *amnat*: "raw amoral power that may be used for either good or evil and which is accumulated and maintained by sheer force" (Jackson 2010, 33). The illegitimacy of amoral power is revealed through the emergence of sickness, famine, and misfortune, as the use of force necessary to put such a regime in power inevitably disrupts the cosmic balance indispensable to the attainment of dharmic perfection. The legitimacy of good governance is couched in terms of dharmic moral terms as an a priori good, and as that which needs no a posteriori justification. The power of those with *panya*, the capacity to act in tune with, or be one with dharma, simply is.

The historian Thongchai Winichakul (2008, 20–21) argues that the term *democracy* has been used in Thailand to refer not to a contested field in which the public debates and decides based on a rule of numbers, but to the framework through which those with *panya* intervene in the name of the people against self-interested political forces abusing and manipulating the populace. Historically, the Thai monarch has served this role, cast as the *dhammaraja* who steps in as the moral authority above politics and as the symbolic figure who speaks for his or her people against the excesses of corrupt politicians or power-hungry generals. Present-day royalist groups like the People's Democratic Reform Committee (PDRC) thus draw on such an image of the king as divine ruler and father of the nation against inherently untrustworthy politicians. According to Thongchai, the strength of the monarchy in modern Thai politics stems from the notion that, without the king as the referee, corrupt politicians will twist the spirit of democracy to their own ends at the expense of the people.

The authority of health experts such as Yok and others at the TCH thus rides on a history of democracy that posits that, should those with *panya* ensure "clean politics," the national environment and its people will be healthy and prosperous. This act of cleansing, however, mobilizes the denigration of those cast as lacking *panya*. How can the vote of an individual with the *panya* of a buffalo be counted equal to that of someone with real knowledge? The notion that there are good people who are beyond or above politics makes the contest of legitimacy that characterizes political participation unnecessary. The good people have already obtained their legitimacy from universal, apolitical sources of goodness, wisdom, and nature; they need no vote.

It is easy to dismiss Yok's argument as simply a political ploy supporting class conflict (Hewison 2012), a divide between rural and urban interests (Fong 2013), or as the effect of a struggle between competing elite groups (Connors 2012). But doing so would be to dismiss an entire cosmology of knowledge and power as authoritarian window dressing. For, as Benedict Anderson (1972) argues, narrowing down what counts as political theory to ideas of power in the West not only relegates all other traditional political concepts to be "cultural" variations on a general theory but also precludes inquiry into how these traditions live on to shape contemporary politics.

GOOD PEOPLE

The TCH office sat above a small street market where vendors like Praew sold snacks and drinks from their carts. Owing to TCH's role as a center for networking between other organizations, the offices were small, given the breadth of programs in which TCH participated. Different experts (like Yok) worked on community-level health-promotion programs, ranging from those specializing in the problem of drug and alcohol abuse to teams that assisted in analyzing social determinants of health at the policy level. Overlooking the street and the carts was the office's common room, with beige couches and a new espresso machine.

As I sat in the room with Yok and Tom, Yok's colleague, I looked down to the street. The sight of the vendors so soon after the outburst over Praew bothered me, and I brought Praew up again. "You don't understand," declared Yok. This time, however, she expanded on what she had said in her car that day in hushed tones. As we looked down onto the street together, she characterized those supporting Thaksin as suffering from anxiety. This suffering, she said, came from engaging in risky activities such as compulsive gambling, migrating to the city to seek better wages, holding unattainable desires premised on a rise in social status or class, and pursuing profit-oriented actions destructive to their health and to the environment in general. Popular religious practices associated with lottery playing also fell into this category of risky and speculative action driven by desirousness, and Praew represented exactly the type of individuals the TCH wanted to target in their push to promote mental immunity.

Tom, fiddling with the coffee in the espresso machine, piped up: "They have yet to open their eyes! They don't understand how dangerous greed can be. Caught up in this political fight, they can't stop thinking about demanding this and that from the country without once stopping to think, 'Why am I demanding?'

They can never be happy if they can't understand what it means to have sufficiency [*pho phiang*]."

Tom worked with environmental activists on the impact of environmental degradation on health, and he often referred to the royal sufficiency economy theory to explain how ecological crises affecting national health were fundamentally a problem of moral overreach by greedy developers or overdesirous consumers. Moreover, he saw ecological damage, the loss of health, and the current political conflict as revealing how the cosmos itself—nature, biology, and social harmony—protested against the promotion of entrepreneurial greed by Thaksin, and that a return to good governance by good people was of a vital necessity.

In their respective programs, Tom and Yok both promoted *panya* as the basis for mental immunity against greed, as well as a means of knowing when needs have been sufficiently met. But while giving credit to the Thai monarch for having already warned his subjects of the repercussions of advanced capitalism (cf. Handley 2006) even before the promotion of the HiAP initiative by the WHO, Tom, Yok, and their colleagues at the TCH also took great pride in the fact that the WHO had recognized their activities as part of a global intervention in the name of the common good. Yok distinguished this sort of international attention from those pro-democracy groups that, according to Yok, evaluated Thai forms of governance against a privileged and universalized Western standard ("following the asses of the foreigners"). Instead, Yok and her colleagues viewed foreign WHO experts as "experts just like us," experts who understood the secret of their struggle. Tom summarized their position succinctly in a metaphor: "Children always resist when you need to give them an injection. But all good doctors know that a little unpleasantness is necessary in order to save lives."

"Good doctors know," said Tom, but such a need to declare the righteousness of his authority carried the inverse effect of calling attention to its limits. The need to keep referring to individuals like Praew as "idiots" or, here, as "children" emerges at the limits of the power to convince, to legitimate Tom's and Yok's righteous place within the hierarchy of *panya* without themselves appearing susceptible to the desire to impress and use force (*amnat*) in the political realm.

It is in light of such a world in which there exists correct knowledge, accessible only to those with the wisdom to see it, that I turn to the Dharma Gallery, where I saw an art exhibition to which Yok took me in May of 2012. I had been pestering her with questions about dharma, *panya,* and how they affect one's mental immunity. Instead of answering my questions, however, Yok offered to take me to see the gallery. Yok led me up the escalator to the elevated skywalk linking the malls at Ratchaprasong intersection, a walkway that led over the site where, on May 19, 2010, the military had shot at Red Shirts, pro-democracy protesters, who had gathered on the street below.[9] The Dharma Gallery now occupied the place where snipers had hidden two years earlier. Even so, the night before our visit, Red Shirts had held a rally in memory of those killed and injured, and from the skywalk, we could see red pools of candle wax, each marking a place where someone had been shot. While neither Yok nor the gallery explicitly mentioned the clash, the timing of the exhibition and its location vis-à-vis the planned Red Shirt commemoration seemed deliberate, as did Yok's choice to take me there that day.

Yok followed my gaze down onto the street, but then encouraged me to read aloud the following from the plaque leading to the gallery:

> Dharma is not just about going to the temple. It is about the everyday life of every individual. It is about happiness. It is about losing strong emotions such as want, greed, anger, and attachment. Dharma is with us in a traffic jam. It is with us in the fitting room. It is with us when we decide to buy. Dharma is with us everywhere, but we are not open enough to see it because we are not mindful in our everyday life.

Tapping at the last sentence, Yok said,

> It is just like *my king* [in English] said, "The only change for the better is through mindfulness of dharma." Dharma is about feeling sufficient in your-self and not comparing what you have with your neighbor. We help indi-viduals to be more attentive to how desire turns into suffering, and suffering into mental illness and social disorder. We try to protect the public from politicians with influence by teaching them that there are consequences to ignoring the law of dharma.

Yok made clear whom she meant by "the public" in need of protection by aiming her comments at the stained street below: "We don't want to be ruled by people who only want to do so for their own political or economic advantage. When Thaksin came into office, farmers and small business owners supported him because they thought that he would make them rich. But they actually got into more debt than before. Wanting him back just shows you how sick they are."

Yok defined sickness here as desire that "turns into suffering, and suffering into mental illness and social disorder." Thus political ambition and the frustration borne out of political disenfranchisement here manifest as symptoms of one's refusal to accept the natural order of things. As with the effort that goes into staving off the flow of the river to create dams, to cite one of Tom's favorite examples, going against nature comes with consequences. In this sense, rule under good people who follow the proper order of things ought to produce intended outcomes with minimal effort. That effort becomes necessary therefore reveals more about the qualities of the individual expert (that is, the expert is doing something wrong) than about the fact that rule by the good, or the notion of an absolute good, is itself a political perspective.

CLEANSING POLITICS

Yok's and Tom's characterization of legitimate individuals as those who can, with minimum effort, gain the confidence of others has its parallels in one of the most popular stories of the Buddha in Thailand. In this story, the Buddha is meditating in a grove when a divine being, Mara, approaches him. Mara attempts to lure the Buddha away from his meditations by promising him worldly power and a life of luxury and riches. The Buddha refuses, and when an angered Mara summons his minions to harm the Buddha, the Buddha lightly touches the ground with his fingertip. His holy touch wakens Mae Thorani, the earth goddess, who rises and wrings from her hair all of the lustral water that the Buddha had poured in religious devotion throughout all of his lives. The flood destroys Mara and his minions.

This destruction comes at minimum effort. No force other than the touch of the Buddha's finger brings forth the flood, since nothing more necessitates the release of water accumulated through his own rites of devotion. It is the earth goddess in the act of wringing out her hair that is enshrined on the seal of the Democrat Party, the political party most fervently advocating the military and opposing Thaksin.

Links between this story and the proper workings of dharma in the present-day conflict are commonplace. The Thai intellectual and Thaksin opponent Sulak Sivaraksa made the parallel between Thaksin and Mara explicit in the days leading to his ouster (Kitiarsa 2006, 4), and he invoked dharma as the means of his defeat (Sulak 2006).[10] It was a narrative that many at TCH repeated when I asked about their varying positions on Thai politics. For opponents of Thaksin within the health community, the military coup of 2006—a coup rumored to have occurred at the

Figure 1. The seal of Thailand's Democrat Party.

behest of the palace—constituted a necessary evil. Thaksin was swept aside for having resisted dharma, and the political world was washed clean, ready for a new foundation.

But even supporters of the military such as Yok found it hard to justify the deaths and injuries caused to so many people, as the necessity of force made all too clear that merely claiming to speak from the perspective of dharma was not in itself convincing to an increasingly skeptical public. What was to be an a priori good not only failed to speak for itself but also relied on brute force for its implementation. I see the deferrals and roundabout ways in which experts explained the philosophy and mission of the TCH to me as themselves symptoms of contradictions that they cannot ignore.

The struggle by experts to present themselves as those with dharmic wisdom also manifested in other ways. Later, long after our visit to the Dharma Gallery, during a TCH-sponsored information session for youth on the importance of understanding the sufficiency economy as it relates to health and immunity to excessive consumerism, Yok was stunned when a participant asked her to explain again just how they were to know when need and want become moral overreach. Yok had just explained the importance of mindfulness to the group, and so the response to her address in the form of "how?" visibly upset her. In front of twenty politely waiting adolescents, I saw Yok's cropped hair swerve to and fro as she turned her head from the young inquirer to her two other colleagues. When the silence became awkward, one of Yok's colleagues stepped in and stated: "When you feel the desire to buy, or feel tempted to get the latest cell phone, for instance, you should repeat the name of the Buddha. Saying his name, 'Bud-dha [*phut- tho*],' 'Bud-dha [*phut-tho*],' 'Bud-dha [*phut-tho*],' like this multiple times, that should help you get over your temptation and help you think of more important things."

If adolescents who came to TCH through associated community projects disturbed Yok's calm, less accommodating audiences presented an even bigger challenge. Later, in private, when discussing the difficulty of convincing Thaksin's adult supporters of the health dangers inherent in their political views, Nui, another health expert, said in frustration: "*Everything* is political now, and it doesn't matter if you know the *truth*, they won't listen. You can't reason with them. If you want a buffalo to move, you have to strike it. That is the problem."

In the next and final section, I expand on Nui's supposed problem to examine in detail how what health experts took to be good governance, a governance driven by the natural necessities of health (with the backing by the WHO), paradoxically mobilized a conservative politics, and what the deployment of HiAP in Thailand might reveal about the risks of relying on health experts to speak for the global common good.

THE DOUBLE BIND OF ANTIPOLITICS

Calling someone a buffalo marks that individual as a person with minimal capacity for self-mastery who lives only to gratify his or her senses. With no wisdom to distinguish right from wrong, such persons threaten harm to themselves, the environment, and the greater world in the process of satisfying their excesses. In a context where "everything is political" (itself a political or politicized statement), Nui believes that buffalo cannot be reasoned with; they follow only that which promises them the most benefits. One can only make them move in the "right" direction by striking them. This recourse to violence reveals not only what Nui sees as the limit of the buffalo's capacity for reason but also the limit of those who claim to have access to a truth beyond all social truths. Only those, as Hannah Arendt (1972) argues, with no power to produce consent must rely on brute force to impose what they consider right.

In play is a logic of exception that undermines health experts' ability to speak from the apolitical, authoritative standpoint of public health. As beneficiaries of the regime that forcibly ousted a popularly elected prime minister and violently suppressed a popular protest, experts' claim to speak for dharma and to act in the name of a transcendental moral law to return peace, harmony, and health to the nation has met with strong challenges. While health experts gained an expanded role in defining what counts as good governance since the interim military government of 2007 that ousted Thaksin, their legitimacy falters beyond the legally given capacity to tautologically claim their authority as just ("I am just because I possess the *panya* that allows me to know I am just"). Contrary to the global ambitions of the WHO to posit health outcomes as a politically neutral basis on which to evaluate public policy, the deployment of the HiAP in Thailand in ways that render certain segments of the population as buffalo has been anything but neutral.

According to Claude Lefort (1986), the notion of legitimacy in democratic regimes relies on the perception that such authorizing power belongs to everyone and thus to no one in particular. Power, then, comes from an "empty place" (Lefort 1986, 17) that no figure could fill without the risk of appearing to be an illegitimate usurper. The legitimate is in a constant state of contestation, as this lack of authoritative guarantee at the core of democratic regimes allows for multiple claims and counterarguments. The notion of rule by an unelected council of good people elides this struggle by covering over this empty place with a transcendental notion of the good, accessible only to those with *panya*.

Health experts have long played a significant role in moments of exception when threats to population health and conditions of existence call for coercive measures to place individuals in quarantine, to regulate nutritional intake, or to enforce discipline in the name of hygiene. But the use of health to bring elected governments into check, and in the Thai case, even to advocate for their removal altogether raises the political significance of experts to a new level. Yet as we see, Thai health experts fail to completely convince others that they speak on behalf of the common good and, when challenged, advocate increasingly violent and coercive means to convince a skeptical public of the legitimacy of their actions. Where the WHO sees the adoption of HiAP in Thailand as the growing relevance of this initiative worldwide,[11] failing to see the incommensurable differences that appear in the Thai iteration of HiAP risks giving credence to the type of rule by good people promoted by conservative political forces in Thailand. Following Isabelle Stengers's argument, different ontological worlds demarcate the realm of politics (what entities count within it) and nature (as accessible via science or *panya*) in different ways, thus challenging our assumptions about what constitutes the world and how we ought to be within it for the better. Difference, according to Stengers, provides the possibility to imagine a radically new form of politics, an antidote to the hegemonic frameworks under which we currently live. What the case of HiAP in Thailand reveals, in contrast, is that the encounter with difference does not always open onto a new emancipatory horizon. Different ontological horizons in which wisdom, morality, and health make sense allow us to imagine other possibilities of being, but we must not forget that this encounter with otherness can also open onto new horrors.

ABSTRACT

This article rethinks the presumed translatability of the World Health Organization's (WHO) health promotion models and explores the unintended consequences of their global export. Specifically, I focus on the Thai military government's adoption (2006–2008) of the Health in All Policies (HiAP) initiative, which redefined health outcomes as the standard universal measure against which the success of national public policy ought to be evaluated. Through my fieldwork at state-owned Thai health organizations, I track how a dharmic concept of wisdom (panya), one that links the capacity to make healthy choices with differential levels of enlightenment, undergirds the Thai adoption of HiAP, with political implications that are unrepresentable in nondharmic political worlds. I analyze the ramifications of framing a political intervention within the apolitical bioscientific register of medical necessity, and explore the effect that global health movements have on the status of political legitimacy and national political conflicts. [global health; cosmopolitics; knowledge practices; political legitimacy; experts; Thailand]

NOTES

Acknowledgments I thank the three anonymous reviewers and *Cultural Anthropology*'s editorial collective: Dominic Boyer, James Faubion, and especially Cymene Howe, who helped guide this article to its completion. I am also deeply indebted to Hoon Song, Jeremy Fernando, Ulrika Backebo, and David Rojas for offering invaluable theoretical insights and critical commentary. Finally, I wish to thank Andrew Alan Johnson for sharing with me his wealth of knowledge on Thai popular religion, and for his support throughout.

1. TCH and the individuals to whom I refer on a personal basis are all protected here under pseudonyms.
2. *Phumikhumkanjit* has become a popular concept among many NGOs, mobilized in the context of anticonsumerism drives, efforts to stop farmers from being swindled by con artists selling "miracle seeds," and as a part of the promotion of the Thai king's sufficiency economy (Walker 2010).
3. These movements, in their latter form, took the name of the People's Democratic Reform Committee (PDRC), although the Thai name literally translates as the "People's Committee for Absolute Democracy with the King as Head of State" (*Khaosod English* 2013).
4. While Thailand is ostensibly multireligious, Theravada Buddhism is hegemonic. Roughly 95 percent of Thais identify as Buddhist, the Thai state casts itself as the guardian of religion (understood to be Buddhism), and the Thai monarch, the legal head of state, is required to be Buddhist. In Thai public discourse, Buddhism is seen to be synonymous with being ethnically and nationally Thai.
5. For instance, in everyday Buddhist practice, *panya* represents the highest of the three steps toward enlightenment, with the others being moral conduct and the practice of meditation (Crosby 2014, 55).

6.   Here, Tambiah uses the term *dhamma*, which is written as *dharma* (Sanskrit) in the Pali spelling and as *thamma* in Thai.
7.   By framing this in racial terms, Yok may have been attempting to establish solidarity with me, another non-*farang*, who might be more sympathetic.
8.   Accusations that those who disagree with mainstream or elite discourses are somehow inherently foreign abound in Thai nationalist discourse (Johnson 2013).
9.   This clash between Red Shirt protesters who demanded elections and those advocating the repeal of *lèse-majesté* laws resulted in close to one hundred civilian deaths and more than one thousand injured (Sopranzetti 2012).
10. Sulak has, in the ten years since, become an advocate for democratic rule and an opponent of the current military government.
11. HiAP was first developed in Finland and promoted within the European Union under Finland's E.U. presidency.

REFERENCES

Anderson, Benedict
     1972   "The Idea of Power in Javanese Culture." In *Culture and Politics in Indonesia*, edited by Claire Holt, 1–70. Ithaca, N.Y.: Cornell University Press.
Arendt, Hannah
     1972   *Crises of the Republic*. San Diego, Calif.: Harcourt.
Asad, Talal
     2003   *Genealogies of Religion: Discipline and Reasons of Power in Christianity and Islam*. Baltimore, Md.: Johns Hopkins University Press.
Connors, Michael
     2012   "Notes towards an Understanding of Thai Liberalism." In *Bangkok May 2010: Perspectives on a Divided Thailand*, edited by Michael Montesano, Pavin Chachavalpongpun, and Aekapol Chongvilaivan, 97–107. Singapore: Institute of Southeast Asian Studies.
Crosby, Kate
     2014   *Theravada Buddhism: Continuity, Diversity and Identity*. Oxford: Wiley-Blackwell.
de la Cadena, Marisol
     2010   "Indigenous Cosmopolitics in the Andes: Conceptual Reflections Beyond 'Politics.'" *Cultural Anthropology* 25, no. 2: 334–70. http://dx.doi.org/10.1111/j.1548-1360.2010.01061.x.
Descola, Philippe
     2013   *Beyond Nature and Culture*. Chicago: University of Chicago Press.
Evans, Timothy
     2010   "Foreword." In "Implementing Health in All Policies: Adelaide 2010," edited by Ilona Kickbusch and Kevin Buckett, 2. Adelaide: Department of Health, Government of South Australia. http://www.who.int/sdhconference/resources/implementinghiapadel-sahealth-100622.pdf.
Fassin, Didier
     2008   "The Humanitarian Politics of Testimony: Subjectification through Trauma in the Israeli–Palestinian Conflict." *Cultural Anthropology* 23, no. 3: 531–58. http://dx.doi.org/10.1111/j.1548-1360.2008.00017.x.
     2011   *Humanitarian Reason: A Moral History of the Present*. Berkeley: University of California Press.
Fong, Jack
     2013   "Political Vulnerabilities of a Primate City: The May 2010 Red Shirts Uprising in Bangkok, Thailand." *Journal of Asian and African Studies* 48, no. 3: 332–47. http://dx.doi.org/10.1177/0021909612453981.
Foucault, Michel
     1994   *The Birth of the Clinic: An Archaeology of Medical Perception*. Translated by A. M. Sheridan. New York: Vintage.

Gethin, Rupert
    2004   "He Who Sees Dhamma Sees Dhammas: Dhamma in Early Buddhism." *Journal of Indian Philosophy* 32, no. 5: 513–42. http://dx.doi.org/10.1007/s10781-004-8633-6.
Gupta, Akhil
    1998   *Postcolonial Developments: Agriculture in the Making of Modern India*. Durham, N.C.: Duke University Press.
Handley, Paul
    2006   *The King Never Smiles: A Biography of Thailand's Bhumibol Adulyadej*. New Haven, Conn.: Yale University Press.
Hetherington, Kregg
    2013   "Beans Before the Law: Knowledge Practices, Responsibility, and the Paraguayan Soy Boom." *Cultural Anthropology* 28, no. 1: 65–85. http://dx.doi.org/10.1111/j.1548-1360.2012.01173.x.
Hewison, Kevin
    2012   "Class, Inequality and Politics." In *Bangkok May 2010: Perspectives on a Divided Thailand*, edited by Michael Montesano, Pavin Chachavalpongpun, and Aekapol Chongvilaivan, 141–60. Singapore: Institute of Southeast Asian Studies.
Jackson, Peter
    2010   "Virtual Divinity: A Twenty-First Century Discourse of Thai Royal Influence." In *Saying the Unsayable: Monarchy and Democracy in Thailand*, edited by Søren Ivarsson and Lotte Isager, 29–60. Copenhagen: Nordic Institute of Asian Studies Press.
Johnson, Andrew Alan
    2013   "Moral Knowledge and its Enemies: Conspiracy and Kingship in Thailand." *Anthropological Quarterly* 86, no. 4: 1059–86. http://dx.doi.org/10.1353/anq.2013.0052.
    2014   *Ghosts of the New City: Spirits, Urbanity, and the Ruins of Progress in Chiang Mai*. Honolulu: University of Hawai'i Press.
Khaosod English
    2013   "Khaosod English's Note on Translation of Anti-Government Leadership Title 'PCAD.'" December 24. http://www.khaosodenglish.com/detail.php?newsid=1387872575.
Kickbusch, Ilona, and Kevin Buckett
    2010   "Implementing Health in All Policies: Adelaide 2010." Adelaide: Department of Health, Government of South Australia. http://www.who.int/sdhconference/resources/implementinghiapadel-sahealth-100622.pdf.
Kickbusch, Ilona, and David Gleicher
    2012   "Governance for Health in the Twenty-First Century." Copenhagen: World Health Organization Regional Office for Europe. http://www.euro.who.int/en/publications/abstracts/governance-for-health-in-the-21st-century.
Kitiarsa, Pattana
    2006   "In Defense of the Thai-Style Democracy." Paper delivered at the Asia Research Institute, National University of Singapore, October 12.
Lakoff, Andrew
    2010   "Two Regimes of Global Health." *Humanity: An International Journal of Human Rights, Humanitarianism, and Development* 1, no. 1: 59–79. http://dx.doi.org/10.1353/hum.2010.0001.
Lefort, Claude
    1986   *The Political Forms of Modern Society: Bureaucracy, Democracy, Totalitarianism*. Cambridge, Mass.: MIT Press.
McCargo, Duncan
    2005   "Network Monarchy and Legitimacy Crises." *Pacific Review* 18, no. 4: 499–519. http://dx.doi.org/10.1080/09512740500338937.

Nguyen, Vinh-Kim
> 2010   *The Republic of Therapy: Triage and Sovereignty in West Africa's Time of AIDS.* Durham, N.C.: Duke University Press.

Pandolfi, Mariella
> 2003   "Contract of Mutual (In)Difference: Governance and the Humanitarian Apparatus in Contemporary Albania and Kosovo." *Indiana Journal of Global Legal Studies* 10, no. 1: 369–81. http://www.repository.law.indiana.edu/ijgls/vol10/iss1/13/.

Pasuk Phongpaichit, and Chris Baker
> 2009   *Thaksin.* Chiang Mai: Silkworm Books.

Petryna, Adriana
> 2002   *Life Exposed: Biological Citizens after Chernobyl.* Princeton, N.J.: Princeton University Press.

Prawase Wasi
> 2000   "'Triangle that Moves the Mountain' and Health Systems Reform Movement in Thailand." *Human Resources for Development Journal* 4, no. 2: 106–10. http://www.who.int/hrh/hrdj/en/index6.html.

Rasanathan, Kumanan, Tipicha Posayanonda, Maureen Birmingham, and Viroj Tangcharoensathien
> 2012   "Innovation and Participation for Healthy Public Policy: The First National Health Assembly in Thailand." *Health Expectations* 15, no. 1: 87–96. http://dx.doi.org/10.1111/j.1369-7625.2010.00656.x.

Redfield, Peter
> 2005   "Doctors, Borders, and Life in Crisis." *Cultural Anthropology* 20, no. 3: 328–61. http://dx.doi.org/10.1525/can.2005.20.3.328.
> 2012   "Humanitarianism." In *A Companion to Moral Anthropology*, edited by Didier Fassin, 451–67. Malden, Mass.: Wiley-Blackwell.

Sopranzetti, Claudio
> 2012   *Red Journeys: Inside the Thai Red-Shirt Movement.* Chiang Mai: Silkworm Books.

Stengers, Isabelle
> 2005   "The Cosmopolitical Proposal." In *Making Things Public: Atmospheres of Democracy*, edited by Bruno Latour and Peter Weibel, 994–1003. Cambridge, Mass.: MIT Press.

Sulak Sivaraksa
> 2006   "Removing Thaksin Mindfully." *ThaiDay*, March 13. http://www.manager.co.th/IHT/ViewNews.aspx?NewsID=9490000033982.

Surin Maisreikrod
> 2007   "Learning from the 19 September Coup: Advancing Thai-Style Democracy?" *Southeast Asian Affairs*: 340–59. http://www.jstor.org/stable/27913340.

Tambiah, Stanley
> 1977   "The Cosmological and Performative Significance of a Thai Cult of Healing Through Meditation." *Culture, Medicine and Psychiatry* 1, no. 1: 97-132. http://dx.doi.org/10.1007/BF00114812.

Tejapira, Kasian
> 2006   "Toppling Thaksin." *New Left Review* 39: 5–37. http://newleftreview.org/II/39/kasian-tejapira-toppling-thaksin.

Thailand National Health Commission Office
> 2007   "Phraratchabanyat: Sukhaphap Haeng Chat [Thai National Health Act], B.E. 2550." http://www.acfs.go.th/km/download/act_healthy_2550.pdf.

Thongchai Winichakul
> 2008   "Toppling Democracy." *Journal of Contemporary Asia* 38, no. 1: 11–37. http://dx.doi.org/10.1080/00472330701651937.

Ticktin, Miriam I.
> 2011   *Casualties of Care: Immigration and the Politics of Humanitarianism in France.* Berkeley: University of California Press.

Walker, Andrew
    2006   "Prawase Wasi's Sufficiency Democracy." *New Mandala*, November 29. http://asiapacific.anu.edu.au/newmandala/2006/11/29/prawase-wasis-sufficiency-democracy.
    2010   "Royal Sufficiency and Elite Misrepresentation of Rural Livelihoods." In *Saying the Unsayable: Monarchy and Democracy in Thailand*, edited by Søren Ivarsson and Lotte Isager, 241–66. Copenhagen: Nordic Institute of Asian Studies Press.
World Health Organization (WHO)
    2010   "Adelaide Statement on Health in All Policies: Moving towards A Shared Governance for Health and Well-Being." Report from the International Meeting on Health in All Policies, Adelaide 2010. http://www.who.int/social_determinants/publications/countryaction/adelaide_statement_hiap/en/.
World Health Organization (WHO), and the Ministry of Social Affairs and Health, Finland
    2013   "The Helsinki Statement on Health in All Policies." Adopted at the 8th Global Conference on Health Promotion, June 10–14. http://www.who.int/healthpromotion/conferences/8gchp/statement_2013/en/.

CIRCULATING IGNORANCE: Complexity and Agnogenesis in the Obesity "Epidemic"

EMILIA SANABRIA
Ecole Normale Supérieure de Lyon
http://orcid.org/0000-0002-5595-7905

I log into Skype with the usual hesitancy—is 2 p.m. GMT noon or 1 p.m. in France? I am joining the monthly Executive Committee (EC) call of the World Public Health Nutrition Association (WPHNA), along with colleagues in Australia, Brazil, Ghana, Norway, South Africa, and the United Kingdom. The agenda is full, owing to the upcoming International Conference on Nutrition (ICN2).[1] For nearly a year, the association, along with others, has been engaged in the delicate exercise of proposing modifications to the draft Framework for Action that United Nations (UN) member states will endorse at ICN2. Today we discuss the loss of a footnote pertaining to the technical definition of a "healthy diet." One prominent anti-sugar advocacy group wants to see this defined as a diet in which only 5 percent of calories come from added sugar.[2] There are a few weeks to go still, but ICN2's political reach already feels compromised. Agenda point 3 of our meeting asks whether the association should sign a letter to appear in the *Lancet* expressing its support for a global convention on nutrition, one modeled on the Global Framework Convention on Tobacco. The hope is that ICN2 may lead to a legally binding international framework to address global malnutrition, which in the twenty-first century includes competing rates of hunger and obesity. Today, our discussion turns on how the term *nonstate actors* adopted by the UN lumps together BigFood corporations, health agencies, patient associations, and civil society organizations defending small-scale farmers or human rights. "Busi-

CULTURAL ANTHROPOLOGY, Vol. 31, Issue 1, pp. 131–158, ISSN 0886-7356, online ISSN 1548-1360. © *by the American Anthropological Association. All rights reserved. DOI: 10.14506/ca31.1.07*

ness," one senior member of the EC notes, is being granted "inappropriate access" to the meeting, and using this undue influence to lobby against a legally binding framework convention. Everyone shares anecdotes about behind-the-scenes lobbying they have observed in their various positions. Much of it pertains to semantics: pushing for individual responsibility where market regulation is discussed, advocating a need for "just more food" when nutritional quality or changes to the food system are invoked.[3] The WPHNA is fairly unique in its approach. Although it is mainly constituted of medically trained nutritionists, it subscribes to a vision that sees nutrition as a political as much as a biological phenomenon. For the WPHNA executive, this implies critically engaging with the way in which scientific evidence is deployed in the field of nutrition and questioning the role BigFood plays in addressing global malnutrition.

IGNORANCE, DESIGNED AND PERVASIVE

This article examines the things that are said to be un/known about obesity and the way in which attributions of knowledge or ignorance circulate within the field of public health nutrition. I have been struck by experts' focus on knowing more and building better evidence bases, even as they reflect on how much is not known about obesity. What does this focus on knowing obfuscate? The knowledge constructed in expert meetings and scientific forums provides the contours of possible public health interventions addressing obesity. Such framings recast not just what is known (or not yet known) but also what is knowable. My article draws on recent work on the social construction of ignorance (Croissant 2014; Geissler 2013; Kelly and Beisel 2011; McGoey 2012; Pinto 2015; Proctor 2011) to argue that the field of evidence in obesity science is fashioned in a way that deflects attention (and responsibility) away from questions of food production, distribution, and marketing and continues to frame the problem as one of individual responsibility. I analyze the variegated forms of un/knowing that arise from my observations concerning the operational problems of contending with complexities and uncertainties in the field of obesity science to attend to the politics at stake in the maintenance of distinctions between knowledge and ignorance.

Recent work in social theory has turned attention to how unknowing is not simply the absence of knowledge; rather, it may be actively produced by social practices. The term *agnotology* has been coined to refocus attention away from what we know and how we know to what we do not know and why (Proctor and Schiebinger 2008). It broadens the focus given to the social construction of knowledge to include analyses of the social production of ignorance. Linsey

McGoey's (2007) analysis of "strategic ignorance" shows, for example, how willful blindness on behalf of the pharmaceutical industry constitutes a strategy used to exonerate it from the need to take action. Uncertain, complex, contradictory, or competing scientific facts may be mobilized as political capital or rhetorical tools that shift blame, as those communicating ignorance are excused (Oreskes and Conway 2011). Earlier analyses of *agnogenesis*, or the production of ignorance (Pinto 2015, 296), focused on the instrumental production of ignorance for corporate profit. While important in revealing the impact of the neoliberalization and industrialization of scientific research (Hess 2015), such studies implicitly assume that this is bad science and that transparency would reduce scientific ignorance (Frickel and Edwards 2014; Pinto 2015). Yet ignorance is a somewhat inevitable and at times positive feature of scientific activity and organizational labor (Croissant 2014; Gross and McGoey 2015). The more guileless production of ignorance resulting from organizational processes is—or can be—thoroughly embroiled with willful intent to create strategic opportunities from this decoupling of facts (Heimer 2012). Recent work on ignorance departs from the normative assumption that science deals in certainty and points to the fact that the very process of scientific research, from experimental design to data analysis and publication norms, have been shaped from within by decades of industry-funded research. Ignorance reigns not (only) because transnational corporations secretly produce doubt but also because the epistemic form that science has acquired— its evidentiary norms, reductionist underpinnings, and emphasis on causality and quantification—render many relations invisible (Kleinman and Suryanarayanan 2015). David Hess (2015) proposes the notion of "undone science" to move past accounts that locate the instrumentalization of uncertainty in vertical relations between scientific elites and disempowered publics or their governments. Undone science refers to those known unknowns that civil society organizations highlight as having potential public benefit but that industrial elites may actively seek to elide through their influence on what Hess (2015, 142) calls "the political opportunity structure of research funding." As Manuela Pinto (2015, 310) notes, at stake is a discussion of the epistemic and social goals of science, against which practices of ignorance construction can be measured.

Governments, corporations, or international agencies often appeal to available evidentiary regimes to support their actions, but such appeals to the neutrality of evidence prove highly problematic. Critical scholars are calling attention to the fact that scientific evidence concerning public health interventions constitutes only one voice in a much larger conversation. They systematically review the repertoire of actions adopted by corporations to mold or landscape the field of evidence and strategically orient scientific debate and policy options (Hawkes and Buse 2011, Moodie et al. 2013; Proctor 2011; Stuckler et al. 2012; Ulucanlar et al. 2014). The intricate links between transnational food corporations and nutrition experts in key governmental and UN decision-making roles across the globe are well established (e.g., Gornall 2015; Moodie et al. 2013). What is more difficult to ascertain is exactly how this connection shapes the knowledge that researchers are producing or inflects the decisions they make as experts. One analysis found that industry-funded studies (or those reporting conflicts of interest) were five times more likely to report a conclusion of no positive association between soft-drink consumption and weight gain than those with no declared industry funding (Bes-Rastrollo et al. 2013). Robert Proctor (2011) documents how the tobacco industry has not just corrupted scientific knowledge about tobacco risk but shaped it from within, through decades of ties between industry and research. Each piece of industry-sponsored research may appear perfectly unbiased at the micro level, but the scale of the tactic becomes evident when such "purchased engagement with public health" is multiplied globally (Gornall 2015). Similarly, writing on the pharmaceutical industry's use of scientific ghostwriting, Mario Biagioli (forthcoming) shows how, taken individually, each peer-reviewed piece is technically not fraudulent, though the net cumulative effect shifts the knowledge base in a direction favorable to corporate interests.

Rather than discrediting the veracity of the evidence produced in industry-research partnerships, this article shows how the consensus forged in conferences and policy spaces concerning the uncertainty and complexity of obesity's determinants creates a continued deflection of responsibilities back to the purported knowledge deficiencies of individual eaters. There are stakes in narrating these forms of ignorance—those imputed or strategically kept out of public debate by agrofood business lobbies—together. Keeping the stories apart produces an absence that obscures the labor of making them appear unrelated. I bring together a series of ethnographic observations from policy spaces, scientific forums, and international advocacy groups in which the downplaying of industrial responsibilities and the overemphasizing of individual responsibilities to know about healthy eating becomes particularly clear. By bringing these variegated forms of nonknowledge together, the article examines the deflections of responsibility at play between individuals deemed ignorant and a food industry highly active in downplaying its role in the obesity epidemic. I present a range of analyses arguing that this represents a deliberate strategy on the part of corporate actors.

My intervention here also means to move beyond this observation to show how the structuring of the field of evidence, the possibility of reliably showing causal relations between the political and socioeconomic determinants of malnutrition and measurable health indexes is largely compromised not simply by the absence of good evidence but also because the existing parameters of good science cannot straightforwardly reveal such relations. This is because the configuration of the knowable is increasingly defined in terms of whether knowledge is actionable (as determined by the logic of evidence-based medicine eloquently described by Vincanne Adams [2013]). Obesity, like many of today's complex problems, results from phenomena spanning multiple scales and determined by myriad nested interactions, from the political economies of market regulation to the modes of agricultural production, the biochemistry of appetite regulation, urban planning, changing family structures, meal patterns, and labor forms. Yet despite growing recognition of the problem's heavy overdetermination (e.g., U.K. Government Office of Science 2007), public intervention—and the science produced to guide or validate such intervention—remains wedded to a mode of reading and intervening that has limited purchase on the complexity with which it contends. The epistemic regimes that dominate the field of public health (and many other areas of public policy) frame complex problems in a manner that reduces them to what is manageable, even when such framings are contested or shown to be inadequate. Complex conditions resist explanation within extant modes of knowing. Writing on how it is that we continue to ignore many of the effects of toxics, Kim Fortun (2012, 452) suggests that this inattention derives from a tendency to rely on established idioms and ways of thinking, although these do not grasp the problems at hand. For example, ignorance is produced when the idioms and thought styles of mechanics are imposed on toxics. No evidence of harm emerges "because the evidence deemed necessary is at odds with the condition it is meant to represent." This state of affairs demands our urgent and critical engagement with the specific meaning of evidence.

OBESITY AND THE FRENCH PARADOX

Obesity rates did not rise as rapidly in France as elsewhere. In the wake of the so-called globesity epidemic, many experts puzzled over this seemingly French paradox: how could the French remain slim despite their gastronomic traditions, three-course meals, hundreds of cheeses, and *boulangeries* full of irresistible pastries? Yet over the last decade, French obesity rates have caught up with those of France's European neighbors. As a consequence, three major public health initiatives were launched to tackle noncommunicable chronic diseases associated with high body-mass indices (BMIs). Such initiatives often revolve around the idea that controlling weight involves willpower and choice; they also tend to focus on nutrition education and information. Within this model, people receive information, are expected to understand it, and to change their behavior accordingly. As Deborah Prentice (2015, 266) puts it: "Ignorance is a popular explanation for dysfunctional behavior." Health education interventions are often limited to a fairly unidirectional process of information transfer from a knowledgeable educator to a purportedly ignorant individual. This approach implicitly assumes that knowledge makes for a sufficient condition to bring about modified behavior, overlooking the possibility that economic conditions, work rhythms, access to healthy foodscapes, or the commensal dimension of eating might constrain the application of knowledge about nutrition.

Obesity has been made into a highly visible issue globally. Think of the news reports and documentaries depicting the headless obese bodies thought to populate contemporary landscapes or the exponential growth curves depicting global obesity trends and rising rates of cardiovascular disease. The BMI surreptitiously provides a numerical valence to what is apparently plain to see. It provides clinicians with a tipping point, albeit one whose global standardization led millions to move from *overweight* to *obese* overnight, without gaining so much as a pound. As elsewhere, French public health programs targeting obesity characterize it as an epidemic, although the epidemiological data to support this claim remains disputed (Gard 2011). The surveillance tools at work in French preschools now enable health workers to identify "future *obèses* [obese persons]" even before they move out of the normal weight range. This feat of making the future obese child visible is accomplished with a simple measurement tool with which all French children are now screened. It involves mapping the so-called adiposity rebound, which is a rise in BMI that occurs between the ages of three and seven years. An early adiposity rebound is said to constitute a risk factor for obesity later on in life. As one school nurse told me: "It's a marvelous tool; you can literally see the future *obèse* before he gains the weight." But what do such representations obscure? Clare Herrick (2009, 57) points to the disjuncture between the complexity and uncertainty surrounding obesity's etiology and the apparent display of confidence in advancing evidence of ever-rising rates of obesity, making for a unique health crisis that has attracted hyperbolic public attention.

I draw on materials gathered in the context of my research on alimentary health in France (Sanabria 2015; Sanabria and Yates-Doerr 2015) and on a retrospective ethnographization (see Ingold 2014) of my encounters with colleagues at the WPHNA and in my (French) workplace, where I was hired to carry out anthropological research in the field of health education. This article refracts a series of global questions concerning the circulation of ignorance in the construction of evidentiary regimes of nutritional interventions through a range of materials collected in France and through my participation in global forums such as the WPHNA. As such, I do not purport to provide an ethnographic description of obesity in France as much as to situate the problem within a specific ethnographic setting.[4] The issue I attend to is difficult to locate as it is raised by a subgroup of vocal but globally dispersed critical public health nutrition advocates, with some of whom I have been collaborating since I joined the WPHNA's Executive Committee in 2013. If anything, what is specific to the French situation is the *absence* of the debate from the public arena. My article draws on observations gathered at numerous French policy meetings, expert workshops, and conferences on how to change *les comportements alimentaires* (eating behaviors), as well as on a review of published literature on public health nutrition interventions.

BEYOND KNOWLEDGE AND ITS ABSENCE: Health education and behavior change

The French National Program for Nutrition and Heath (PNNS) identifies "information education communication" (IEC) as its main strategic lever to shape food behaviors. Yet despite considerable investment in such campaigns, obesity rates continue their progression, leading some to suggest that this represents a weak strategy in the face of our strong biological drive to seek out and enjoy calorie-dense foods (Brownell and Gold 2012; Kessler 2009). Today, the idea that education through the conveying of messages could impact health behaviors seems quaint. Traditionally, health education was premised on a hierarchical model of knowledge transfer in which ignorant individuals were deemed incapable of making appropriate health decisions. The WHO's 1986 Ottawa Charter highlighted the importance of making all governmental policy—from urban planning to housing, employment, and transport—"healthy." Yet the majority of governments have taken the easy (and cheaper) route of reducing health promotion to health education and social marketing (Bergeron, Castel, and Nouguez 2013; Nutbeam 2005; Whitehead and Irvine 2011). Despite the emerging recognition that informing has not worked, IEC models of health education remain entrenched and continue to mobilize attention among experts. In the absence of a magic bullet, targeting health behaviors through education is seen as the sole option.

This point was put quite bluntly to me during a research meeting that explored possible lines of collaboration to identify, in one senior nutritionist's words, how best to *éduquer les comportements alimentaires* (educate health behaviors) to prevent obesity. The meeting followed a tour of a ward in a major hospital in the south of France where "morbid" obesity is tackled. With little success, as the intern noted, given that the patients "*qui échouent là* [who wash up here]" return to the same real-life problems after the ward, where they cannot apply health recommendations. More used to working in Brazilian public hospitals than French ones, I was stunned to observe contrasts not unlike those I had so often witnessed in Brazil: the blatant disparities between thin, well-to-do, white middle-class health professionals and the patients on the wards, who were of mixed rural and immigrant origins and whose stories and bodies attested to lives lived in precarity. "Until we get better epidemiological support for bariatric surgery, all we can do is *éduquer nos obèses* [educate our obese persons]," the chief consultant (who receives, as many French nutritionists do, funding from the Fondation Nestlé and other, less explicitly named corporate entities) concluded.

The medical team is acutely aware of the social dimensions of the problem. "Some [patients] don't even have a dining table!" the intern exclaimed. These patients just microwave their food and eat in front of the television (which, in France, is often referred to as an Americanization of eating). Social inequalities, maximizing the calorie per euro ratio, and lack of education constituted the main determinants of the issue, in the medical practitioners' view. This insight in some respects represents a positive step, laying the groundwork for better cross-disciplinary understanding between medical professionals and anthropologists. But as my colleague and I returned to the stories we had just heard, which revealed more patient knowledge of nutritional recommendations than doctors often recognize and which pointed to the challenges of eating a balanced home-cooked diet when working *les trois-huits*[5] or struggling to resist foods that were simply everywhere, we were cut short by the consultant: "It's all well and easy for you to evoke the endless determinants and say it's more complicated, but we have people dying of obesity and we need answers we can put into practice."

One series of answers sought by nutritionists surrounds how to motivate behavior change through education, and social scientists such as myself have been called on to help operationalize this. As might be expected, the particular set of meetings I am describing ended without us identifying a common rationale. But it made me appreciate afresh the clinician's sense of urgency and the disjuncture between the knowledge we as anthropologists produce and the kind of knowledge that might be required in the day-to-day life of the clinic. Literacy, knowledge acquisition, information, and education are relatively interchangeable in these contexts. Yet changed behavior does not flow, linearly, from information transfer. Critical health pedagogues have shown that reducing education to information transfer does little more than attribute ignorance to others, rendering them passive recipients of pedagogical endeavors (Fitzpatrick and Tinning 2014). Although French nutritional health educators increasingly recognize the insufficiency of information transfer alone, developing interventions that extend beyond it risks being dismissed as cumbersome, expensive, or based on uncertain evidentiary regimes. In the schools in which I have observed nutritional education, these endeavors seldom amount to more than testing a student's ability to list food groups and rehearse the health messages dispensed in national food guidelines (and made known to young people principally through the health warnings on the "junk" foods heavily marketed to them). "It's a bit of a lost battle," one school nurse told me as we discussed the challenges of nutritional education in the corridor while the students played an online game about nutrition as part of their civics and health education curricula. Although growing consensus exists about the need for a change in nutritional behaviors, how it is to be achieved (according to whose definition and with what means) remains an open question.

As I circulate through spaces where the work of rendering obesity interventions (measurably) implementable is carried out, I find myself further removed from the urgencies of tackling morbid obesity or navigating euphemisms to avoid stigmatizing overweight adolescents in the classroom. One morning I attend an expert meeting in Paris on nutrition and chronic disease, where a senior civil servant from the Assurance Maladie (the health branch of France's social security system) is giving a speech that thoroughly confuses health promotion and disease prevention. Monsieur Dupont spoke of promoting individual responsibility for health, "not to place the blame on obese people but to enable them to become stewards of their own health." Dupont has developed a program called Active Health Coaching. Coaching, in France, evokes to many left-wing defenders of public health the worst of neoliberal ideologies, with its individualization of responsibility and its privatization of structural and societal issues. His tone at the meeting is deliberately provocative, implicitly targeting such leftist critiques: "We spend 11 million [euros] on diabetes alone. We're driving into a wall. That's OK, but not while we're honking our horn and not with me at the wheel." Active Health Coaching is still in its trial period, but it signals an interesting move in the French social security system.

I later met with several Active Health Coaching program managers in the pristine Assurance Maladie headquarters in Versailles. There are blurred rationales underlying the program's development, I realized, as we sipped oversweetened coffee from disposable plastic cups. Economics transpires behind the language of empowerment; "I know it's not politically correct to say so when you work for the Assurance Maladie, but we need to start saving," Dupont told me. Coaching is done in groups, a local program manager explained, because it creates a "ripple effect" and because it is cheaper than individual coaching. Information remains crucial: members who sign up for the Active Nutrition program go through a motivational interview in which they commit to four obligatory "information workshops." The interview serves to weed out "those for whom we can't do anything," the manager clarified, so that they do not take up a "space that can be given to a motivated *obèse*; this is public money after all." Public money invested into expensive real estate, with modern shop fronts and dedicated hostesses "to shake off the dusty image of the Assurance Maladie," another manager boasted. Not everyone shares this vision of change, of course. As one Assurance Maladie employee from the much less prosperous Saint-Denis neighborhood noted: "They are opening flashy agencies and personalized e-coaching with dubious behavior-change experts, while closing local branches and suppressing face-to-face contact in the places where it is most needed."

As elsewhere, neuromarketing and nudging are on the rise in French public health circles (e.g., Oullier and Sauneron 2010). *Neuroprévention*, as it is dubbed, draws on the "new" behavioral economics to reveal that individuals are also driven by unconscious factors (Rice 2013). The "naive informational model of health education has failed," a senior health economist stated during the opening session of a meeting of French policymakers gathered to identify new levers for change in nutrition. After a welcome buffet featuring the event's industrial sponsor's new "healthy," vacuum-sealed, diabetic-friendly breakfast bar (but no fruit, another attendant noted with a wink), the meeting kicked off with a talk by a neuroscientist and the director of France's largest marketing research institute. He presented data on the importance of unconscious processes in driving behaviors modeled on "real-life shopping experiments." Consumers make choices in a fraction of a second, he informed us, without any cognitive engagement. "To target reason is to miss the decision [making]." It is telling of the shifts underway that the meeting's organizers would have a marketing director address an assembly of policymakers, doctors, and researchers gathered to identify levers for change in nutrition. As the director told us: "I help my clients [PepsiCo, Danone, Unilever, and Kraft, according to his declaration of interests] sell more. The ethics are your bit."

Unconscious drives occupy a curious place between knowledge and its absence. Such an intrusion (as behavioral economists often present it) of the pre-rational has a complicated relation to knowledge and lack thereof. It is based on a distinction, introduced by Daniel Kahneman (2011), between two systems of knowing: one rational and logical, the other intuitive and perceptual. Health education and most obesity-prevention strategies focus on the rational system, which processes new information against existing knowledge. Yet the intuitive system takes new information at face value, such that Deborah Prentice (2015, 267) suggests it is an open question as to whether this system can experience ignorance. The second system always knows something, even if the knowing is biased, partial, or skewed. "Misknowledge" (Prentice 2015) operating at this level interferes, in the view of behavioral economists, with the rational mind's capacity to translate knowledge into action. Public health interventions have essentially targeted the rational mind, providing it with information that in the emergent competing view cannot be operationalized because of the irruption of precognitive drives. Here, we have an interplay between forms of unconscious knowing, on the one hand (such as the affective drives seen to impede rational decision-making capabilities) and forms of strategic ignorance, on the other. This is all the more troubling when we consider that tools developed to sell more calorie-dense foods are now being marketed to public health experts to redress the deleterious impact of the massive increase in consumption of these foods. Considering that the food industry's budget to deploy these marketing tools is nearly tenfold that invested annually by governments in health promotion, the battle may not just be lost but in fact unwinnable.

A CIVIC (INDIVIDUAL) RESPONSIBILITY FOR HEALTH?

Sheila Jasanoff (2005, 258) proposes the term *civic epistemologies* to refer to how publics know things in common. Such public knowing varies between national contexts as knowledge is presented, tested, and put to use in public arenas. The concept of civic epistemologies poses public life as a "proving ground for knowledge claims and as a theater for establishing the credibility of public actions." The expert meetings and conferences I describe here can be thought of as theaters of civic epistemologies. They are not policymaking spaces as such, for this labor takes place elsewhere, in ministerial cabinets. Nor can they really be conceived as spaces of public accountability, for the publics that they bring together consist of experts, research funding agencies, policymakers, and health professionals vested in addressing nutrition-related health issues. These spaces collectively enact a problem space around obesity, and they outline the contours of possible interventions. As such, they are spaces in which the constitutive dimensions of civic epistemologies about obesity are enacted. The knowledges that circulate here draw eclectically on various disciplines and do not map neatly onto those at work in the more formal scientific arena. Claims about rendering specific interventions operational become legitimized through an active investment in such spaces. It is in and through them that a specific (French) rendition of the individual's civic responsibility for health is constructed and enlivened.

On a rainy winter morning, a group of representatives from the PNNS, the Plan Obésité (Obesity Plan), the Assurance Maladie, and the Mutualité Française,[6] came together with academic researchers in the Parisian headquarters of a leading nonprofit health insurance company to discuss the relative costs of nutrition-related chronic conditions, as well as the contours of different strategic interventions. The Mutualité Française's representative began her presentation by stating that more than 8 million French people are supported under a chronic disease regime. While this represents only 12 percent of the population, it accounts for more than 65 percent of national health costs. At stake, she poignantly argued, is the continued existence of France's social security model: "If costs continue to rise, our system of solidarity will be called into question." As a spokesperson for the French nonprofit *mutuelle* system of health insurance, she was no neutral commentator on the importance of addressing social inequalities and the sustainability of France's model of social solidarity. From her point of view, the unsustainable costs incurred because of chronic disease made overweight people a direct threat to France's social contract. It seemed ironic to hear this defender of social equality speak of "the problem that the obese lay on our system." Likewise, the representative from the Direction Générale de la Santé of the Ministry of Health and Social Affairs noted the costs of obesity-related disease: "15 billion [euros] a year weighs heavily on public accounts. We can reduce this with preventative *education* targeting the obese." In the long list of burdens "the obese" apparently place on society, the toll they take on solidarity and social cohesion makes for a striking addition. This language points to lines of fracture among who is amenable to solidarity, who is included, and how it is gauged.

In *Cruel Optimism*, Lauren Berlant (2011, 98) invites us to consider the distribution of agency assumed in national instantiations of public health imaginaries. She interrogates the paradoxical coexistence of an "attrition of the subject" and of normative notions of agency that assume the subject will, can, or should care for herself. Berlant describes how liberals (in the U.S. sense of the term) seek to reclaim the state as a reparative resource in the face of a deregulated market circulating unhealthy commodities, while conservatives denounce such measures as those of a "communist" or "nanny" state. This approach provides an interesting foil to the situation I am describing. Viewed from France, the U.S. debates around Obamacare are almost incomprehensible. In France, North American calls to charge obese persons more for their health care are often held up as emblematic of national differences in relations between the state and its citizens. This renders the statements that circulated at the expert meeting described above striking, as they point to an attrition of the French social contract in relation to obesity. In the French context, the problem is framed not in terms of paying for those who have brought ill health on themselves, but rather in terms of an intolerance toward obesity-incurred health costs threatening French social security.[7]

There are important stakes in how a problem and its solution are framed. What counts as part of the story of obesity is highly political. Having outlined how many public health interventions continue to hold individuals responsible, I now examine how the field of evidence is landscaped to enhance the promissory value of certain interventions over others. I suggest that strategic ignorance (McGoey 2012) may purposefully obscure or overemphasize the relative implementability or efficacy of interventions and show that this often serves the purpose of deflecting responsibilities back onto individuals.

COMPLEXITY, UNCERTAINTY, AND THE SCALAR LOGICS OF PUBLIC HEALTH NUTRITION

A common feature of the presentations given in policy circles on chronic disease or obesity prevention is the graphic representation of factors affecting health outcomes and the scales at which interventions should be designed. Many of the models used in these contexts are variations of the socio-ecological framework of health.

These models give a visual representation of the classic set of categories that appear in the literature on health promotion. The models depict concentric circles and place the individual at the center of consecutive layers of interpersonal, community, organizational, or policy influences. They obscure interactions between these predefined spheres and reveal the importance of the modern, rational individual decision-maker for public health. Many accounts of the complex problem of malnutrition cannot be accommodated by these models and their reified

Figure 1. One variant of the socio-ecological framework of health promotion. Uncredited slide.

categories. One such account considers the growing availability of processed hyperpalatable foods in urban environments as a major factor in the rise of obesity. Hyperpalatability refers to the fine-tuning of foods by the industry to enthrall the senses, override satiety, and motivate eaters to pursue more (Kessler 2009). This phenomenon collapses the scalar relations between categories such as body, individual, environment, or political-legal regulation. Here macroeconomic forces—such as trade agreements, pricing mechanisms, or the massive entrance of transnational food and beverage companies into developing world markets— directly target the biochemistry of appetite regulation. That is, they methodically elicit the irruption of what behavioral economists refer to as precognitive drives. In the cybernetic models used to think the relations between eaters and the environments in which they source foods, nutrients, fat cells, the gastrointestinal tract, brain regions, and pleasure receptors undermine eaters' capacities to make rational choices (Sanabria 2015). For example, in Figure 2 (variations of which increasingly appear in the expert meetings I attend), the environment influences metabolism through mechanisms such as availability, palatability, taste, and social habits. Feedback loops set by a central "metabolic brain" link it to the internal milieu, graphically represented by free-floating organs. I argue that, at present, only the first type of graphic representation informs public action.

Hannah Landecker (2013) asks after the "knowledge effects" of the growth of metabolic disorders such as those associated with obesity worldwide. She argues

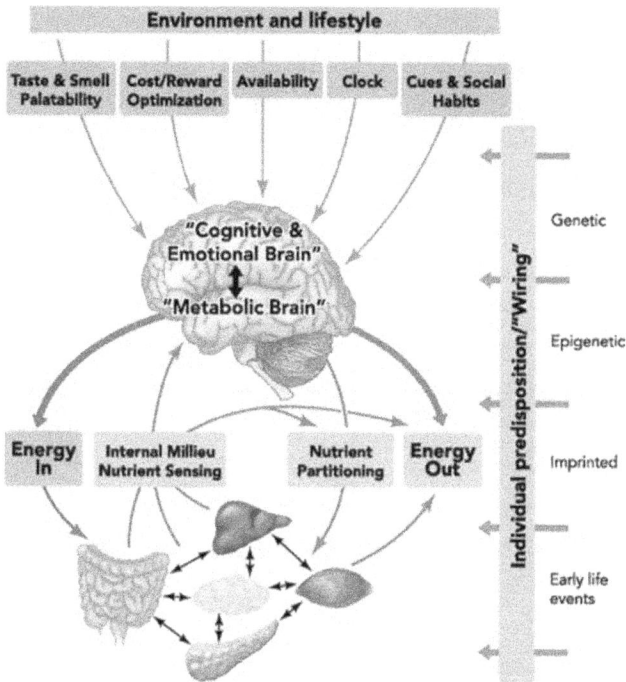

Figure 2. Schematic diagram of the major factors determining the neural control of appetite and energy balance regulation. Figure from "Neural Systems Controlling the Drive to Eat: Mind Versus Metabolism," by Zheng Huiyuan and Hans-Rudi Berthoud, http://dx.doi.org/10.1152/physiol.00047.2007.

that the efforts to comprehend and treat metabolic disorders are transforming our knowledge of life. The shift she traces between industrial and postindustrial metabolism makes for one way to read the changes in the graphic representations of obesity mobilized here. "Fat knowledge," or the knowledge effects of obesity, has brought about a shift in the conceptual language of metabolic research, away from the language of manufacturing and energy toward that of regulation, signal, and information (Landecker 2013, 511). Landecker (2013, 516) points out that the conditions for the growth of postindustrial metabolic fat knowledge were set by the logics of industrial metabolism and the "fattening effects of industrialization." Likewise, Julie Guthman (2015) shows how the imbalance of food production and food consumption poses a limit to capitalist accumulation. The food industry addresses this imbalance through competitive marketing, increased food processing, and substitutionism, as well as by inducing people to eat more.[8] The changes made to the material constitution of foods that exist primarily to "resolve a particular limit to capitalism" (Guthman 2015, 9) have many as yet unknown effects on eaters' metabolisms and the sustainability of local food systems.

The question is whether (and how) such effects could become knowable. As we saw at the outset, obesity's complexity spans phenomena operating at multiple scales. The problem of relating these often incommensurable scales in a manner that can guide interventions addressing obesity appears acutely at relevant scientific gatherings. A recent European Congress on Obesity (ECO) held in France brought together more than 2,500 international delegates around a multistream scientific program that included high-profile industry-sponsored satellite sessions. The scientific program included presentations on the clinical management and prevention of obesity, bariatric surgery, adipose tissue physiopathology, epigenetics, epidemiology, psychiatry, health economics, and social psychology. Attending such an event, one is struck by the complexity of the processes described at each scale. What relations are crafted between the ontologically different entities held in the various models, from brain parts to blood sugar measures, from experiences of hunger to the spatial politics of food distribution, from metabolic hormones to agrarian policies or reforms to the health-care system (both notable absences from ECO)? The tangible angst surrounding obesity is linked to the nature of the problem it appears to present. Putting all of these scales together gives rise to an almost absurdly complex representation. For instance, the Foresight report (U.K. Government Office of Science 2007) included the Obesity System Map, which attempts to represent this complexity. The map reveals the difficulty inherent in making policy on the basis of the proliferation of factors recognized as affecting dietary health outcomes.

Stanley Ulijaszek (2015) remarks that the Obesity Systems Map explicitly frames obesity as a complex issue that requires multiple sites of intervention beyond individual-focused health education. Whether or not this complexity exceeds that of other health problems (which also span biochemical, social, behavioral, and environmental phenomena), what is notable about the field of obesity is the way in which the arena reflexively grapples with its own complexity. In his analysis of the Obesity Systems Map, Ulijaszek draws on Chunglin Kwa's (2002) analysis of the ways in which science has approached complexity. Kwa differentiates between two models of complexity in science: the romantic and the baroque. In this schema, romantic framings of complexity are founded on the idea of hierarchical levels of organization integrated into a functional whole. Romantic complexity thus aims to provide a coherent model of complex systems by mapping the relations between constitutive elements. The baroque sensibility, on the other

Foresight
Obesity System Map

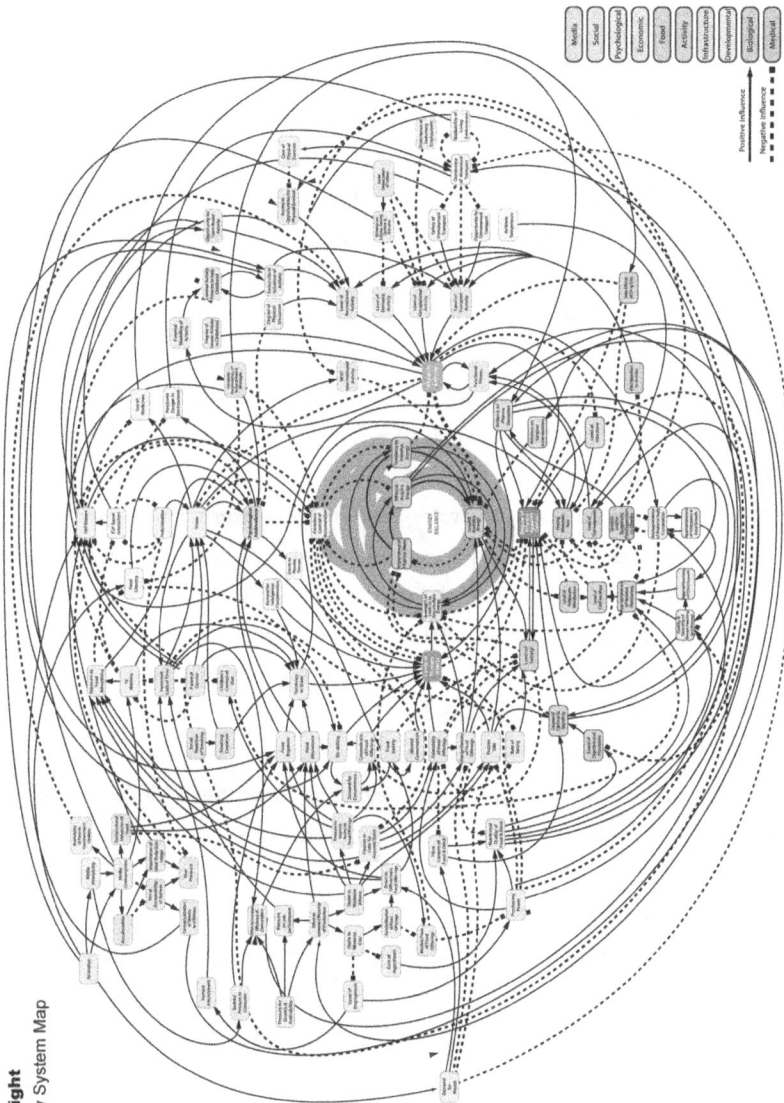

Figure 3. The Foresight Obesity Systems Map. Image by the Foresight Programme, U.K. Government Office of Science.

hand, views complexity as endless and impossible to know fully (Law 2004). Within baroque complexity, it is not possible to arrive at an emergent overview of the determinants and factors affecting a complex system given the lack of final coherence and the existence of only partially mappable connections and uncertain relations between different factors. In Kwa's (2002, 47) words, uncertainty in the baroque reading of complexity is ontological rather than epistemological. Ulijaszek shows how the complexity of obesity's determinants became reduced to a romantic framing, which places the energy balance at the center of the model, obscuring or displacing other possible framings (such as gene-environment inter-actions, food production, and distribution or macroeconomic factors influencing food choice). In his view, this resulted from the British Government Office for Science explicitly charging the Foresight Project with producing a view of obesity control that could be politically tractable (Ulijaszek 2015). This makes evident the relation between framings of complexity, definitions of the knowable (and, by extension, what is not known or ignored), and the (state) politics of opera-tionalizing knowledge.

At stake is how to make emerging knowledge—overburdened by its own complexity—operational. This requires rendering the effects of interventions cal-culable in accord with the logics of bureaucratic management. For example, Charlotte Biltekoff (Biltekoff et al. 2014, 22) argues that "charismatic nutrients" have helped render nutritional problems (such as micronutrient deficiencies, ex-cess lipids, or simple carbohydrates) calculable. Charismatic nutrients index more than nutrition, in that they also carve out an evidentiary space for advocates to rally (wittingly or not) behind specific nutritional interventions in a context where nutritional experts need to "satisfy increasingly quantification-oriented parame-ters." Much of the scholarship in the area of evidence-based policy focuses on the difficulties of knowing complex realities, but less has focused on the way in which complexity and uncertainty are both productive and actively produced. In the final section, I examine how certain facts concerning obesity or public health nutrition interventions come to rally more support and visibility than others.

FROM SCIENTIFIC UNCERTAINTY TO STRATEGIC IGNORANCE

In their analysis of the effects of corporate behavior on public health, Moodie and colleagues (Moodie et al. 2013, 671) propose the term *industrial epidemic* to refer to the spread of disease caused by "corporate disease vectors." The authors express concern over the call for multisectoral action, to include the private sector and industry, by the UN's High-Level Meeting on Non-Communicable Diseases.

This call makes public-private partnerships central to the development of public health policy. Public-private partnerships are often heralded as holding the potential to improve health globally, but Moodie and colleagues (Moodie et al. 2013, 670) point out that the unhealthy commodities actively promoted by the private partners constitute major drivers of global noncommunicable disease (NCD) epidemics. They therefore conclude that these industries should play no role in the formation of NCD policy and that "public regulation and market intervention are the only evidence-based mechanisms to prevent harm caused by the unhealthy commodity industries." Likewise, a group of 150 organizations made a declaration (Public Interest Civil Society Organizations and Social Movements Forum 2014) at the aforementioned International Conference on Nutrition in Rome, urging member states to ensure the proper regulation and accountability of transnational corporations whose practices interfere with the enjoyment of the human right to adequate food. In particular, they called attention to the fact that agroindustrial food systems have contributed to various forms of malnutrition at stake in their discussions and argued that there is a need to protect the policy space of governments against conflicts of interest introduced by inappropriate relationships with "powerful economic actors." Corporate influences on public policy have become the object of an emerging subfield of public health concerned with systematically analyzing the effects of corporate behavior on health. Moodie and colleagues (Moodie et al. 2013) methodically review the ways in which industries avoid regulation and shape policy agendas through a range of techniques. These include biasing research findings, co-opting policymakers, lobbying to oppose public regulation, circulating blame-the-victim approaches to health promotion, and denouncing so-called nanny-state interventions. "As an alternative to regulatory measures," Moodie and colleagues (Moodie et al. 2013, 674) explain, "industries promote ineffective individually-targeted information and educational approaches." Examining the incursion of market actors into French public health programs, Henri Bergeron, Patrick Castel, and Etienne Nouguez (2013, 285) note that the framing of obesity in the current version of the PNNS proves even less unfavorable to industrial interests. As the communications director of one agroindustrial health promotion partner told them, "education about consumption behaviors" is a positive solution to public health problems, while "regulatory or legal constraints," such as "abusive taxation or the banning of advertisement," do not prove effective. Such a statement is astounding and points to how the notion of efficacy has itself been transformed by the kind of evidentiary regimes that are in place after decades of industry-funded research. In a workshop hosted by Lille's

Institut Pasteur Nutrition Service in 2013, the then-director of the French Advertising Regulation Authority was invited to a roundtable discussion on childhood obesity. He stated that the industries he represented awaited solid *preuves scientifiques* (scientific evidence) linking product advertisements to children with increased rates of obesity. In the absence of such causal demonstrations, he saw no reason for industry to unilaterally assume the responsibility for "all of society's ills." Obesity is primarily "an educational problem," he concluded, alluding to parental responsibilities. While the director's position was entirely predictable, what surprised me was the complete lack of response from his copanelists and from the assembly of more than 150 health professionals and educators. As my colleagues at the WPHNA often remark, the burden of proof weighs more heavily on the side of those who contest the status quo around how evidence is mobilized for policy.

Selda Ulucanlar and colleagues (Ulucanlar et al. 2014) propose the term *evidential landscaping* to describe how transnational tobacco corporations misrepresent scientific evidence. They systematically review strategies deployed by the tobacco industry to change the evidential landscape within which the policy debate is conducted, which include misquoting published evidence, mimicking scientific critique, and introducing and promoting alternative research, in particular behavioral studies of individuals rather than assessments of population-scale interventions. Examples of evidence landscaping in the field of obesity research include the recurrent tipping of the balance of blame toward sugars, fats, or sedentary behavior. These research agendas have been linked, respectively, to dairy or sugar consortia that fund research programs downplaying the deleterious health impacts of their products, as one senior nutritionist explained to me in an interview. In a presentation given at the annual conference of a large French public-private research consortium on the levers for nutritional behavior change, a senior civil servant from the Direction Générale de la Santé outlined the changing role of the PNNS since its inception in 2001. While "informing" and "educating" remain central, new policies "implicating stakeholders" (a euphemistic term for the private sector) have been added. He emphasized how this new policy instrument served as a guarantee of the "scientific validity of nutritional information." By signing voluntary agreements to improve the nutritional profile of their products (such as by lowering salt or sugar content), industrial stakeholders can use the PNNS logo in their advertisements. When questioned by a member of the audience about how health claims were assessed—given the controversial nature of such knowledge—the civil servant responded that there was "no controversy over what a good diet includes." He added that it was essential to move past conspiracy thinking and that the PNNS considered the food industry *incontournables* (indispensable) stakeholders in the promotion of healthy eating. The tone was tense and the chair rapidly moved the debate to a technical discussion about measuring the efficacy of PNNS interventions. The voluntary PNNS agreements have the advantage of being simultaneously cheap for the state and remarkably unaggressive toward the food industry (Bergeron, Castel, and Nouguez 2013). Voluntary self-regulation has been heavily critiqued for its inefficiency (see, especially, Moodie et al. 2013). In French health policy circles, a widely circulating public secret (cf. Taussig 1999), discussed over coffee between sessions, is that the state can do very little to tackle obesity given that the agroindustry remains the nation's largest employer. As a cardiologist I interviewed explained: "*C'est la crise* [it's a time of crisis], and governments are terrified of delocalization. They can't do much because the agroindustrial lobbies are too powerful." While this dilemma is not specific to France, what seems notable here is the absence of debate around conflicts of interest and lobbying practices in public health nutrition.[9]

The emphasis placed on measures of efficacy and quantified *évaluations d'impacts* (impact evaluations) in these expert circles is striking given the inefficiency of individual-focused IEC interventions. Take the concept of the obesogenic environment. Presentations on the subject are principally concerned with the methodological difficulties of modeling how urban settings shape eating behaviors. One health geographer presented her exploratory results at the aforementioned conference on the levers for nutritional behavior change and opened with a tellingly cynical remark: "I don't have a Conflict of Interest slide because industry isn't interested in geographers yet, but I love Ferrero Rochers." She went on to present research on the use of GPS to "objectively measure people's exposures to their environments." The project purports to map people's daily trajectories through urban spaces to evaluate the impact of food offerings on individual consumption behaviors. Yet things get tricky when establishing indicators or proxies for un/healthiness. The speaker noted that, in North American obesogenic environment studies, proximity to a supermarket is taken as a proxy for healthy eating, an assumption that did not carry through to the French context, in which supermarkets remain associated with unhealthy eating. Beyond revealing the at times arbitrary nature of such indicators, particularly as they travel, the case of this presentation demonstrates the promissory value that quantifiable interventions hold, even when they are founded on methodologically dubious frameworks.

CONCLUSION

Risks caused by individual behaviors have been an overstated concern in public health. Individual behavior has been identified as a critical locus of intervention, largely because these interventions are cheap and comparatively easy to implement. But this approach obscures a range of things, such as the contested nature of the knowledge transferred and the ways in which uncertainty may not simply be an inherent product of complexity but can also be strategically produced. I have highlighted the disproportion between exhortations to healthy eating aimed at individual consumers and the remarkable laissez-faire that characterizes how the food and drink industries are invited to voluntarily limit fat, sugar, or salt in their products. In a world of uncertainties and contested knowledges, knowing does not constitute a clearly identifiable endpoint. Knowledge does not proceed linearly from the absence of knowledge (or ignorance) to knowing. The focus on knowing latent in health education is based on a presumption of ignorance that overshadows the variegated forms of not-knowing at play in the field of public health nutrition. New social marketing versions of health education emphasize individual responsibility to consume in particular ways. These campaigns tend to be conducted at the expense of truly multisectoral regulatory interventions across agricultural and nutritional policy domains. Interventions in public health nutrition often operate on a mechanistic model of goal realization. At stake here is the capacity to intervene in an operational manner, as well as to define the kinds of knowledges that enable intervention. Where the public health response to the problem of obesity is concerned, the difficulty of implementing measurably effective interventions is both a problem for action and an endless resource to fuel further action (Sanabria and Yates-Doerr 2015).

Carlo Caduff (2014, 304) argues that while the attempted escape from the "knowledge machine" of late liberalism constituted an important move, simply turning to its underside— unknowing—locks social science into a dialectics of the un/known. I have traced the loopings that operate between regimes of knowing and unknowing not so much to know more about unknowing as to reveal the politics of ascribing knowledge or its absence to specific groups or evidence-making practices.

I have also aimed to consider how such circulations affect possible registers of public action. In mapping the relations between complexity, uncertainty, and knowledge in public health, my concern has been to consider the spaces for intervention carved out in the field of obesity. The problem of obesity's complexity conceals an assumption about the possibility of developing efficient interventions through the accumulation of evidence and the computing, scaling up, or translating of this evidence into replicable practices of prevention or care. The implicit idea here is that we need more evidence, more knowledge, and more powerful computational tools and models to link the types of evidence produced, from the genetic to the individual to the community scale to the realm of global policy.

An important epistemological question remains concerning the kinds of things that *can* be known and the relation between knowledge and action. Interrogations along these lines have much to gain by considering not only what can be known and what can be established as a valid regime of proof, but also what is actively made unknown or unknowable. The evidentiary exigencies around the implementation and evaluation of public health nutrition interventions are such that crucial phenomena are ignored or rendered irrelevant. This is not because we do not know enough, as is often claimed in public health nutrition conferences, but because existing forms of scientific evaluation make it impossible for certain things to be known, for certain relations to be causally established.

Rather than questioning the forms that evidentiary practices have taken— as in the request for *preuves* (proof) of causal linkages—we are witnessing a diffuse, but increasingly consensual rhetorical move toward the language of uncertainty. Working alongside my colleagues at the WPHNA, I find myself wondering about their desire to build sounder scientific evidence for the socially and environmentally sustainable alternatives that we hope to see reshape the current profit-driven food system. How, I wonder, can a knowing specific to ethnographic practice be leveraged to inflect how the knowable is framed in public health? I have argued here that making noncausal and nonlinear relations visible is something that the practice of ethnography is uniquely equipped to do. Ethnography can see through contemporary habits of framing complex conditions, untangling with its exacting specificity the tightly coupled technical (and ideological) systems typical of what Kim Fortun (2012) has called late industrialism.

ABSTRACT

This article examines what is said to be un/known about obesity and the ways in which attributions of knowledge or ignorance circulate in the field of public health nutrition. Risks caused by individual behaviors have been an overstated concern in public health. Obesity, like many of today's complex problems, is determined by myriad nested interactions spanning the political economies of market regulation, modes of agricultural production, the biochemistry of appetite regulation, and chang-

ing family structures. Yet public intervention—and the science produced to validate it—remains wedded to a mode of intervening that has limited purchase on the complexity with which it contends. This article draws on scholarship on the social construction of ignorance to argue that the field of evidence in obesity science is fashioned in a way that deflects attention (and responsibility) away from questions of food production and marketing and continues to frame the problem as one of individual responsibility. Rather than discrediting the veracity of evidence produced out of industry-research partnerships that increasingly dominate public health research, this article examines how the field of evidence has been structured by these relations. It argues that the demonstration of causal relations between political and socioeconomic determinants of malnutrition and measurable health indexes is largely impossible, not simply because of the absence of good evidence but because the existing parameters of good science cannot straightforwardly reveal such relations. This, in turn, is due to the configuration of the knowable in terms of whether knowledge can be made operational. [obesity; ignorance; scientific evidence; complexity; France]

NOTES

Acknowledgments   My thinking on scientific evidence, complexity, conflicts of interest, and strategic ignorance owes much to the exchanges in which I am lucky to be engaged with colleagues at the World Public Health Nutrition Association. The ideas developed here germinated in the context of the "Producing Knowledge, Governing Populations" conference held at the Ecole Normale Supérieure de Lyon in September 2013, and I am particularly grateful to Charlotte Brives and Frédéric Le Marcis for the sustained conversations that grew out of this event. The argument was much improved thanks to the feedback I received at the Centre de Sociologie des Organisations seminar, Sciences Po, Paris (October 2014) and the "Knowledge/Value, Dark Data and Absences" workshop held in Exeter (December 2014). I am particularly grateful to the insightful and engaged comments that Dominic Boyer, Anita Hardon, Kaushik Sunder Rajan, and Emily Yates-Doerr provided on earlier drafts of this article.

1. This meeting of the Food and Agriculture Organization and the World Health Organization was held in Rome in November 2014. It brought together United Nations representatives, civil society organizations, and the agrofood industry.
2. This footnote, along with others that provided technical definitions of healthy diets, were scratched in the final ratified declaration after the United States and several European delegations raised concerns about wording.
3. These were the words of the Nigerian minister for agriculture at ICN2.
4. Situating the French response to obesity within a comparative analysis of international policy responses to the issue lies beyond the remit of this article. Such a project would need to engage with the imaginaries produced through geographically localized representations of national specificities (think of the "Mediterranean diet," the "French paradox," the "Americanization of the food system," and so on) as they circulate in international spaces.
5. *Les trois-huits* refers to a system of three eight-hour shifts that enables factories to function twenty-four hours a day but is deeply disruptive to chronobiological systems as workers oscillate between day and night shifts several times a week.
6. *Mutuelles* are not-for-profit organizations that provide health insurance to meet health costs not covered by the state national security system.
7. Even the extreme-right party le Front National defends access to national health services for all "French." The concept of social security itself is not questioned.

8.   Substitutionism involves substituting farm-based commodities with manufactured ones. It has been taken to new levels as emulsifiers, transfats, and high-fructose corn syrup stand in for plant and animal foods, lowering quality and cost while increasing profit margins (Guthman 2015, 8).

9.   The French political system is founded on the ideal that no institutions come between the state and its citizens. This has impeded the development of transparent consultation procedures by which the roles of intermediate organizations that do lobby parliamentarians are spelled out.

REFERENCES

Adams, Vincanne
    2013   "Evidence-Based Global Public Health: Subjects, Profits, Erasures." In *When People Come First: Critical Studies in Global Health*, edited by João Biehl and Adriana Petryna, 54–90. Princeton, N.J.: Princeton University Press.
Bergeron, Henri, Patrick Castel, and Étienne Nouguez
    2013   "Éléments pour une sociologie de l'entrepreneur-frontière. Genèse et diffusion d'un programme de prévention de l'obésité." *Revue Française de Sociologie* 54, no. 2: 263–302. http://dx.doi.org/10.3917/rfs.542.0263.
Berlant, Lauren
    2011   *Cruel Optimism*. Durham, N.C.: Duke University Press.
Bes-Rastrollo Maira, Matthias B. Schulze, Miguel Ruiz-Canela, and Miguel A. Martinez-Gonzalez
    2013   "Financial Conflicts of Interest and Reporting Bias regarding the Association between Sugar-Sweetened Beverages and Weight Gain: A Systematic Review of Systematic Reviews." *PLOS Medicine*, December 31. http://dx.doi.org/10.1371/journal.pmed.1001578.
Biagioli, Mario
    Forthcoming   *Strange Appropriations: Plagiarism and Ghostwriting in Science.*
Biltekoff, Charlotte, Jessica Mudry, Aya H. Kimura, Hannah Landecker, and Julie Guthman
    2014   "Interrogating Moral and Quantification Discourses in Nutritional Knowledge." *Gastronomica* 14, no. 3: 17–26. http://dx.doi.org/10.1525/gfc.2014.14.3.17.
Brownell, Kelly D., and Mark S. Gold
    2012   *Food and Addiction: A Comprehensive Handbook*. Oxford: Oxford University Press.
Caduff, Carlo
    2014   "Pandemic Prophecy, or How to Have Faith in Reason." *Current Anthropology* 55, no. 3: 296–315. http://dx.doi.org/10.1086/676124.
Croissant, Jennifer L.
    2014   "Agnotology: Ignorance and Absence or Towards a Sociology of Things That Aren't There." *Social Epistemology* 28, no. 1: 4–25. http://dx.doi.org/10.1080/02691728.2013.862880.
Fitzpatrick, Katie, and Richard Tinning
    2014   *Health Education: Critical Perspectives*. Oxford: Routledge.
Fortun, Kim
    2012   "Ethnography in Late Industrialism." *Cultural Anthropology* 27, no. 3: 446–64. http://dx.doi.org/10.1111/j.1548-1360.2012.01153.x.
Frickel, Scott, and Michelle Edwards
    2014   "Untangling Ignorance in Environmental Risk Assessment." In *Powerless Science? The Making of the Toxic World in the Twentieth Century*, edited by Soraya Boudia and Nathalie Jas, 215–33. New York: Berghahn Books.
Gard, Michael
    2011   "Truth, Belief, and the Cultural Politics of Obesity Scholarship and Public Health Policy." *Critical Public Health* 21, no. 1: 37–48. http://dx.doi.org/10.1080/09581596.2010.529421.

Geissler, P. W.
  2013   "Public Secrets in Public Health: Knowing not to Know while Making Scientific Knowledge." *American Ethnologist* 40, no. 1:13–34. http://dx.doi.org/10.1111/amet.12002.
Gornall, Jonathan
  2015   "Sugar: Spinning a Web of Influence." *BMJ* 350, February 11. http://dx.doi.org/10.1136/bmj.h231.
Gross, Matthias, and Linsey McGoey, eds.
  2015   *Routledge International Handbook of Ignorance Studies*. London: Routledge.
Guthman, Julie
  2015   "Binging and Purging: Agrofood Capitalism and the Body as Socioecological Fix." *Environment and Planning A* 47. http://dx.doi.org/10.1068/a140005p.
Hawkes, Corinna, and Kent Buse
  2011   "Public Health Sector and Food Industry Interaction: It's Time to Clarify the Term 'Partnership' and Be Honest about Underlying Interests." *European Journal of Public Health* 21, no. 4: 400–403. http://dx.doi.org/10.1093/eurpub/ckr077.
Heimer, Carol A.
  2012   "Inert Facts and the Illusion of Knowledge: Strategic Uses of Ignorance in HIV Clinics." *Economy and Society* 41, no. 1: 17–41. http://dx.doi.org/10.1080/03085147.2011.637332.
Herrick, Clare
  2009   "Shifting Blame/Selling Health: Corporate Social Responsibility in the Age of Obesity." *Sociology of Health & Illness* 31, no. 1: 51–65. http://dx.doi.org/10.1111/j.1467-9566.2008.01121.x.
Hess, David J.
  2015   "Undone Science and Social Movements: A Review and Typology." In *Routledge International Handbook of Ignorance Studies*, edited by Matthias Gross and Linsey McGoey, 141–54. London: Routledge.
Ingold, Tim
  2014   "That's Enough about Ethnography!" *Hau: Journal of Ethnographic Theory* 4, no. 1: 383–95. http://dx.doi.org/10.14318/hau4.1.021.
Jasanoff, Sheila
  2005   *Designs on Nature: Science and Democracy in Europe and the United States*. Princeton, N.J.: Princeton University Press.
Kahneman, Daniel
  2011   *Thinking, Fast and Slow*. New York: Farrar, Straus, and Giroux.
Kelly, Ann H., and Uli Beisel
  2011   "Neglected Malarias: The Frontlines and Back Alleys of Global Health." *Biosocieties* 6, no. 1: 71–87. http://dx.doi.org/10.1057/biosoc.2010.42.
Kessler, David A.
  2009   *The End of Overeating: Taking Control of our Insatiable Appetite*. New York: Rodale.
Kleinman, Daniel Lee, and Sainath Suryanarayanan
  2015   "Ignorance and Industry: Agrichemicals and Honey Bee Deaths." In *Routledge International Handbook of Ignorance Studies*, edited by Matthias Gross and Linsey McGoey, 183–91. London: Routledge.
Kwa, Chunglin
  2002   "Romantic and Baroque Conceptions of Complex Wholes in the Sciences." In *Complexities: Social Studies of Knowledge Practices*, edited by John Law and Annemarie Mol, 23–52. Durham, N.C.: Duke University Press.
Landecker, Hannah
  2013   "Postindustrial Metabolism: Fat Knowledge." *Public Culture* 25, no. 3: 495–522. http://dx.doi.org/10.1215/08992363-2144625.

Law, John
    2004   "And If the Global Were Small and Noncoherent? Method, Complexity, and the Baroque." *Environment and Planning D* 22: 13–26. http://dx.doi.org/10.1068/d316t.
McGoey, Linsey
    2007   "On the Will to Ignorance in Bureaucracy." *Economy and Society* 36, no. 2: 212–35. http://dx.doi.org/10.1080/03085140701254282.
    2012   "Strategic Unknowns: Towards a Sociology of Ignorance." *Economy and Society* 41, no. 1: 1–16. http://dx.doi.org/10.1080/03085147.2011.637330.
Moodie, Rob, David Stuckler, Carlos Monteiro, Nick Sheron, Bruce Neal, Thaksaphon Thamarangsi, Paul Lincoln, and Sally Caswell
    2013   "Profits and Pandemics: Prevention of Harmful Effects of Tobacco, Alcohol, and Ultra-Processed Food and Drink Industries." *Lancet* 381, no. 9867: 670–79. http://dx.doi.org/10.1016/S0140-6736(12)62089-3.
Nutbeam, Don
    2005   "What Would the Ottawa Charter Look Like if It Were Written Today?" *Reviews of Health Promotion and Education Online*. http://www.iuhpe.org/rhpeo/reviews/2005/19/index.htm.
Oreskes, Naomi, and Erik M. Conway
    2011   *Merchants of Doubt: How a Handful of Scientists Obscured the Truth on Issues from Tobacco Smoke to Global Warming*. New York: Bloomsbury.
Oullier, Olivier, and Sarah Sauneron
    2010   "Nouvelles approches de la prévention en santé publique. L'apport des sciences comportementales, cognitives et des neurosciences." Paris: Centre d'Analyse Stratégique. http://www.ladocumentationfrancaise.fr/rapports-publics/104000139/.
Pinto, Manuela Fernández
    2015   "Tensions in Agnotology: Normativity in the Studies of Commercially Driven Ignorance." *Social Studies of Science* 45, no. 2: 294–315. http://dx.doi.org/10.1177/0306312714565491.
Prentice, Deborah A.
    2015   "Targeting Ignorance to Change Behavior." In *Routledge International Handbook of Ignorance Studies*, edited by Matthias Gross and Linsey McGoey, 266–73. London: Routledge.
Proctor, Robert N.
    2011   *Golden Holocaust: Origins of the Cigarette Catastrophe and the Case for Abolition*. Berkeley: University of California Press.
Proctor, Robert, N., and Londa Schiebinger, eds.
    2008   *Agnotology: The Making and Unmaking of Ignorance*. Stanford, Calif.: Stanford University Press.
Public Interest Civil Society Organizations and Social Movements Forum
    2014   "Declaration to the Second International Conference on Nutrition (ICN2), Rome, 21 November 2014." *Development* 57, no. 2: 135–40. http://dx.doi.org/10.1057/dev.2014.85.
Rice, Thomas
    2013   "The Behavioral Economics of Health and Health Care." *Annual Review of Public Health* 34: 431–47. http://dx.doi.org/10.1146/annurev-publhealth-031912-114353.
Sanabria, Emilia
    2015   "Sensorial Pedagogies, Hungry Fat Cells and the Limits of Nutritional Health Education." *BioSocieties* 10, no. 2: 125–42. http://dx.doi.org/10.1057/biosoc.2015.5.
Sanabria, Emilia, and Emily Yates-Doerr
    2015   "Alimentary Uncertainties: From Contested Evidence to Policy." *BioSocieties* 10, no. 2: 117–24. http://dx.doi.org/10.1057/biosoc.2015.17.

Stuckler, David, Martin McKee, Shah Ebrahim, and Sanjay Basu
  2012   "Manufacturing Epidemics: The Role of Global Producers in Increased
          Consumption of Unhealthy Commodities including Processed Foods, Alcohol,
          and Tobacco." *PLOS Medicine* 9, June 26. http://dx.doi.org/10.1371/
          journal.pmed.1001235.
Taussig, Michael
  1999   *Defacement: Public Secrecy and the Labor of the Negative.* Stanford, Calif.: Stanford
          University Press.
U.K. Government Office of Science
  2007   "Tackling Obesities: Future Choices." Foresight Programme. https://www.
          gov.uk/government/collections/tackling-obesities-future-choices#project-
          report.
Ulijaszek, Stanley
  2015   "With the Benefit of Foresight: Reframing the Obesity Problem as a Complex
          System." *BioSocieties* 10, no. 2: 213–28. http://dx.doi.org/10.1057/biosoc.
          2015.16.
Ulucanlar, Selda, Gary J. Fooks, Jenny L. Hatchard, and Anna B. Gilmore
  2014   "Representation and Misrepresentation of Scientific Evidence in Contemporary
          Tobacco Regulation: A Review of Tobacco Industry Submissions to the UK
          Government Consultation on Standardised Packaging." *PLOS Medicine*, March 25.
          http://dx.doi.org/10.1371/journal.pmed.1001629
Whitehead, Dean, and Fiona Irvine
  2011   "Ottawa 25+—'All Aboard the Dazzling Bandwagon'—Developing Personal
          Skills: What Remains for the Future?" *Health Promotion International* 26, S2:
          ii245–52. http://dx.doi.org/10.1093/heapro/dar072.